STUDIES IN
SELECTIVE
CREDIT
POLICIES

STUDIES IN SELECTIVE CREDIT POLICIES

EDITED BY

Ira Kaminow

James M. O'Brien

FEDERAL RESERVE BANK
OF PHILADELPHIA

October 1975
Library of Congress Catalog Card Number: 75-5010
International Standard Book Number: 0-915484-01-3
Printed in the United States of America.

Single copy free. Additional copies are available from the Department of Research, Federal Reserve Bank of Philadelphia, Philadelphia, PA 19105 at $2 each.

Cover design by Arthur J. Johnson

Interior design by Anne W. Churchman

CONTENTS

PART 2

FOREWORD

Selective credit policies have periodically been embraced by policymakers and their constituents to achieve a wide variety of objectives. Frequently the goals sought have been laudable. But all too often advocates have moved ahead without the kind of guidance that can be provided by systematic economic research. In large part this was because of a marked lack of such research into many open issues related to selective credit policies.

It was with this lack in mind that the Federal Reserve Bank of Philadelphia undertook a major and ongoing project to investigate credit allocation techniques. The papers in this volume are among the first to come out of this project. It is my hope that they will add to our understanding of these frequently advocated but imperfectly understood policy tools.

David P. Eastburn
President

August 1975

PREFACE

This volume contains papers completed under the Philadelphia Federal Reserve Bank's Project on Selective Credit Policies.

Early in the Project, it was decided to establish a systematic inventory of the work that had already been done on selective credit policies and credit allocation techniques. As a result, four specialists in the area were each asked to survey a particular aspect of the literature. Among its other attributes, this group comprises a rather broad and more or less representative range of opinion and viewpoints on selective credit policy issues. It is the work of this group that constitutes Part 1 of the current volume.

Apart from sponsoring the survey articles, the Bank encourages economists who are in residence at its Research Department to work on questions related to the general area of selective credit policies. The papers in Part 2 are drawn from such work.

It is still too early to extract from the Project many new conclusions directly applicable to problems of policymakers. The Project, in its earlier stages, has not been designed to achieve this end, but rather to gain general insights into the issues surrounding selective credit policies and perhaps establish a framework for further study. In this regard, we offer the first piece in this volume, "Issues in Selective Credit Policies: An Evaluative Essay," as an interim indication of the Project's progress in evaluating the various issues.

It is appropriate in this space to acknowledge those who have helped us with the volume and the total project. This we do with great enthusiasm. We are greatly indebted to David P. Eastburn, President of the Federal Reserve Bank of Philadelphia, who first suggested the Project on Selective Credit Policies and whose continuing support has been crucial to its success. Mark Willes, who served as Project Director until he became the Bank's First Vice President, did much to mold the project and define its nature.

Our thanks also to Edward G. Boehne and Kathleen Holmes for representing the Project's interests when Bank resources were being allocated and used. Robert Ritchie ably and conscientiously provided stylistic editing of the contributions and with Ronald Williams oversaw the production process. Finally, we express our gratitude to our coauthors, the contributors, who have all been extremely cooperative through the entire process from first outline to final draft.

IRA KAMINOW
JAMES M. O'BRIEN

August 1975

COPYRIGHT NOTICES

Issues in Selective Credit Policies: An Evaluative Essay*

IRA KAMINOW
JAMES M. O'BRIEN

This essay mirrors in its general intent the objectives set for the book and for the broader project on selective credit policies[1] of which this volume is a part. These objectives are (1) to record and evaluate what economists know about selective credit policies, (2) to identify gaps in our understanding of these policies, and (3) to move toward narrowing the gaps. While the essay relies heavily on the other contributions, it is not designed to be a summary of the rest of the book. Rather, we have tried to use the perspective provided by those contributions as well as other work connected with the project, including discussions, proposals, and papers in progress, to examine and organize the issues surrounding selective credit policies.

* The authors would like to acknowledge helpful comments received from the research staff of the Federal Reserve Bank of Philadelphia and, particularly, detailed discussions of certain issues with Donald J. Mullineaux, Donald L. Raiff, and Anthony M. Rufolo. Needless to say, the views expressed here reflect those of the authors and not necessarily the Bank's research staff.

[1] A project sponsored by the Federal Reserve Bank of Philadelphia. By selective credit policies we mean any policy which is principally designed to alter the mix or, possibly, ownership distribution of financial assets and liabilities.

IRA KAMINOW and JAMES M. O'BRIEN

Three important issues are the subjects of this essay. The first concerns the goals of selective credit policies. These policies have been widely advocated as devices to reallocate real resources by altering credit flows. However, it would seem that credit and resource allocation are only proximate goals. That is, they are not ultimately desired for their own sakes but rather to forward higher level goals such as economic efficiency, social stability, and equality of opportunity. The first section of the essay is devoted to a discussion of the links between the proximate and ultimate objectives of selective credit policies. While it is difficult to get a quantifiable grip on ultimate goals, we do suggest ways in which conceptualization of their links to proximate goals might be improved.

The second section of the paper concerns the ability of selective credit policies to achieve the proximate objective of resource allocation. Much remains to be done before we can reach a definitive conclusion on this issue. However, partly because it is possible to borrow from other work on credit flows and partly because there is available literature of a direct applicability, probably more is known about this area of selective credit policies than any other.

The last issue discussed is the income or wealth incidence of credit allocation policies. There is also some literature here which can be useful, but it is not extensive. It is our view, however, that the literature on corporate income tax incidence, with appropriate modification, may help to answer questions related to the incidence of selective credit policies.

I. GOALS OF SELECTIVE CREDIT POLICIES

The surveys in this volume provide a fairly complete list of the various objectives which have been cited by advocates of selective credit policies. We do not propose here to discuss all of them or even to deal comprehensively with any one of them. Instead we will emphasize important issues which we feel have either been slighted in earlier studies or where we have disagreements with the views of some of our predecessors. The

2

discussion will be organized around three groups: the reallocation of real resources consistent with broad national objectives, the correction of credit market imperfections, and the control of sectoral impacts of business cycles and countercyclical policies. The organization of ultimate goals into these three classes has followed major categories that have developed in the literature and are not necessarily the most logical division of goals.

Resource Allocation Goals. In discussing selective credit policies, economists have suggested that a basic aim of such policies is the allocation of resources among different activities. At least in part, this objective derives from a purported inability of commodity markets to yield a socially desirable mixture of output (see, for example, Silber's discussion in this volume).[2] While numerous issues are associated with this goal, our main concern here is the criteria for determining the socially desirable composition of output and its relation to selective credit policies.

It would seem to us that resource allocation is not an ultimate concern of society. That is, we care about the output mix only because it influences the attainment of higher-order goals which might include Pareto optimality, equality of opportunity, social stability, etc. Yet the literature on resource allocation policies (and particularly selective credit policies) focuses mostly on the proximate goals of resource allocation or, more specifically, the attainment of more housing, more municipal services, and so on. This emphasis on proximate objectives manifests itself in one of two ways. In some analyses, ultimate goals are totally or largely ignored and the relation of resource allocation

---

[2]References to Silber, Young, Penner, Smith, etc. apply to studies in this volume by the respective authors. Also, see Lester C. Thurow, "Proposals for Rechanneling Funds to Meet Social Priorities," in *Policies for a More Competitive Financial System: A Review of the Report of the President's Commission on Financial Structure and Regulation*, Conference Series No. 8 (Federal Reserve Bank of Boston, 1972), pp. 177-89; and Lester C. Thurow in U. S., Congress, Senate, Committee on Banking, Housing and Urban Affairs, *Selective Credit Policies and Wage-Price Stabilization*, 92d Cong., 1st sess., 31 March, 1 and 7 April 1971, pp. 145-49. For studies concerned with housing programs, see Henry J. Aaron, *Shelter and Subsidies: Who Benefits from Federal Housing Policies?* (Washington: Brookings Institution, 1972); David Laidler, "Income Tax Incentives for Owner-Occupied Housing," Arnold C. Harberger and Martin J. Bailey, eds., *The Taxation of Income from Capital* (Washington: Brookings Institution, 1969), pp. 50-76; and Jerome Rothenberg, *Economic Evaluation of Urban Renewal: Conceptual Foundation of Benefit-Cost Analysis* (Washington: Brookings Institution, 1967).

3

policies to the proximate objectives tends to serve as the criterion for judging the worth of these policies. In those discussions in which ultimate goals are considered, the analysis is usually organized around specific proximate objectives. Thus, we are much more apt to find articles that seek to explain which ultimate objectives can be advanced by more housing (or education, or public transportation, etc.) than we are to find articles that ask what resource mix is most conducive to achieving one or more ultimate goals.

There are several reasons that might help to explain the focus on proximate objectives. First, popular and legislative concerns with resource allocation policies seem to have this focus.[3] Second, it is more difficult to quantify ultimate goals. It is easier to examine and specify the links between selective credit policies and the output of particular commodities than the links between these policies and, let us say, economic efficiency.

We do not necessarily fault the literature for its concentration on proximate objectives. Scientists should answer questions raised by policymakers and their constituents. And it may indeed be better to concentrate on issues which can be resolved with the tools available than on more important issues which cannot be so resolved. Nonetheless, the concentration on proximate objectives causes difficulties which might legitimately temper the enthusiasm with which judgments on the merits of credit or other reallocation policies are sometimes made. These difficulties might also provide an incentive for a research strategy that, over the long haul, focuses more on the ultimate goals in their own right.

First, consider those analyses which tend to judge the value of selective credit policies in terms of their ability to alter the output mix and not ultimate goals.[4] The limitation of this approach is clear. There is no reason to take for granted the links

---

[3] While discussions by legislators and the popular press often ostensibly deal with support for this or that sector, it seems fair to suggest that real concerns are with what we refer to as ultimate goals rather than commodities *per se*. For example, most discussions are couched in terms of achieving "a more equitable situation" or of "helping the needy," etc.

[4] See, for example, Jacob Cohen, "Integrating the Real and Financial Via the Linkage of Financial Flow," *Journal of Finance* 23 (1968): 1-27; D. C. Rao, "Selective Credit Policy: Is It Justified and Can It Work?" *Journal of Finance* 27 (1972): 473-79; and Richard G. Davis, "An Analysis of Quantitative Credit Controls and Related Devices," *Brookings Papers on Economic Activity*, No. 1 (1971): 65-96.

between ultimate and proximate objectives. If the presumed links don't hold, conclusions on the desirability of selective credit policies based on the policies' ability to advance proximate goals can be incorrect. The case for subsidizing housing is illustrative. Three ultimate goals have been alleged to be served by housing subsidy programs: the capturing of significant externalities,[5] the achievement of greater equality of opportunity,[6] and the furtherance of social stability.[7] Analysts of these housing goals argue that their achievement necessitates a more equal distribution of housing among different income groups, a reduction in the existence of slums and a reduction in racial discrimination.[8] Selective credit policies which, say, effectively shifted the composition of capital in favor of a larger housing stock may not effectively redistribute housing toward lower income groups, reduce slums or impact on racial discrimination in the housing market. Thus, such policies may be effective in the narrow sense of influencing the allocation of resources but not in the broader sense of furthering the chosen set of ultimate goals. At some point it would seem necessary to come to grips with the issue of the efficacy of selective credit policies in the broader context.

Now consider those studies that do look at ultimate goals but only as they relate to specific proximate objectives, such as more housing. Our difficulty with this approach is that it appears to yield misleading, if not incorrect, answers to the question of appropriate resource-allocation policies. Two factors suggest this. One is the necessity of a basic arbitrariness in the selection of commodities to examine. Thus, it may be the popular concern with housing, ecology, etc., that prompts economists to inquire into the possible social gains from policies aimed at these goods. Moreover, as fashions change, so, too, may the list of goods coming within the economist's purview. The second factor is

---

[5] Rothenberg, op. cit., and Aaron, op. cit.

[6] John F. Kain, "What Should Housing Policies Be?" *Journal of Finance* 29 (1974): 683-89.

[7] Laidler, op. cit., p. 53.

[8] As might be surmised from these conditions, it is still a much debated issue as to precisely what role housing, or more housing *per se*, plays in the achievement of ultimate goals. Indeed, some would argue that the basic issue is one of the distribution of income and that housing subsidies are simply a politically feasible method for redistributing income to low-income groups. Kain and Frank deLeeuw address themselves to this debate in their separate essays, "What Should Housing Policies Be?" *Journal of Finance* 29 (1974): 683-98 and 699-721.

that, considered in isolation, any good might appear to warrant some sort of governmental consideration. It is not particularly surprising, for example, that we can find externalities associated with housing. We might reasonably expect to be able to do this for other goods that we have yet to consider. Thus, without even denying the social attributes sometimes suggested for housing, the *relative* importance of these attributes may still be highly uncertain.

We would argue that a more neutral way to approach the issue is the strategy suggested earlier: What output mix best achieves our ultimate goals—economic efficiency, social stability, equality of opportunity, etc.? This approach should help to bring the achievement of ultimate objectives to the fore and decrease the emphasis on particular commodities. In competing for favoritism in research and, possibly, governmental attention, all goods would tend to start on the same footing. Moreover, it would force us to recognize the importance of our ignorance concerning the absolute or relative social merits of many (or most?) goods and, hence, the uncertainty that is likely to accompany the optimality of any resource-reallocation proposal. In these respects, this strategy is also likely to increase attention to the potential appropriateness of a "no-resource-reallocation" policy.

In concluding, we fully recognize the difficulties of pursuing a research approach which shifts the emphasis away from (specific) proximate objectives and toward ultimate objectives. And, given the current state of economic knowledge, we do not wish to imply that present practices should be abandoned. But we do suggest that the shortcomings of these practices should color policy conclusions and that, over the long haul, the suggested alternative strategy might provide a better guarantee that policy recommendations would indeed further ultimate goals.

Credit Market Imperfections. In addition to correcting for believed shortcomings of commodity markets, selective credit policies have been suggested to offset credit market imperfections.[9] These imperfections are defined in the traditional sense

---

[9] See, for example, the essays of Penner and Silber; Thurow in *Selective Credit Policies and Wage-Price Stabilization*, pp. 145-49; Thurow, op. cit., pp. 177-89; and Rothenberg, op. cit., p. 51.

that certain characteristics of credit markets produce deviations from Pareto optimality conditions. Imperfections mentioned most often appear to relate to the existence of nonprice credit rationing on the part of institutional lenders and the "customer relationship."[10] It is argued that these "imperfections" tend to discriminate against specific activities (for example, housing) and specific borrowers (for example, small businesses).

Recent studies appear to establish more firmly not only the existence of nonprice credit rationing but even the possibility that it is a part of equilibrium-lending behavior.[11] However, to conclude from this that selective credit policies are a proper response to such practices would seem to be premature.

In the presence of uncertainty of return or transactions and search costs, there is nothing inherently suboptimal about large customers receiving "preferential" treatment, long-term customer relationships, or the use by lenders of such nonprice terms as the "loan-to-value ratio" in evaluating individual loan applications. If anything, what should be explained is why such nonprice considerations would not, so to speak, have a price. Yet, the only rigorous explanation for postulating the inability of the interest rate mechanism to be the (final) arbiter of credit allocation relies on the uncertainty of loan repayment and lender maximization of profit (or risk-adjusted profit).[12] Neither of these underlying postulates need be market imperfections in the Pareto sense. Of course, this need not deny that there are

---

[10] The term nonprice credit rationing is used in the sense employed in the literature on credit rationing: A situation where the demand for loans exceeds the supply at the existing loan rate (see Dwight M. Jaffee and Franco Modigliani, "A Theory and Test of Credit Rationing,"*American Economic Review* 59 [1969]: 851). For the initial and defining study of the "customer relationship," see Donald R. Hodgman, *Commercial Bank Loan and Investment Policy* (Champaign: University of Illinois, Bureau of Economic and Business Research, 1963).

[11] A review of theoretical and empirical work is presented in Benjamin M. Friedman, *Credit Rationing: A Review*, Staff Economic Study (Washington: Board of Governors of the Federal Reserve System, 1972). See also William L. Silber and Murray E. Polakoff, "The Differential Effects of Tight Money: An Econometric Study,"*Journal of Finance* 25 (1970): 83-97; Duane G. Harris, "Some Evidence on Differential Lending Practices at Commercial Banks," *Journal of Finance* 28 (1973): 1303-11; Duane G. Harris, "Credit Rationing at Commercial Banks: Some Empirical Evidence," *Journal of Money, Credit and Banking* 6 (1974): 227-40; and Duane G. Harris, "Interest Rates, Non-Price Terms, and the Allocation of Bank Credit," *Southern Economic Journal* 40 (1974): 428-33.

[12] See Donald R. Hodgman, "Credit Risk and Credit Rationing," *Quarterly Journal of Economics* 65 (1960): 258-78; and Jaffee and Modigliani, op. cit., section 1, especially proposition 1.3.

other causes of interest rate rigidities and, consequently, non-price credit rationing—particularly over short or cyclical periods. But, to date, we appear to have little more than casual speculation concerning these alternative sources of loan rate stickiness (aside from usury ceilings).[13] There would, therefore, seem little to go on in evaluating the optimality or non-optimality of credit market solutions.

Nonprice credit rationing, customer relations, and so on deal with purported credit market imperfections which are at least partly believed to be inherent in free-market processes. Both supporters and critics of selective credit policies cite Government regulations as another market imperfection. Financial market restrictions singled out most often are regulations on deposit and loan rates. This gives rise to the argument that even if unfettered credit markets are efficient, selective credit policies may be a second-best solution in actual credit markets.[14]

The important and valid point of this contention is that it reduces the relevance of the efficiency of free markets in judging the desirability of credit policies in already regulated markets. This is so because the inefficiencies of one regulation may be offset by a second. Still, it seems to us that the significance of free-market efficiency is not completely eliminated. If unregu-

---

[13] Along these lines, we might note the common tendency to cite oligopolistic lending practices as helping to explain loan rate rigidities and the customer relationship. (See Thurow, "Proposals for Channeling Funds to Meet Social Priorities," op. cit., pp. 177-89; Donald R. Hodgman, "The Deposit Relationship and Commercial Bank Investment Behavior," *Review of Economics and Statistics* 42 (1961): 257-68; Edward J. Kane and Bruce G. Malkiel, "Bank Portfolio Allocation, Deposit Variability, and the Availability Doctrine," *Quarterly Journal of Economics* 79 (1965): 125; and Jaffee and Modigliani, ibid). Again, this citation would seem to be more in the way of casual suggestion than resulting from any serious presentation of theory or evidence to support the position. The analytical models developed to explain credit rationing and the customer relationship generally are quite compatible with a high degree of atomistic-type lending behavior (albeit with regulatory constraints and long-run profit concerns). Moreover, the observation of loan rate sluggishness and "deposit leadership" (a bank changing its loan rate which is later followed by others) may reflect competitive market behavior under demand uncertainty and disequilibrium rather than the oligopolistic pricing procedure that is often suggested. See Edmund S. Phelps et al., *Microeconomic Foundations for Employment and Inflation Theory* (New York: W. W. Norton and Company, 1970) and Kenneth J. Arrow, "Toward a Theory of Price Adjustment," Moses Abramovitz, ed., *The Allocation of Economic Resources* (Stanford, Calif.: Stanford University Press, 1959), pp. 41-51. The issue of defining economic efficiency during periods of disequilibrium is discussed below.

[14] See Thurow, "Proposals for Rechanneling Funds to Meet Social Priorities," op. cit., pp. 177-89.

lated credit markets were to represent a superior level of economic efficiency, then it is insufficient to argue simply that properly designed selective credit policies will improve the efficiency of existing credit markets. In this situation it also becomes important to know how the attainment of a "local" optimum relates to the attainment of a more "global" optimum—that is, unregulated markets. If, for example, introducing more regulations reduces the likelihood of ever attaining a situation of free credit markets, the gains of a second-best solution would be uncertain.

Moreover, second-best gains must net out any new inefficiencies which the regulations might create. These new inefficiencies would include the possibility of subsequent regulation designed to yield "third-", "fourth-", etc.-, best solutions as problems with the initial legislation became apparent. The whole set of new regulations might combine to be inferior to the initial level of economic efficiency. The potential relevance of this possibility is suggested by the impressionistic conclusions of some economists that credit policies once instituted tend to expand.[15] In short, while the existence of regulatory or other market imperfections opens the door to second-best solutions in the form of selective credit policies, there must still be an attempt to show that such policies can be expected to produce even a constrained optimum.

Finally, we note a specific second-best argument concerning usury ceilings that have been established by state governments. In this case, the decentralized nature of authority may make it more difficult than otherwise to eliminate these regulations. This could add greater force to the argument that regulatory imperfections can be "undone" only by a corresponding credit policy at the Federal level—for example, one that subsidized mortgage or other selective credit flows during periods of high interest rates. This argument for selective credit policies raises

---

[15] For a detailed study of West European experiences, see Donald R. Hodgman, *National Monetary Policies and International Monetary Cooperation* (Boston: Little, Brown and Company, 1974). For considerations of some U.S. experiences, see Edward J. Kane, "Short-Changing the Small Saver: Federal Government Discrimination against the Small Saver during the Vietnam War," *Journal of Money, Credit and Banking* 2 (1970): 513-22; and James M. O'Brien, "Federal Regulation of Stock Market Credit: A Need for Reconsideration," *Business Review* of the Federal Reserve Bank of Philadelphia, July-August 1974, pp. 23-33.

questions about the appropriate division of authority between Federal and state governments. But there is the additional point that state and local financial regulations are far from uniform, and it may be exceedingly difficult to design a selective credit policy at a national level sufficient to overcome this hetero-geneity. That is, credit market imperfections associated with usury ceilings are likely to be highly specific to particular localities or regions and conceivably might not be amenable to corrections of national selective credit policies.

On the whole, arguments concerning the existence of credit market imperfections would at present appear to provide little basis for selective credit policies. This is not to deny that credit market imperfections exist, but that claims to specific imperfec-tions or suggestions that credit policies will improve the func-tioning of credit markets appear to be little more than casual speculation rather than the result of serious analytical study. The popularity of the view that credit markets are subject to significant malfunctions does, however, indicate the need for serious research on this issue.

Efficiency and Countercyclical Policy. Apart from the general efficiency questions that have been discussed above, there are issues of efficiency which bear on the relation between selective credit policies and countercyclical policies. By and large, these issues are not unique to selective credit policies, but relate to the more general question of the efficiency consequences of the sectoral impacts of cycles and macroeconomic policies. They may be put into two related categories. First, certain policies which are designed to affect the aggregate of labor and com-modity markets are considered to have "adverse" impacts on subsets of these markets. An example of this phenomenon is the claim that restrictive monetary policy would be more efficient if it bore less heavily on housing production and more on the production of other commodities. Second, it has been suggested that particular commodity and labor markets have cycles of their own which may or may not coincide with general business cycles and that the existence of these cycles is ineffi-cient because of factors such as a "bunching" of production over time.

10

Selective credit policies enter these two issues because they have been widely suggested as devices to improve the workings of markets during cycles and periods in which countercyclical policy was applied. The discussion below does not relate particularly to the efficiency of selective credit policies but to the logically prior issues of the efficiency aspects of cycles and countercyclical policy and hence the value of redressing any inefficiencies whether by selective credit policies or other means. Much of the discussion earlier in this section which was specific to selective credit policies bears on the particular role of these controls in relation to cyclical issues.

Typical discussions of efficiency issues surrounding the sectoral dimension of cycles are loosely broken down into a two-stage optimization problem.[16] First, a loss function containing macro variables (for example, gross national product, the rate of inflation, etc.) is considered to be minimized. Then, constrained by the solution to the "macro" problem, the optimal sectoral impacts are determined based on "micro" efficiency criteria. These criteria are usually direct transplants of standard Pareto criteria for pure exchange or fixed-income economies. More specifically, it is argued that for each level of national income (and in particular for each level or path of national income determined by purely macroeconomic considerations), there exists a set of optimal sectoral distributions of the available product. The set satisfies the usual marginal conditions and in the simplest case may be taken as the contract curve in an

---

[16] Most discussions of these issues contain the elements we outline below although they are often loose and not as structured as the summary presented here. We acknowledge the danger that in trying to structure the discussion we have overdrawn the issues. While it appears to us that we have captured the essence of the discussions, the reader may nevertheless want to bear this danger in mind. For illustrations of these discussions, see Lyle E. Gramley, "Short-Term Cycles in Housing Production: An Overview of the Problem and Possible Solutions," *Federal Reserve Staff Study: Ways to Moderate Fluctuations in Housing Construction* (Washington: Board of Governors of the Federal Reserve System, 1972), pp. 1-67; Thomas Mayer, "Financial Guidelines and Credit Controls," *Journal of Money, Credit and Banking* 4 (1972): 360-74; Peter Fortune, "Discussion," *Credit Allocation Techinques and Monetary Policy*, Conference Series No. 8 (Federal Reserve Bank of Boston, 1973), pp. 42-49: and William L. Silber, "The Excess Burden of Monetary Policy: A Discussion of the Hodgman and Mayer Papers," *Journal of Money, Credit and Banking* 4 (1972): 414-18.

Edgeworth-box diagram. Once the optimization criteria are so established, there follow some estimates of how actual experience compares with the optimal distribution and finally some discussion of how to minimize the gap between actual and ideal.

Many economists suggest that the gap can be minimized if allocational decisions are left to market forces. They argue that at most the authorities should try to stabilize the macro economy. Others claim that, if a discretionary stabilization policy is pursued, it is logically impossible to leave the allocational problem solely to the market. Adherents of this view argue that different mixes of macro-policy tools which can achieve the same macro objectives will have different sectoral impacts. And, since authorities make a choice on the mix of macro tools, they must necessarily be making a choice on the sectoral impacts.[17] Following this view, the decision is not *whether* to intervene at the sectoral level, but *how*. Of course, it is still possible to reject selective credit policies because they are inappropriate vehicles for sectoral intervention in a cyclical context but not because such intervention itself is inappropriate.

It is our belief that neither view is correct. However, the view that *laissez-faire* is logically incompatible with stabilization policy does suggest an important insight—that sectoral impacts should not be ignored in establishing the optimization criterion for stabilization policies. Its error is the belief that policymakers can arbitrarily choose the mix of policy tools they use to minimize the macro-loss function. Put otherwise, it presumes that policymakers have one or more extra policy tools available to achieve macro objectives. Actually, however, it is more likely that there are no "extra" policy tools so that the mix of tools which will minimize the macro-loss function is unique. There are two reasons for this. First, society has several objectives and

---

[17] This is stated most explicitly in Rao, "Selective Credit Policy: Is it Justified and Can It Work?" pp. 473-79, as reported in Silber's study in this volume. However, this view follows closely in the tradition of writers such as Guttentag who argue that sectoral impacts can be improved by appeal to heavier reliance on fiscal policy to achieve desired countercyclical goals. For additional illustrations of this view see quotations in Young's essay.

it is not obvious that it has more tools than goals.[18] Second, as Young reminds us in his paper, there are no extraneous policy tools in a world of uncertainty regardless of the number of goals relative to tools. Thus, it is logically *possible* for policymakers to follow a unique optimum stabilization policy (in the sense of minimizing the macro-loss function) and leave the allocational problem solely to the market.

However, the problem with a "let-the-market-take-care-of-the-sectors" view is the essential arbitrariness of arguing that intervention is appropriate at the "macro" level but not at the sectoral or "micro" level. There are strong currents in economic thought which are moving to blur the previously sharp distinction between macroeconomics and microeconomics. If it is possible to improve on the market solution in the aggregate of labor markets, it may be possible to improve on it in other markets as well.[19]

Cycles and countercyclical policy are being extensively explored from the perspective of market disequilibrium in the context of a Walrasian framework. That is, economic slowdowns are viewed as conditions of excess supply in the labor market and corresponding excess demands elsewhere. From this vantage point, the stabilization problem is not one of too high (low) production resulting from excess (inadequate) demand in a Keynesian sense. It is instead one of sustained disequilibrium in markets that results from sticky relative prices.[20] Consequently, countercyclical policy is seen as an attempt to accelerate or implement attainment of a general Walrasian equilibrium. The sectoral efficiency problem of countercyclical policy is, thus, not one of optimally distributing a fixed product among alternative uses but rather one of finding the optimal path back to general equilibrium.

The advantage of looking at the problem this way is that it points out the basic similarity between "micro" and "macro"

---

[18] According to the theory of economic policy, in a world of certainty there are extraneous policy tools only if the number of tools exceeds the number of goals.

[19] Yet, the arguments against sectoral intervention may also be used to argue against intervention at the "macro" level (as indeed they have been).

[20] We do not mean to imply here that we are talking about substantively different problems, but merely different ways of viewing the same problem.

cyclical problems. Both result from the inability of markets to adjust quickly to a notional equilibrium.[21] They differ from each other only in terms of the level of aggregation. If sticky relative prices mean that markets in the aggregate require assistance in adjusting, it might well imply that certain specific markets need assistance as well. Thus, sectoral impacts of cyclical phenomena will depend more on which relative prices are sticky than on traditional welfare criteria. The "invisible hand" does not put everything into place at once. It is in this sense that selective credit policies can be suggested to overcome stickiness and rigidities in certain credit markets.

A related advantage of viewing the problem within a market disequilibrium framework is that it forces examination of the efficiency aspects of the entire cyclical and countercyclical policy process simultaneously. This compares with the two-step procedure in which the optimal "macro" policy is frequently analyzed. The more traditional procedure ignores possible efficiency losses in selecting "macro" variables without reference to "micro" implications.

Unfortunately, viewing the problem from the market disequilibrium perspective presents a number of problems. We cannot rely as easily on the traditional theory of welfare economics since our concern has shifted to the efficiency of the path of adjustment to equilibrium. Moreover, the optimal mix of monetary and fiscal policy becomes far more complex to determine because we cannot limit criteria of success to a few easily quantifiable, highly aggregated variables such as the variance in national product. Instead, we must consider a range of disaggregated impacts of policy. In addition, we are likely to face complicated feedback and simultaneity problems. Young has pointed out that the introduction of additional instruments changes the optimal fiscal policy/monetary policy mix insofar as purely macro criteria are concerned. That is to say, introduction of a new instrument (such as selective credit policies) in order to handle sectoral problems will alter the macroeconomic impact of traditional monetary and fiscal policies.

---

[21] See Herschel I. Grossman, "Money, Interest, and Prices in Market Disequilibrium," *Journal of Political Economy* 79 (1971): 943-61.

In sum, we must conclude that the state of the art must be considerably advanced before making any statements regarding efficiency criteria of countercyclical policy. It may be possible to argue for or against a "micro" interventionist policy during cycles (whether selective credit policies or others), but we believe it cannot be done simply on the basis of optimally distributing a highly aggregated measure of national product. Concentrating on aggregates may be an appropriate abstraction for some problems of macroeconomics, but hardly when the very issue is sectoral impacts.

II. THE ISSUE OF EFFICACY

Quite apart from the question of whether selective credit policies should be used to allocate real resources is whether they can be so used. Whether credit policies can achieve their resource distributional goals is, of course, an empirical question.

Some Issues Involved in Testing the Efficacy of Selective Credit Policies. The simplest and most direct test of the ability of selective credit policies to influence the flows of real resources is the use of a reduced-form econometric model. Such a model can be used to test whether changes in a specified instrument (the selective credit policy) have "caused" changes in resource allocation or the level of production in the intended directions and over the intended time period. However, reduced form tests of the ability of selective credit policies to influence real resources have not been very popular. This is partly because it is not always possible to use them. Reduced form tests, for example, cannot handle anticipated structural changes. In particular, it is impossible to test the likely impacts of a proposed policy in the absence of a structural model. Once we open the analysis to include tests of policies within a structural framework, the range of questions to be resolved broadens markedly. Three have turned out to be of particular significance in the existing literature: (1) the appropriate transmission mechanism, (2) the value of general as opposed to partial analysis, and (3) the

15

usefulness of "incomplete tests" (that is, tests that examine only some of the links connecting policy instruments and policy goals).

With rare exceptions—such as the papers by Rao-Kaminow and Wood in this volume—there have been few attempts at rigorous study of the transmission mechanism linking controls and their intended resource distributional goals. However, while the theoretical development remains primitive, two loosely defined views can be discerned. According to one view, credit controls work directly through flows of funds. This view argues that within any portfolio, the demand for particular assets depends on the level of certain corresponding liabilities in that portfolio. It implies that the liability side of the portfolio is first determined, and then the asset side. So, for example, Jacob Cohen writes:

What is then needed is financial market analysis in which interest rates and financial flows mutually determine each other. From the solution for financial markets, financial flows then become explanatory variables in expenditures equations.[22]

The asymmetrical nature of this approach—which even in equilibrium makes liability demand a function of prices, but asset demand a function of the quantity and mix of liabilities— seems peculiar and difficult to justify on theoretical grounds. There exists, however, another variant of the flow-of-funds view which seems somewhat more plausible. We might call this variant the selective credit availability doctrine. This view mirrors in its theoretical underpinnings the more general credit availability doctrine. In the general doctrine, credit availability is seen as a constraint on the demand for assets which are financed through credit. Extending it to the selective case, the demand for particular kinds of assets will be constrained by the availability of particular kinds of finance or liabilities. In this view, the quantity of liabilities enters the demand for assets only when there is disequilibrium in credit markets[23]—that is, only when the demand for certain types of credit falls short of

---

[22] Cohen, op. cit., p. 2.
[23] See Guttentag for a more complete statement of this view.

the supply at existing market prices. Hence, selective credit policies work to relax (tighten) constraints on desired (undesired) assets.

The alternative to the flow-of-funds view is based on the more traditional notion that the demand for goods and the means of finance are determined simultaneously. The variables that determine these demands are relative prices (including interest rates) and some initial scale condition such as endowment or net worth. Demand and supply equations for both financial and real assets are "solved" by the market to determine equilibrium prices and quantities. In this view, selective credit policies work by shifting demand or supply functions and hence altering the final equilibrium rates and quantities.

The two views can be reconciled in principle. Selective credit availability can be viewed as a disequilibrium notion, which is relevant over short periods. The more traditional view can be seen as providing the equilibrium solution and therefore is perhaps relevant over longer-run periods. Thus, for example, imperfections in credit markets, information costs, and response lags can permit credit availability to constrain asset purchases in the short run. In the longer run, normal market pressures work to remove these constraints and force traditional equilibrium.

This proposed reconciliation is similar to that exploited in macroeconomic analysis. There, a distinction is frequently drawn between "effective" and "notional" aggregate demand. Effective aggregate demand is constrained by income so that increases in income yield higher levels of demand. "Notional" demand, however, recognizes that an individual's income is ultimately subject to his decision-making process and not a parameter which must be passively accepted. Income serves as a constraint only as long as fundamental market forces, such as relative price adjustments, do not have a chance to work themselves out.[24] Notional demand, however, is relevant to the "true" equilibrium after market forces have completely worked through.

---

[24] Beyond that period, factors such as the quantities of human and nonhuman capital become the relevant constraints.

Ray Fair and Dwight Jaffee have extended the equilibrium-disequilibrium framework to flow of funds models in which interest rates cannot be counted on to equilibrate financial markets immediately.[25] In our view, an equilibrium-disequilibrium flow-of-funds model of this sort can be integrated into an analogous expenditure model. In such a model, effective asset demands would depend on credit constraints in disequilibrium but these constraints would disappear in the equilibrium state when notional demands become relevant.

Thus, we believe it is possible to think of and construct an integrated system in which credit availability and the more traditional view both operate. Determination of the relevant time periods is, of course, an empirical question and an important one. In the extreme, the disequilibrium period can be so short or the period required to reach equilibrium so long as to be empirically irrelevant. So, extremists can reject the empirical plausibility of one or the other notion without rejecting its theoretical possibility. However, it is certainly possible to switch between the two views according to the policy in question and the relevant time horizon, and there is no need to associate particular analysts exclusively with either view.

Another question to be resolved in analyzing or testing the efficacy of selective credit policies—and one that has not always been squarely faced—is the relative value of general versus partial analysis. In establishing a structural model to test the impact of policies on goals, one must decide the extent to which attention can be limited to one or two markets of direct concern while ignoring interactions and feedbacks with other markets. In some cases, a prior judgment can be made that a simple partial framework gives a good first approximation because interactions are relatively unimportant and/or slow and hence not "worth the candle" of taking them into account. In other cases, however, there may be a significant danger that these partial impacts will be totally and quickly wiped out if the analyses are extended to include all reverberations through the economy.

---

[25] Ray C. Fair and Dwight M. Jaffee, "Methods of Estimation for Markets in Disequilibrium," *Econometrica* 40 (1972): 497-514; Dwight M. Jaffee, "The Specification of Disequilibrium in Flow of Funds Models," mimeographed.

18

A final but important point in evaluating the literature on the ability of selective credit policies to affect real resource allocation is the value of "incomplete" tests. It is possible to think of the structure which connects the instruments to the goals of policy as a series of "links." For example, we might view a simple selective availability mechanism as being divisible into three "links." The first link is that between the instrument and the availability of a particular kind of credit. The second is the connection between the availability of credit and demand for particular commodities. The third is the relation between the commodity demands and the output mix. By "incomplete" test we mean a test that examines the validity of only some but not all the links connecting instrument to goal. Incomplete tests cannot by themselves provide evidence sufficient to demonstrate the ability of controls to alter the real resource mix, and as such are not entirely satisfactory. The missing links must be filled in either by appeal to evidence accumulated elsewhere or prior—but untested—expectations. As we will see, the issue of the value of "incomplete" tests arises because of the paucity of empirical work addressed specifically to selective credit policies.

The Literature. The four articles in this volume that survey the existing literature on selective credit policies provide a rather comprehensive discussion of the current state of statistical evidence as it bears on the efficacy issue. Moreover, the survey authors themselves represent a range of views on the three questions we have just discussed and in this sense comprise something of a microcosm of the profession. This disparity of views accounts in no small way for the fact that they reach different conclusions about whether selective credit policies can influence the real resource mix. Guttentag and Smith seem to be most certain that selective credit controls can have a substantial and predictable impact on the allocation of real resources. Penner is more doubtful of their efficacy, and Silber does not believe appropriate evidence has been accumulated to make a judgment. There does, however, seem to be some agreement that the longer controls remain in force, the greater will be the feedbacks and the less effective will be the controls.

Aside from the direct conclusions on the efficacy of credit policies, however, one thread seems to run through the survey articles. The empirical evidence on the efficacy question leaves much to be desired. Most evidence on the efficacy is based on incomplete tests—tests that examine only some of the links between instrument and goal. Instances of complete tests of actual or hypothetical controls are extremely rare. Only a few papers were reported by Smith and Silber as attempts at comprehensive studies addressed specifically to issues of the impact of selective credit policies on real resource allocation. The reported papers conclude that controls can influence real resource allocation. But Silber, and to a lesser extent Smith, express some reservations about the studies. The balance of the evidence in the survey articles is based on incomplete tests and tests not directly designed to examine the effects of selective credit policies. In arriving at conclusions regarding efficacy, the contributors were forced to fill in missing pieces and "sew" together conclusions from various papers.

While Guttentag (for housing) and Smith (for consumer goods) agree on the efficacy of selective credit policies, they differ on transmission mechanisms. Guttentag favors the selective availability view which pervades his paper. The bulk of his evidence and discussion is related to the links between selective credit controls and the credit mix. A linkage between the credit mix and real demands is apparently presumed. Smith, in contrast, emphasizes a more traditional view. He bases his conclusion in part on the linkage between the demand for consumer durables and various credit terms. The evidence supplied by Smith presumes at the minimum some linkage between selective credit policies and credit terms paid by the consumer.

The value of the evidence provided by Guttentag and Smith (on links between credit terms and real demands) can only be assessed in the context of the prior views of the reader. There must be some consistency of views between the author and the reader in terms of the appropriateness of the favored transmission mechanism and the validity of supplying the "missing links" if the evidence is to be viewed as useful.

20

Two theoretical papers in this volume shed some light on this issue. Wood argues that credit restrictions on business firms will redistribute production and investment over time in a predictable way and "there is little danger that firms will be able to escape completely from the effects of anticipated [or unanticipated] controls even if account is taken of new financial institutions and instruments that may be devised to assist the evasion of these effects." This conclusion, rigorously derived, is consistent with Guttentag's view that credit restrictions impinge on real resource allocation. More narrowly, it supports a portion of his transmission mechanism by which housing can be encouraged by discouraging corporate investment through corporate borrowing restraints.

Rao-Kaminow raise some questions about the relevance of both the Guttentag and Smith evidence. Rao-Kaminow conclude that one cannot necessarily draw equilibrium efficacy conclusions on the basis of partial analysis. In particular, with respect to Smith, they argue it is possible to envision a model in which real demands depend on credit terms (that is, the interest elasticities are non-zero) but in which selective credit policies do not alter the real resource mix (or at least not in the predicted way). That is, Smith's evidence on the (partial) relation between credit terms and real demands ignores various market adjustments and feedbacks so that by itself the evidence is not conclusive. However, as we noted, it is possible—especially in the absence of other evidence—to take the view that the second and subsequent round impacts change the conclusions very little, particularly over some suitably short time horizon.

With respect to the Guttentag paper, the Rao-Kaminow analysis can be used to show that it is possible to imagine a world in which real flows do not mirror financial flows.[26] It should be pointed out that since Rao-Kaminow use a (somewhat) general equilibrium analysis, it is not as applicable to short-run dynamic problems as is the Wood study which is dynamic but partial. Wood deals with distributing various ac-

---

[26] This conclusion does not apply directly to the paper but may be surmised from the discussion in section II-G of Rao-Kaminow.

21

tivities over time and emphasizes microfirm behavior at the expense of market behavior. The Rao-Kaminow study, however, is static and general: it has no time dimension and emphasizes market adjustments.

We noted that there is a serious lack of papers dealing explicitly and comprehensively with the links between instruments and proximate goals of selective credit policies. In analyzing taxation and credit policies, Penner attempts to solve the problem by connecting links that have been forged independently. Thus, he devotes part of his survey to the evidence linking instruments to the cost of capital and then discusses the evidence or the links between the cost of capital and real investment.

The paper suggests that links between instruments and the cost of capital and between the cost of capital and real investment hold. However, the approach can be viewed as making the best of a weak literature; it is of necessity somewhat naive because it merely "adds up" partial responses and, as a result, ignores feedbacks. In this respect, it is similar to the Smith evidence and subject to the same criticism and defense we discussed there. Penner, however, seems less willing to accept uncritically the partial evidence imposed on him by the literature. He points out how second and subsequent round portfolio adjustments may (and he believes will) work to limit the impact of selective credit policies even if the partial effect might be strong. It is because of these impacts that Penner is somewhat skeptical on the effectiveness of selective credit policies in reallocating resources.

The principal framework of the survey article by Silber and the empirical estimates presented by O'Brien are in the general equilibrium spirit. The emphasis in these papers is on substitutability among assets and liabilities. Once measured empirically, the degree of substitutability can be "plugged" into theoretical models such as those found in Rao-Kaminow to determine the likely impact of selective credit policies after feedbacks have had a chance to work. These papers are among the few attempts to try systematically to apply empirical estimates on asset substitutabilities to the efficacy of selective policies.

The evidence reported in the Silber and O'Brien papers suggests that substitutabilities among financial assets may be low.[27] This is a necessary condition for certain types of controls to be useful in reallocating resources. In the spirit of the approach of these two papers, however, no conclusion can be drawn on the efficacy of controls from this evidence alone, and neither Silber nor O'Brien draws such conclusions. Indeed, among the authors of survey articles in this volume, Silber is the least certain on the efficacy issue, withholding judgment until more comprehensive and better designed research is forthcoming.

In concluding, the evidence accumulated on the ability of selective credit policies to influence the real resource mix has tended to be indirect and incomplete. Not infrequently, it has been necessary to borrow conclusions from work designed to answer other questions. There is a great deal of work that needs to be done before all the holes are filled.

Yet, of that evidence that has been accumulated, little contradicts the view that the selective credit policies can have a predictable impact on real resource allocation. To a large extent, therefore, the debate over the efficacy of controls comes down to the question of how much weight the bits of evidence collected so far can support. Those who believe selective credit policies work seem to view the partial evidence as adequate and, at least over a sufficiently short (but empirically meaningful) period of time, portfolio adjustments and other feedbacks are secondary. Those who do not believe controls work even over relatively short periods of time place much weight on the likelihood that these feedbacks reverse the conclusions of simple partial analysis.

III. THE ISSUE OF INCIDENCE

Selective credit policies will likely have differential impacts on the income and wealth of individuals. As suggested in the

---

[27] Silber's time-series evidence may refer more to short-run asset behavior. O'Brien's evidence on household asset behavior, however, is based on cross-section data.

first section and in the discussions by Guttentag, Penner, and Silber, income or wealth incidence could be an important issue in judging the merits of these policies. Indeed, in the minds of the general public, it could be overriding. Despite its importance, there are still relatively few studies which have dealt with the incidence of selective credit policies.[28]

Theoretical Issues. Attempts to measure the incidence of selective credit policies have generally sought to determine changes in income yielded by the asset(s) at which the policies are directly aimed. These yield studies have tried, implicitly or explicitly, to estimate the asset's yield change and the new equilibrium quantity. The distribution of income gains or losses among, say, different income classes is then estimated from the ownership distribution of the asset. A variant of this approach is to determine the new equilibrium (yield and quantity) and then proceed to calculate the appropriate areas under the demand and/or supply schedules. Gains and losses are determined by the difference between these areas and those under the respective curves in the old equilibrium. The advantage of this latter approach is the inclusion of changes in consumer or producer surpluses in the calculating of welfare changes. A disadvantage is the greater difficulty in making such calculations—the need to know or hypothesize entire portions of the supply and demand schedules.[29]

---

[28] Studies which have considered the incidence of selective credit policies include studies on the tax exemption of municipal bonds such as David J. Ott and Allan H. Meltzer, *Federal Tax Treatment of State and Local Securities* (Washington: The Brookings Institution, 1963) and on the deposit interest-rate ceiling such as Kane, op. cit., pp. 513-22. Studies of housing subsidy incidence have also considered, directly or indirectly, the incidence of mortgage subsidies. See, for example, Henry J. Aaron, "Income Taxes and Housing," *American Economic Review* 60 (1970):789-806; Henry J. Aaron, *Shelter and Subsidies;* Laidler, "Income Tax Incentives for Owner-Occupied Housing," Harberger and Bailey, eds., op. cit., pp. 50-76; and Laurence J. and Michelle J. White, "The Tax Subsidy to Owner-Occupied Housing: Who Benefits?" University of Pennsylvania, 1975, mimeographed. While concerned primarily with the efficacy of mortgage subsidy programs, Penner and Silber, "The Interaction between Federal Credit Programs and the Impact on the Allocation of Credit," *American Economic Review* 63 (1973): 838-52, also has incidence implications for such programs. For a study of the cost of Federal Credit programs, see Murray L. Weidenbaum, "Subsidies in Federal Credit Programs." in U.S., Congress, Joint Economic Committee, *The Economics of Federal Subsidy Programs,* 92d Cong., 2d sess., 8 May 1972, part 1, pp.106-19.

[29] While most studies use the former approach, Laidler, op. cit., pp. 50-76; and White and White, op. cit., were concerned with the welfare gains and losses as measured by the areas under the demand curve.

We might first note that it is somewhat surprising that little consideration has been given to asset value changes in incidence analysis.[30] Credit policies are also likely to impact on the capital value of assets, and the consequent incidence effects need not be determinable from those of asset yield changes. Policies which, say, raise asset yields may lower their capital value, implying potential gains for asset purchasers but possibly capital losses for initial owners. Thus, analysis which is restricted to the effects of asset yield or income changes will generally not be enough to give a complete picture of incidence.

However, we believe that a conceptually more important shortcoming of incidence studies is the use of a partial equilibrium approach. As a rule, the procedure has been to examine incidence only for the market being directly affected by the policy. It is assumed the only displacement from equilibrium is that produced by the subsidy- or tax-induced shift in that market's demand or supply curve.[31] There are several potentially important limitations to this approach. One is the usual problem of failing to take account of "secondary" shifts in the demand and supply curves of the subsidized or taxed market resulting from equilibrium changes in other markets. Since these "secondary" shifts may be important, ignoring them in calculating gains or losses is quite arbitrary.[32]

A second limitation stems from incidence depending on changes in the sum total of income from all assets (and labor), not just the subsidized or taxed asset. Conclusions, for example, that home owners benefit from housing credit subsidies will be incomplete until the effects of the program on other sources of income are also determined. This point is emphasized by the fact that subsidies must be financed from some source(s) of

---

[30] For an exception, see White and White, op. cit.

[31] For example, if the selective credit policy is a subsidy to mortgage purchasers, the policy effects are essentially assumed to be captured by an outward movement in the mortgage demand curve directly produced by the subsidy. See for example, the theoretical frameworks specified in Penner and Silber, op. cit., Aaron, "Income Taxes and Housing," op. cit., pp. 789-806; Aaron, *Shelter and Subsidies;* and Laidler, op. cit., pp. 50-76.

[32] This is not to say that there has been no recognition of this general equilibrium consideration but, rather, that there is presently a lack of formal attempts to incorporate it into conceptual frameworks or empirical work.

income (or tax revenues must be dispersed). Thus, for example, it might be possible that significant gainers from housing credit subsidies could be significant losers from some other source(s) of income.

A significant departure from this partial equilibrium approach is the corporate income-tax studies based on Harberger's general equilibrium analysis.[33] With some modifications, Harberger's framework may be applicable for analyzing the incidence of selective credit policies. One useful change would be to allow for the existence of different types of assets—rather than simply positing the existence of a homogeneous factor of production called capital which, like labor, can be employed in several uses. Introducing different (that is, imperfectly substitutable) assets would allow for consideration of different incidence impacts across wealth owners. A related suggestion is the need to introduce finance into the analysis. In analyzing the incidence of selective credit policies, one could very well want to distinguish equity from debt capital and borrowers from lenders.

Furthermore, as implied earlier, it would be beneficial to allow for changes in the prices of assets. Harberger explicitly assumed capital mobility and perfectly competitive markets. This ensures that in equilibrium the average rate of return to capital will equal its marginal rate which, in turn, implies that asset prices will not vary as we move from one equilibrium to another.[34] By relaxing either the assumption of perfect capital mobility or perfect competition, we can expect that movements to a new equilibrium will alter both asset yields and prices.[35]

---

[33] Arnold C. Harberger, "The Incidence of the Corporation Income Tax," *Journal of Political Economy*, 70 (1962): 215-40.

[34] To see this, denote P_1 the current equilibrium market price of a unit of asset i after some exogenous shock; P_0, the initial price; R, the average (perpetual) return to asset i per dollar of investment; and r, the current market rate of return or yield on asset i. Using the equilibrium condition that the market value of an asset will equal the present value of its return we can derive $P_1/P_0 = R/r$. For Harberger, R = e where e is the marginal value product of capital. Since in the long run equilibrium r = e, asset prices would be fixed in a Harberger-type model.

[35] For an attempt at a multiple asset analysis of incidence see James M. O'Brien, "The Incidence of Selective Subsidization and Taxation of Asset Income: A Multi-Asset Approach," unpublished manuscript, 1975.

Empirical Evidence. Despite the suggested shortcomings of the studies dealing with the incidence of housing (mortgage) and municipal bond subsidies, their empirical conclusions are not without interest. Generally, these studies indicate that such subsidies go primarily to upper-middle or upper-income classes.[36] However, this result appears to be due to the fact that existing programs may not be well-suited for income redistribution, and is not necessarily a general property of selective credit policies. For example, because deposits are more equally distributed than mortgage debt,[37] a selective credit policy (such as deposit rate ceilings) which benefits mortgage debtors at the expense of depositors will redistribute income from lower- to upper-income groups. And credit subsidies effectively paid for by Federal income taxes (including tax exemptions) will do little to redistribute income because assets and debts are usually distributed toward upper-income groups at least as much as Federal income taxes.[38]

Finally, it should be emphasized that these income incidence results may say relatively little about the distribution of particular assets—such as housing—among income groups. Income and wealth incidence depend on the impacts of subsidies or taxes on asset yields and asset values. However the effect of, say, a mortgage subsidy on the distribution of housing depends

---

[36] We consider here the housing or mortgage subsidies as studied by Aaron, "Income Taxes and Housing," op. cit., pp. 780-806; Aaron, *Shelter and Subsidies;* Laidler, op. cit., pp. 50-76; and Kane, op. cit., pp. 513-22; and the municipal bond tax exemption studies such as Ott and Meltzer, op. cit. The results of several of these studies are discussed by Penner. However, Aaron, *Shelter and Subsidies,* (pp. 74-90), suggested that the FHA mortgage-guarantee program may tend to favor lower-income families. Also these subsidy programs do not include those housing credit programs specifically designed for low-income classes.

[37] Kane, op. cit., pp. 513-22.

[38] Various types of asset and debt distributions among different income classes can be found in the "basic tables" in Dorothy S. Projector and Gertrude S. Weiss, *Survey of Financial Characteristics of Consumers: Federal Reserve Technical Paper* (Washington: Board of Governors of the Federal Reserve System, 1966). For the distribution of Federal income taxes among different income groups, see Richard A. and Peggy B. Musgrave, *Public Finance in Theory and Practice* (New York: McGraw-Hill Book Company, 1973), p. 368. Of course, ultimately determining the incidence of Federal income taxes involves more than just the distribution of taxes among different income groups but should include at least the estimation of the impacts of the taxes on the (before-tax) rates of return to different assets (and labor).

not only on the income distribution effects but also on the elasticities of demand with respect to mortgage yields (and other credit terms) among different income groups. Guttentag, for example, argues that the demand elasticities with respect to mortgage credit terms will be greatest among the lower-income groups. It would seem possible that the various housing credit subsidies could be equalizing the distribution of housing without doing the same for income.

To summarize, incidence conclusions from studies of housing and municipal bond subsidies suggest that benefits may go largely to upper-middle and upper-income groups. This result appears to be more a characteristic of the specific programs than of anything inherent in selective credit policies. However, at best we regard these results as little more than rough first approximations particularly because of a failure to incorporate general equilibrium considerations. It may very well be, of course, that employment of a general equilibrium approach will simply lead to a recognition of the difficulty of making unambiguous conclusions concerning incidence rather than more confidence in any given set of results.

IV. CONCLUSION

Many economists have expressed a general opposition to the use of selective credit policies for the purpose of influencing resource allocation. One may want to argue that this opposition stems more from the *laissez-faire* attitude that permeates much of traditional economic thought than from a serious evaluation of credit policies on their own merits. One theme running throughout our discussion has been the relative lack of systematic research directly addressed to the basic issues surrounding credit policies.

Nonetheless, the paucity of research cuts two ways. While we have no strong confirmation of much of the harm envisioned by opponents, we have little if any demonstration that social gains might be expected from selective credit policies, or that they are the best way to achieve these gains. First, advocates of selective credit policies have failed to indicate in any rigorous manner how these policies will further society's more ultimate goals (such as economic efficiency, social stability, and equality of opportunity). Second, there is even a lack of firm evidence that selective credit policies will have the desired impact on the proximate objectives of resource allocation. While existing studies clearly do not refute the hypothesis that credit policies can predictably alter the composition of credit and output, the evidence is far from satisfactory. Finally, on a conceptual basis, it is likely to be very difficult to determine with any degree of precision the income or wealth distribution of selective credit policies. And, both conceptually and empirically, we have little reason to believe that such policies would be an effective mode for redistributing income—at least with respect to those credit policies which are aimed mainly at altering the composition of output. The result of all this is that we must still rely very heavily on personal preconceptions in concluding on the effects of selective credit policies.

Several points of concern deserve to be singled out for future research. One is the lack of clarity in specifying the ultimate goals of selective credit policies or their relation to proximate goals. This includes the tendency to make the case for or against credit policies merely on their ability to alter the composition of output. There seems no reason to assume that the relation of selective credit policies to their ultimate goals is determined only by their effect on the composition of output. It also includes the current practice of relating ultimate goals to proximate objectives by considering a particular good and asking what social goals might be advanced by Government encouragement (or discouragement) of this good. It would be of interest to see what type of conclusions might result if we changed the procedure to the more logical approach of starting with the ultimate goals and asked what composition of output is best suited for achieving these goals.

Another shortcoming is the casual and, possibly, unjustified borrowing of arguments and conclusions from other areas of economics to support positions for or against selective credit policies. This includes the citation of credit market "imperfections"—credit rationing, customer relationships, and second-best considerations—as arguments in favor of the use of credit policies. It also includes the unwarranted use of the traditional pure-exchange model efficiency criteria in arguing for "the market" as the determiner of the sectoral impacts of stabilization policies. Indeed, we have serious reservations about the general relevance of a comparative-static equilibrium welfare approach to analyzing the efficiency of stabilization policies.

A third general criticism deals with the conceptual issue of employing a partial equilibrium framework for analyzing the efficacy and incidence of selective credit policies. Determining the policy impacts on asset yields and prices, which is critical to these issues, is inherently a general equilibrium (or disequilibrium) problem. Only by examining these issues in a multimarket setting can we ultimately expect to gain a more complete grasp of their determinants.

Given the current intent of Congress to implement some form of credit allocation program, it is appropriate even in the face of all these unresolved questions to ask what policy implications emerge from this evaluation of the issues. From our perspective, the implications for expanding selective credit policies are negative. This stems from our conclusions that there are virtually no clear indications that such policies might improve economic efficiency or otherwise produce social benefits. We have no basis even to reject the possibility that they will have perverse influences. In this connection, we cite the absence of demonstrably beneficial links between proximate objectives and more ultimate goals, and the absence of convincing evidence that selective credit policies can be expected to have predictable or desirable effects on resource allocation or income distribution.[39]

---

[39] Obviously, we can design credit policies so as to increase the probability that they will further, or at least not impede, one or even several objectives. For example, if there is concern for providing benefits to low-income classes, we might subsidize a particular type of credit only for families whose income does not exceed a certain amount. However, we still face the question of what impact this policy has on other objectives of concern, be they ultimate or proximate. And we will still face gaps in existing research in looking for answers such as concern general equilibrium questions. Moreover, if our main concern is with redistributing income, there is the issue of using such an inefficient procedure as selective credit policies.

Yet, we can be fairly confident that credit allocation policies will produce several types of costs. In particular, there are the administrative and enforcement costs (record-keeping, legal counsel, supervision, etc.) borne by regulators and regulated. While economists generally ignore these costs in their formal analyses, this should not be taken to imply that such costs must be insignificant. There would also seem to be a political cost. Selective credit policies, by their nature, impinge upon an individual's freedom of choice. In a democratic society such as ours, this must *in and of itself* be judged as a burden of such policies. We believe that the uncertainty of any gains combined with the presence of these costs argues against the imposition of selective credit policies at this time.[40]

---

[40] It should be noted that this policy judgment does not generally apply to the removal of existing credit regulations. This is so primarily because existing market restrictions have already been "discounted" and therefore their removal will entail costs which must be balanced against any expected gains. We cannot arbitrarily dismiss the adage that "an old tax is a good tax."

PART *1*

JACK M. GUTTENTAG is Robert Morris Professor of Banking at the University of Pennsylvania. He holds a Ph.D. from Columbia University, specializing in financial institutions and real estate finance. He has served as Market Analyst for the Federal Housing Administration and Chief of Domestic Research at the Federal Reserve Bank of New York. Editor of the *Journal of Finance*, he is the coauthor of *New Series on Home Mortgage Yields Since 1951* and author of essays in *Federal Credit Agencies*, *Study of the Savings and Loan Industry*, and *A Study of Mortgage Credit*. He has also published in the *American Economic Review*, the *Journal of Political Economy*, and the *Quarterly Journal of Economics*.

Selective Credit Controls On Residential Mortgage Credit

JACK M. GUTTENTAG

This study examines the literature on selective credit controls on residential mortgages, with the primary intention of summarizing what is known, identifying major issues, and indicating possible fields of further inquiry. Sections I and II provide background "facts" about relevant institutional structures, and compare selective controls with other devices for influencing residential construction. Section III provides a modest analytical framework for examining the various objectives of selective controls. Sections IV-VIII consider each of several possible objectives, indicating in each case the historical background, current relevance, and possible research implications.

I. DEFINITIONS, CONCEPTS, AND INSTITUTIONAL STRUCTURE

Selective credit controls on residential mortgage loans can be defined as the manipulation by the Government of maximum terms on residential mortgage loans for the purpose of influenc-

35

ing the demand for residential mortgage credit, and thereby the flow of real resources into residential construction. Maximum terms may be set by law, or they may be set by regulations within the limits of the law.[1]

The most important terms are maximum allowable interest rate, maturity, and loan-value ratio. Another important term is the maximum ratio of mortgage payment (or total housing expense) to income. However, this term is not constrained by law in the United States, although it is in many foreign countries.

The objectives for which maximum terms are manipulated should be distinguished from the original purposes for setting maximum terms. The law establishes maximum maturities and loan-value ratios for the purpose of limiting lender risk,[2] while maximum interest rates are designed to prevent borrower exploitation. Although these purposes are not the concern of this study, the different objective of controls on the interest rate as compared to controls on the other terms should be noted. In the case of the interest rate the lender is constrained from being "too harsh" to the borrower, whereas in the case of the other terms the lender is prevented from being "too generous." This is fundamentally why the maximum interest rate is a different type of selective control.

Since selective controls involve manipulation of terms, there must be a regulatory agency with power to adjust terms as conditions require. In the case of loan-value ratios and maturities on Federal Housing Administration and Veterans Administration loans, the respective agencies can adjust the maximums within the limits set by law. Since actual maximums today are at or near legal limits, the FHA and VA can restrict maximum terms, not liberalize them. Liberalization requires Congressional action. With some exceptions, the Fed-

---

[1]This has been the conventional definition of selective controls. However, special measures to influence the supply of residential mortgage credit—for example, changing the attractiveness of mortgages relative to other assets—might also be viewed as types of selective controls. Unfortunately, measures of this type are so numerous that extensive treatment of any would transcend the scope of this essay. The author has attempted to the degree possible to indicate the various possibilities, to say something about their general effectiveness, and to provide references to the literature.

[2]On Federally underwritten (FHA and VA) loans, the purpose is to limit risk to the underwriting agencies.

eral Home Loan Bank Board has regulatory authority over maximum terms on conventional loans made by member savings and loan associations.[3] The maximum terms applicable to conventional loans made by other lenders, however, can be changed only by new legislation. Thus, if selective controls were to be imposed today and applied to the entire residential market, new legislation would be required similar to that enacted during 1950, when Congress authorized the Board of Governors under Regulation X to establish maximum terms on FHA, VA, and conventional loans made by all major lender groups.

In the case of maximum interest rates, on FHA and VA loans the Department of Housing and Urban Development has discretionary authority,[4] but rate ceilings on conventional loans are set by state legislation. State agencies in New York and New Jersey have limited discretion to adjust the maximum rate within narrow limits, while in Pennsylvania and Alaska, they use formulas that tie the rate to long-term Government bond yields and the Federal Reserve discount rate respectively.

II. SELECTIVE CONTROLS AND OTHER DEVICES FOR INFLUENCING RESIDENTIAL CONSTRUCTION

The accompanying Table shows how selective controls fit within a broad classification of policy measures to influence the flow of residential mortgage credit. While the Table is not meant to be exhaustive, it will help to define the scope of the paper, and clarify the importance of the symmetry of policy tools.

The focus of this study is changes in maximum mortgage terms (I-A), which are designed to affect the *demand* for

---

[3]Maximum loan-value ratios and maturities are subject to legal limits in the case of nonamortized loans and loans made under some special programs, while all residential loans are subject to maximum size limits which constrain loan-value ratios on high-value properties.

[4]This authority, which resides in the Secretary of HUD, involves a "temporary" supersession of the statutory limit of 6 percent. The expiration date for this authority, which has been pushed forward several times, is now June 30, 1977.

A Classification of Proposed Measures to Influence the Flow of Residential Mortgage Credit

Measure[*]	*Effect on Mortgage Credit Flows*
I. Measures to influence the demand for residential mortgage credit	
A. Manipulating maximum terms on residential mortages	Policy-asymmetrical in short run
B. Interest-rate and other subsidies paid to borrowers[1]	Expansionary in long run, policy-symmetrical in short run
II. Measures to influence the supply of residential mortgage credit	
A. Structural measures to increase the attractiveness of residential mortgages to private investors[2]	Expansionary in long run, stabilizing in short run
1. Variable rate mortgages[3,4]	
2. Purchasing power mortgages[5]	
3. Contingent participation mortgages[6]	
4. Removal of rate ceilings[4,7,8,9]	
5. Improvement of secondary markets[10]	
6. Increased availability of construction loans[11]	
7. Rate change insurance[12]	
B. Flexible policy measures to vary the attractiveness of mortgages relative to other instruments	Neutral or expansionary in long run, policy-symmetrical in short run
1. Tax credits against mortgages[7]	
2. Variable reserve requirements[13]	
3. Yield supplements paid to mortgage lenders[14]	
C. Structural measures to strengthen savings and loan associations[15]	Not clear
1. Diversification and maturity extension of interest-bearing liabilities[4]	

Measure*	Effect on Mortgage Credit Flows

2. Issuance of demand liabilities[7]
3. Diversification of assets[16, 17]

D. Selective controls on the corporate business sector

    1. Quantitative controls on business credit demands[18] — Policy-asymmetrical in short run

    2. System of price supplements on capital goods[19] — Neutral in long run, policy-symmetrical in short run

    3. Variable tax credit on business investment[4, 20]

E. Flexible Federal mortgage credit programs[21] — Expansionary in long run, policy-symmetrical in short run

    1. Federal National Mortgage Association
    2. Government National Mortage Association
    3. Federal Home Loan Bank System

F. General fiscal policy[22] — Policy-symmetrical in short run

---

*Many of the policy measures listed here have been examined in one or more of the recent Federal Reserve staff studies on residential finance [see *Federal Reserve Staff Study: Ways to Moderate Fluctuations in Housing Construction* (Washington: Board of Governors of the Federal Reserve System, 1972)]. Citations are identified with (FR).

Notes to Table

[1]Good papers on housing subsidy programs are in U. S., Congress, House, Committee on Banking and Currency, *Papers Submitted to Subcommittee on Housing Panels on Housing Demand, and Developing a Suitable Living Environment,* 92d Cong., 1st sess., 1971, part 2. See especially Morton L. Isler, "The Goals of Housing Subsidy Programs," pp. 415-36; Ira S. Lowry, "Housing Assistance for Low-Income Urban Families: A Fresh Approach," pp. 489-523; and Frank de Leeuw, "The Housing Allowance Approach," pp. 541-53.

[2]For a broad treatment, including analysis of some of the standard characteristics of mortgages, see (FR) Alan R. Winger, "An Economic Analysis of Mortgages during Periods of Monetary Restraint: Characteristics and Acquisitions by Lenders," pp. 456-80.

[3]The most comprehensive treatment is (FR) William Poole, Barbara Negri Opper, and R. Frederick Taylor, "The Variable Rate Mortgage on Single-Family Homes," pp. 377-98.

[4]Recommendation adopted by the Board of Governors. See "Ways to Moderate Fluctuations in the Construction of Housing," Report of the Board of Governors of the Federal Reserve System, 3 March 1972, *Federal Reserve Bulletin* 58 (1972): 215-25.

[5]This proposal is spelled out in (FR) William Poole, "Housing Finance under Inflationary Conditions," pp. 355-76.

[6]This proposal is discussed in (FR) Bernard N. Freedman, "Contingent Participation Mortgages on Single-Family Homes." pp. 160-76.

[7]Recommendation adopted by the Hunt Commission. See *The Report of the President's Commission on Financial Structure and Regulation* (Washington: Government Printing Office, 1971).

[8]Recommendation adopted by the Commission on Mortgage Interest Rates. See *Report of the Commission on Mortgage Interest Rates to the President of the United States and to the Congress* (Washington: Government Printing Office, August 1969).

[9]The case *against* removal of rate ceilings is contained in Jack M. Guttentag, "Changes in the Structure of the Residential Mortgage Market: Analysis and Proposals," *Study of the Savings and Loan Industry*, 4 vols. (Washington: Federal Home Loan Bank Board, 1969), 4: 1479-1559.

[10]Two basic sources are Oliver Jones and Leo Grebler, *The Secondary Mortgage Market: Its Purpose, Performance, and Potential* (Los Angeles: Graduate School of Business Administration, UCLA, 1961); Jack M. Guttentag, "The Federal National Mortgage Association," Commission on Money and Credit, *Federal Credit Agencies* (Englewood Cliffs, N. J.: Prentice-Hall, 1963), pp. 67-158; for a more recent treatment, see (FR) Leo Grebler, "Broadening the Sources of Funds for Residential Mortgages," pp. 177-252.

[11]See (FR) Robert Moore Fisher, "The Availability of Construction Credit for Housing," pp. 127-135

[12]See (FR) Robert Lindsay, "Rate-Risk Insurance for Mortgage Lenders," pp. 301-22.

[13]See (FR) Samuel B. Chase, Jr., "Use of Supplementary Reserve Requirements and Reserve Credits to Even Out the Flow of Mortgage Funds," pp. 97-109; (FR) Richard H. Puckett and James L. Pierce, "Implications of Asset Reserve Requirements or Credits in Bank Asset Selection," pp. 406-19; and (FR) Richard H. Puckett, "Effects of Asset Reserve Requirements on Control of Monetary Aggregates," pp. 399-405.

[14]See (FR) Barbara Negri Opper, "Interest Equalization on Home Mortgages," pp. 323-36.

[15]The most comprehensive discussion and analysis is the four-volume *Study of the Savings and Loan Industry*, directed by Irwin Friend. See, in particular, Irwin Friend, "Changes in the Asset and Liability Structure of the Savings and Loan Industry," 3: 1355-1433; and David I. Fand, "Savings Intermediaries and Consumer Credit Markets," 4: 1435-78. See Leo Grebler, *The Future of Thrift Institutions: A Study in Diversification versus Specialization* (Danville, Ill.: Joint Savings and Loan and Mutual Savings Bank Exchange Groups, 1969). Also, (FR) James B. Burnham, "Private Financial Institutions and the Residential Mortgage Cycle, with Particular Reference to the Savings and Loan Industry," pp. 81-96.

[16]Widespread diversification is recommended by the Hunt Commission. Diversification into consumer loans is recommended by the Board of Governors.

[17]See (FR) James L. Kichline, "Prospects for Institutional Reforms of the Major Depositary Intermediaries," pp. 282-300.

[18]See (FR) Eleanor J. Stockwell, "Quantitative Controls," pp. 420-31.

[19]See (FR) James L. Pierce and Peter A. Tinsley, "A Proposal for a Policy Instrument to Affect Business Investment," pp. 345-54; and (FR) Jan Karcz, "Investment Funds in Sweden," pp. 275-81.

[20]See Roger Craine, James A. Stephenson and Peter A. Tinsley, "Some Evidence on a Fiscal Instrument to Alter Business Investment," pp. 110-26.

[21]See the sources cited in footnote 10. In addition, see James S. Duesenberry, "Appraisal of Selected Policy Instruments Affecting Savings and Loan Associations," *Study of the Savings and Loan Industry* 4: 1591-1618; and Leo Grebler and Tom Doyel, "Effect of Industry Structure and Government Policies on Housing Demand and Cyclical Stability: Study of 1966 Experience," ibid., 3: 1241-1351.

[22]See (FR) W. Beeman, F. Shupp, and H. Wendel, "The Contribution of Fiscal Policy to the Housing Problem," pp. 68-80.

mortgage credit. Most other measures shown in the Table are designed to affect the *supply* of mortgage credit.[5]

A large number of proposals have been advanced in recent years for increasing the attractiveness of residential mortgages relative to other instruments (II-A). All of the proposals shown in the Table were considered in the Federal Reserve Board staff studies but only two appear in the Board's recommendations: authorization of variable-rate provisions on FHA and VA mortgages, and removal of interest-rate ceilings on these mortgages. Proposals of these types are *structural* in the sense that they are not meant to be reversible, nor do they provide any additional policy stabilization tools. In some degree they would have an expansionary effect on residential mortgage flows in the long run while perhaps imparting greater stability to flows in the short run. The latter consideration was uppermost in the minds of the Board in adopting the two proposals noted above.

A second category of measures designed to increase the attractiveness of residential mortgages includes policy-control parameters (II-B). With the possible exception of tax credits, they are designed to be *policy-symmetrical* in the short run, in the sense that the degree of benefit attached to mortgages could be varied over the cycle.[6] Over the long run they could be neutral except for tax credits which are inherently expansionary.

Structural measures to strengthen savings and loan associations (II-C) are designed basically to make these institutions viable in a competitive environment without need for the protective umbrella of Regulation Q. The literature on this subject is now voluminous,[7] and focuses mainly on various types of asset and liability diversification. The Board supports diversification into consumer loans whereas the Hunt Commission proposes very widespread diversification. The impact of such diversification on residential mortgage flows, however, both in the short and long run, remains a controversial issue.

---

[5]Although discussion of these measures exceeds the scope of this study, some broad perspective on them is attempted.

[6]By *policy-symmetrical* this writer means that there is nothing inherent in the mechanism that makes it less useful as a tool of restraint than as a tool of expansion. Needless to say, this does not imply that the tool will in fact be used symmetrically.

[7]See footnotes 16, 17, and 18 in the Table.

Selective controls on the business sector designed to reduce cyclical swings in residential mortgage credit (II-D), were given only passing attention in the literature prior to the Board staff studies. Such controls have two persuasive a priori advantages over most other devices to stabilize the residential sector. First, such measures can be allocatively neutral in the long run (although, of course, they need not be). Other policy tools that can be used for purposes of short-run stabilization, such as tax credits on mortgages or secondary market purchases by FNMA, tend to have a long-run expansionary bias. The second advantage of selective controls on the business sector is that they are likely to be more effective in accomplishing their objective. (The reasons for this are considered in section V.) Perhaps for these reasons four of the Board staff studies were directed to these controls, while Lyle E. Gramley's overview paper also gives them a prominent place.[8]

Three different types of selective controls on business are examined in the Board staff studies. Quantitative controls on business credit, which would be the most analogous to selective controls on residential mortgage credit, are not recommended. Gramley notes that:

... a feasible program of quantitative controls would be likely to make only a limited contribution to reducing cyclical fluctuations in housing activity. It would do so, moreover, at high costs—relative to programs that rely on incentives—in terms of discriminatory effects on individual firms, loss of efficiency, and administrative complexity.[9]

A close reading of the staff paper on quantitative controls by Eleanor J. Stockwell, which provides the basis for Gramley's conclusions, suggests that his negative reaction might even have been stronger.[10]

---

[8]See his "Short-Term Cycles in Housing Production: An Overview of the Problem and Possible Solution," *Federal Reserve Staff Study: Ways to Moderate Fluctuations in Housing Construction* (Washington: Board of Governors of the Federal Reserve System, 1972), pp. 1-67. This essay provides a masterful summary of most of the other staff contributions, along with a judicious weighing of the major policy issues.

[9]Ibid., p. 57.

[10]"Quantitative Controls," *Federal Reserve Staff Study: Ways to Moderate Fluctuations in Housing Construction*, pp. 420-31.

In contrast the staff studies come out very favorably toward a special business investment fund that would be used to vary the price of new capital goods. Gramley notes:

The new policy instrument discussed here would resemble, in spirit, an approach to stabilization that has been employed in Sweden. It would involve the establishment of a business investment fund into which contributions tied to investment expenditures would be made by business firms during some periods and withdrawals, also tied to investment expenditures, would be permitted in others. The unit deposit or withdrawal rate would be determined on the basis of the expected level of aggregate fixed investment relative to the level that would be desirable for economic stabilization. ... The rate of contribution or withdrawal would be equivalent to a percentage mark-up or rebate on the purchase price of new capital equipment, and would have incentive effects on investment comparable to equivalent changes in the prices of capital goods.[11]

The Board did not endorse this proposal, however, but chose the third possibility—the variable-investment tax credit.

One instrument of tax policy, the investment tax credit, has in recent years been employed to influence business investment decisions. By now the investment tax credit is well understood by the business community, by the Congress, and by the general public. Its effects on the rate of business investment have been demonstrated in actual experience.

... Thus, the magnitude of the tax credit could be lowered when excess aggregate demand threatened to generate inflationary pressures, or it would be raised when the economy was in need of stimulus. If the tax credit were adjusted in this fashion, variations in business external financing demands would tend to be reduced, fluctuations in market interest rates would tend to diminish, and these developments could contribute to stabilizing the flow of mortgage credit and housing construction.[12]

Presumably the Board felt that the tax credit could be used as

---

[11]Ibid., pp. 46-47.
[12]"Ways to Moderate Fluctuations in the Construction of Housing," Report to the Board of Governors of the Federal Reserve System, 3 March 1972, *Federal Reserve Bulletin* 58 (1972): 224.

43

effectively as the proposed business investment fund while having the advantage of familiarity. While the staff study of the investment tax credit is more or less favorable, it does not consider administrative and other "practical" aspects. For some reason Gramley did not consider the investment tax credit. Hence, it is not obvious a priori how it stands in terms of efficiency, equity and cost relative to the investment fund proposal.

Regarding Federal mortgage credit programs (II-E), we can again do no better than quote Gramley:

In recent years, the effects on housing activity of fluctuations in the supply of mortgage credit from the depositary institutions have been dampened by large-scale operations of Federally sponsored credit agencies. These agencies have opened an alternative supply of mortgage credit—by issuing their own securities in the money and capital markets and supplying funds either directly, or in the case of FHLB advances to member S & L's indirectly, to the residential mortgage market. The staff study on housing [finance] has explored the potential for broadening still further the reliance upon the securities markets as a source of funds during periods of general credit restraint.

The deliberate use of the Federal housing credit agencies as a first line of defense against cyclical fluctuations in housing production is relatively new. Although the FHLB System was expected to help "regulate the supply of mortgage credit in a way that will discourage building booms and support normal construction year in and year out . . . ," its operations before 1966 were too marginal in scope to have an appreciable impact on the mortgage lending and housing cycle. The intent of the Congress in creating FNMA in 1938, moreover, was to expand the supply of mortgage funds over the long run, principally by helping to develop a secondary market for Government-guaranteed mortgages that would increase mortgage liquidity and acceptability to private lenders.

In the early 1950's, the potential use of the Federal housing credit agencies in an economic stabilization role increasingly became recognized. It was not clear at that time, however, whether these agencies should employ their resources to stabilize housing or to stabilize general economic activity. Given that cycles in housing and in general economic activity tend to be inversely related, the two objectives were frequently in conflict—as they still are.

44

Since the mid-1960s, the concept of the proper role of the Federally sponsored housing credit agencies has changed radically. Stabilization of housing production has emerged as the principal operating objective. The scale of their operations also has changed markedly. Prior to 1965, the amount of funds supplied to the residential mortgage market by these agencies was comparatively small. In 1966, however, funds were poured into 1- to 4-family mortgages by the combined Federal agencies (including FHLB advances to member associations) at a peak annual rate of $5.5 billion in the second quarter—nearly twice the previous peak rate in the second quarter of 1959. And in 1969, the peak annual rate of contribution soared to $11.3 billion in the fourth quarter. The fact that housing declined in both 1966 and 1969 does not indicate that these efforts were unsuccessful. On the contrary, the increase in housing starts financed by FHA and VA mortgages during 1969 and early 1970 attests to the capability of these programs to support housing construction in a period of severe credit restraint.[13]

This is an excellent summary except for the last sentence, which is a non sequitur. The bulge in FHA and VA starts in 1969, even assuming that the agencies were entirely responsible, was probably in large part at the expense of the conventional sector.

In this connection there is no easy way to measure the net contribution of the Federal credit agencies to new construction. One can measure fairly accurately their *gross* contribution by estimating the value of new construction that was directly supported by credit extended by the agencies. This is higher than the agencies' net contribution, however, because (among other reasons) some of the funds raised by the agencies in the capital market would otherwise have been invested in mortgages, while the concentration of agency lending on new construction causes a diversion of private residential credit to existing houses.[14]

Another approach is to include some relevant measure of agency operations in econometric models designed to explain total mortgage flows or total residential construction. Some

---

[13]Gramley, op. cit. pp. 37, 38.

[14]For a more complete analysis of this general problem, see Jack M. Guttentag, "The Federal National Mortgage Association," Commission on Money and Credit, *Federal Credit Agencies* (Englewood Cliffs, N. J.: Prentice-Hall, 1963), pp. 94-104.

45

interesting results along this line are reported by Eugene Brady and Ray Fair, who find that FHLB advances to savings and loan associations are positively correlated with housing activity, but that this is not the case regarding net mortgage purchases by FNMA.[15]

In general we would expect the Federal credit agencies to be expansionary in the long run, to the extent that they grow secularly. In the short run they are policy-symmetrical but their effectiveness as stabilizers is quite limited, relative to, say, selective controls on the business sector. Some reasons for this have already been suggested and will be considered further below.

General fiscal policy (II-F) is, in a sense, the preferred method of dealing with the short-run housing problem. A countercyclical fiscal policy that would obviate the need for wide counter-cyclical swings in monetary policy has the support of the Board, the Hunt Commission, and the Commission on Mortgage Interest Rates. During periods of heavy demands on resources and tight money, for example, a Federal surplus would release funds that could be channeled into mortgages (at the same time the mechanism by which the surplus was generated—a tax rise, for example—releases the real resources needed to expand construction). Unfortunately, general fiscal policy tends to be refractory, for reasons that are well known; if this were not so the pressures for other flexible policy tools to soften the impact of monetary restraint on construction would not have developed.

It will be noted from the Table that, in contrast to other flexible policy tools, selective controls on residential mortgages are policy-asymmetrical. Assuming away enforcement and other administrative problems, such controls can always be effective in principle in restricting credit flows but they may or may not be effective in stimulating credit flows, depending on conditions in the residential mortgage market.[16]

---

[15]See Eugene A. Brady, "An Econometric Analysis of the U. S. Residential Housing Market," and Ray C. Fair, "Monthly Housing Starts," R. Bruce Ricks, ed., *National Housing Models* (Lexington, Mass.: D. C. Heath and Company, Lexington Books, 1973), pp. 1-41, 69-84.

[16]The same is true in the opposite direction for selective controls on business credit demand—namely, in principle they can always be effective in stimulating the flow of residential mortgage credit but they would not necessarily be effective in curtailing it.

III. MAXIMUM TERMS AND MARKET TERMS

Understanding the relationships between maximum terms and market terms is central to any analysis of the possible functions and limitations of selective controls. If there were no legal or regulatory restraints, lenders would apply some of their own restrictions to control risk and ration funds. It is useful to express this in terms of a loan-supply function, where the amount offered in the market is a negative function of the loan-value ratio and maturity, and a positive function of the interest rate.[17] The loan demand function would have opposite signs. In general, any change in terms that increases risk to the lender also makes it easier for borrowers to qualify for credit, or allows borrowers with given qualifications to obtain more credit. Thus, the supply of loans will be lower at higher loan-value ratios because a high loan-value ratio increases the probability that a decline in property value will eliminate the borrower's equity, thereby increasing the risk of default and foreclosure. But, a borrower with given wealth or liquid assets can command a larger loan (and a more expensive house) at a higher loan-value ratio.

It is very useful (and does little violence to the facts) to assume that in the absence of legal or regulatory constraints on terms the interaction of supply and demand in the market would result in a set of market-clearing terms, such that supply would equal demand. These may be called the *market equilibrium terms* or, simply, the *market terms*. Under the assumed conditions, an increase in the supply of (or demand for) mortgage loans will result in a new set of market terms that will be "more liberal" (or "more restrictive") than the previous set.

This is illustrated in the Figure, which shows demand and supply expressed as functions of the loan-value ratio (other terms assumed constant). When supply increases from S to S' the loan-value ratio rises from LV_1 to LV_2.

---

[17]On the concept of a loan-offer function, see Donald D. Hester, "An Empirical Examination of a Commercial Bank Loan Offer Function," Donald D. Hester and James Tobin, eds., *Studies of Portfolio Behavior*, Cowles Foundation Monograph 20 (New York: John Wiley and Sons, 1967), pp. 118-70; and Richard F. Muth, "Interest Rates, Contract Terms, and the Allocation of Mortgage Funds," *Journal of Finance* 17 (1962): 63-80.

Percent

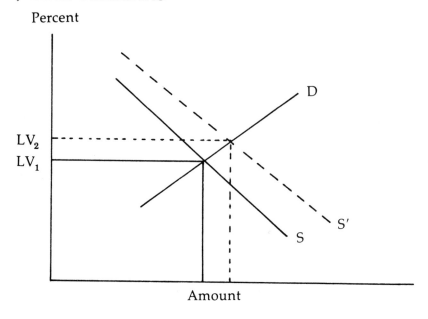

Amount

Maximum terms may or may not be effective in the sense of constraining actual terms, depending on where they are relative to market terms. Thus, when the market loan-value ratio is LV_1 in the Figure, a maximum ratio above LV_1 will not be effective, but a maximum ratio below LV, will be effective.[18] If the maximum ratio is at or above the market ratio, the maximum can be manipulated to curtail but not expand the flow of credit. This is the source of asymmetry in the use of selective controls on residential mortgage credit referred to earlier. In principle at least (ignoring administrative or political problems), it is always possible to make maximum terms restrictive enough to reduce loan volume. Liberalization of terms for the purpose of increasing loan volume, however, will succeed only if existing

---

[18]It is possible, of course, for the maximum loan-value ratio to be effective and the maximum maturity to be ineffective (or vice versa). Where this is the case, a change in the supply of loanable funds may change one term but not the other. An actual case where this occured is described in Jack M. Guttentag and Morris Beck, *New Series on Home Mortgage Yields since 1951* (New York: National Bureau of Economic Research, 1970), pp. 91-92.

48

maximum terms are an effective constraint on loan volume.[19] Otherwise, liberalization will simply allow lenders to do what they are otherwise disposed not to do, thereby accomplishing nothing.[20]

Ineffective maximum terms can become effective either by administrative action making them more restrictive, or by a change in market terms toward greater liberality. Thus, the shift in the supply function of S' would make a maximum loan-value ratio of LV_1 effective. It is possible that liberalization may be ineffective at the time it occurs, yet become effective at a later time when market conditions ease. We have a number of historical examples of such "delayed action" liberalizations.[21]

Selective controls on the demand for business credit involve a similar asymmetry but in the opposite direction insofar as concerns their impact on the residential sector. Assuming away enforcement and other administrative problems, imposition or tightening of such controls can always in principle curtail the volume of business credit, which will expand the supply of residential mortgage credit. Liberalization of maximum terms on business credit will curtail the supply of residential mortgage credit, however, only if maximum terms on business credit are an effective constraint.

Note that whereas an increase in the supply of loanable funds (or reduction in demand) will tend to make a given set of maximum loan-value ratios or maturities more effective, it tends to make a maximum interest rate less effective. This is

---

[19]On this point see David P. Eastburn, "Real Estate Credit Controls as a Selective Instrument of Federal Reserve Policy," (Ph.D. diss., University of Pennsylvania, 1957), pp. 45-46.

[20]Grebler disputes this point citing what he calls a "yardstick effect" of legal terms on the terms offered by lenders. See Leo Grebler, *Housing Issues in Economic Stabilization Policy*, Occasional Paper #72 (New York: National Bureau of Economic Research, 1960), pp. 49-50. If lenders relax loan-value ratios and maturities when market conditions have not changed, however, they must necessarily tighten some other terms (such as the maximum expense-to-income ratio), or introduce some new ad hoc rationing procedures.

[21]"This was true, for example, of the liberalization of mortgage terms on FHA mortgages in 1948, on both FHA and VA mortgages in 1951 and 1952 . . . and on FHA mortgages in 1957. On each of these occasions, the new more liberal maximum terms did become effective at a later time when an increase in the supply of mortgage credit caused an easing in the market. . . . " Jack M. Guttentag, "The Short Cycle in Residential Construction, 1946-59," *American Economic Review* 51 (1961): 287.

because the interest rate enters the demand and supply functions with signs opposite to those of the loan-value ratio and maturity. Assume, for example, initial equivalence of maximum and market terms. If a sharp drop occurs in the supply of mortgage credit and the authorities wish to offset or cushion the effect on construction, reduction in the maximum loan-value ratio and maturity will accomplish nothing, since market terms have become more restrictive than the existing maximums. Since the maximum interest rate has become a constraint, however, a rise in the maximum will keep the decline from being larger than it would be otherwise. In the reverse case where the supply of credit rises and the policy objective is to moderate the rise in construction, all the terms can in principle be used.[22]

IV. PURPOSES OF SELECTIVE CONTROLS:
REDUCING AGGREGATE DEMAND

Any classification of the purposes of selective controls must be somewhat arbitrary. We have attempted the finest classification possible as the best method of identifying useful research projects, recognizing that this creates some obvious overlaps between the different categories.

The five objectives are as follows:

1. Reducing aggregate demand, under conditions where general credit controls are insufficient for some reason;

---

[22]In practice maximum interest rates have not been viewed as a selective device. During periods of monetary restraint when the maximum interest rate on FHA and VA mortgages has been a constraint on loan volume and public policy has been directed toward methods of softening the impact of restraint on the residential sector, there has been great reluctance to raise maximum rates. This reflects the political burden of appearing to sanction high interest rates, plus a well-grounded fear that such rate adjustments would stimulate further increases in market rates. In the few historical periods where expansion in residential construction was viewed as excessive, reduction in the maximum rate below the market rate was not considered as a possible control device—perhaps because other devices were ready at hand.

2. Correcting maladjustments in the housing sector, where conditions in this sector are out of balance with the remainder of the economy;

3. Maintaining structural stability between various sectors of the economy under conditions where marked shifts in demand tend to cause excess demand in some sectors and deficient demand in others;

4. Increasing the share of national resources channeled into residential construction in the long run;

5. Equalizing the distribution of housing resources as between households of varying incomes.

One purpose of manipulating maximum terms is to restrict the demand for housing as a means of controlling excessive aggregate demand, under conditions such that the general tools of monetary policy are for some reason insufficient. This was the main purpose of Regulation X, imposed during the Korean War when the Federal Reserve's power to curb inflationary demands was limited by its commitment to support the Government securities market.[23] Regulation X stipulated more restrictive terms than were being imposed by lenders at that time on a substantial proportion of the loans being made, and this resulted in a decline in housing demand and in construction. Not long after the regulation was imposed, however, the Federal Reserve and the Treasury reached their famous accord, interest rates rose sharply, lender portfolios became less liquid, and the supply of residential mortgage credit declined sharply. This development made Regulation X partially redundant, in the sense that the new market terms largely fell within the limits set by the regulation.[24]

At no time since the Regulation X episode has there been any effort, intent or need to deal with excessive aggregate demand by tightening maximum mortgage terms. For one thing, the

---

[23]To some degree Regulation X may also have had the purpose of curbing excessive expansion in the residential sector (V below). For a further discussion of the background and objectives of Regulation X, see Eastburn, op. cit., pp.128-9, and Jack M. Guttentag, "Some Studies of the Post-World War II Residential Construction and Mortgage Markets, (Ph.D. diss., Columbia University, 1958), pp. 211-13.

[24]See Eastburn, op. cit., pp. 213-16.

Fed's general powers have been viewed as more or less adequate to deal with the problem. Even more important, experience has indicated that general monetary restraint has a severe effect on the residential sector.[25] Even if the overall effect of monetary restraint on aggregate demand is inadequate because of the insensitivity of other sectors to restraint, it probably is neither possible nor desirable to intensify the overall effect by pressing even harder on the residential sector using selective controls. Among the arguments given to support this view are, first, that additional pressure on the residential sector could create unemployment in this sector even in the midst of excessive aggregate demand. Second, it can be argued that the change in maximum terms required would be extraordinarily large, since they would have to more than match the restriction in market terms generated by monetary restraint. The main argument, however, is that a further shift of resources out of the housing sector clashes with current objectives regarding appropriate resource allocation.[26] Thus, it is that the focus of policy has been to find methods by which the effects of monetary restraint on residential construction could be softened rather than intensified. Needless to say, an easing of maximum terms would be useless for that purpose.

So long as the Federal Reserve relies mainly on general credit controls, one cannot conceive of a situation arising that would call for the use of selective credit controls on residential mortgages for the purpose of restricting aggregate demand. Yet conceivably the System could change its basic modus operandi, relying on an array of selective controls instead of on general controls. This possibility will be considered in section VI.

---

[25]The majority opinion is that the effect is "disproportionately severe," while a minority holds that it probably is "appropriately severe." For a discussion of the issues involved in this dispute, see Jack M. Guttentag, "The Federal Reserve and the Mortgage Market: Some Perspectives on the 'Crisis' of 1966," in U. S., Congress, Senate, Committee on Banking and Currency, Subcommittee on Housing and Urban Affairs, *A Study of Mortgage Credit*, 90th Cong., 1st sess., 22 May 1967, pp. 393-406.

[26]Neither of the first two arguments is very convincing. It is not at all clear that unemployment in construction rises significantly when residential construction declines sharply, since there is evidence of ready transferability of resources between residential and other types of construction. Large changes in maximum terms would constitute a further problem, only because of public unwillingness to accept the need for them.

V. CORRECTING "MALADJUSTMENTS" IN THE RESIDENTIAL CONSTRUCTION SECTOR

Selective controls can be used to affect housing demand under conditions where the residential sector is considered to be out of phase with the remainder of the economy. While cases IV and V may not be sharply distinguishable in practice, particularly from a contemporaneous point of view, in principle the distinction is clear enough. The one historical example where selective controls were used mainly for the purpose of reducing the flow of resources into the residential sector occurred in 1955.[27] Terms on FHA and VA mortgages were tightened, and other restrictive measures were taken as well, in order to correct "specific maladjustments in the housing and mortgage markets" associated with very rapid expansion in this sector. This was at a time when the monetary authorities were reluctant to restrain the overall supply of credit too rapidly, for fear of curbing an emerging recovery in general business—the magnitude and strength of this recovery was uncertain at the time.[28] As in the case of Regulation X, however, soon after the restrictive measures were imposed, the capital markets tightened under increasing pressure from the Federal Reserve, residential construction declined more than anyone wished, and the previous administrative actions were reversed, although with little visible effect.

Maladjustments in the opposite direction—namely, excessively severe declines in residential construction—also belong here. Indeed, excessive expansions such as occurred in 1955 elicit much less concern (for obvious reasons) than what are considered excessive contractions, such as occurred in 1953, 1957, 1960, 1966, 1969, and 1973. A wide range of policies aimed at moderating the effects of tight money on residential construction has been discussed. During the 1950s proposed remedies

---

[27]For a detailed discussion of this episode, see Grebler, op. cit., chap. 3.

[28]Grebler notes that "the selective measures can be credited with having had a moderate part in correcting specific maladjustments in the housing and mortgage markets inherited from the previous expansion of residential construction; that is, in helping to avoid general overbuilding and an excessive spread of easy credit terms for home purchase that might have threatened the stability of a large component of the nation's private debt structure." Ibid., p. 64.

focused on the FHA and VA programs, which were the more volatile segments of the market, while in the 1960s more attention was given to the savings and loan industry, reflecting the increasing instability of the savings and loan sector.[29]

In section II some general approaches toward moderating the short construction cycle were summarized and discussed briefly. Now, the usefulness, for purposes of moderating the effects of cyclical tight money on residential construction, of selective controls on the residential sector, and on the business sector, will be analyzed in somewhat more detail.

A simple analytical framework will be used for this purpose. Assume that the Fed maintains a total credit target, which it adjusts in line with developments in the economy.[30] Assume further that total credit can be divided into four basic components—corporate business credit, Federal Government credit, residential credit, and other credit. During a period of monetary restraint the policy objective is to increase residential credit. Each of the ways in which this can be done will now be analyzed.

1. *Increase Total Credit.* If we assume that the Federal Reserve does a good job in adjusting total credit to macroeconomic needs, this approach is undesirable by definition. Granted this assumption, the implication is that our objective is to reallocate credit to the residential sector from other sectors.

2. *Increase Residential Demand.* Reallocation can occur if the demand for residential credit increases and there is some elasticity in other demands. Selective controls on residential mortgages can be liberalized for this purpose, but this approach will not work unless existing maximum terms are an effective constraint, as explained earlier. In fact, during periods of monetary restraint, market terms invariably become more re-

---

[29]In addition to the references cited in the Table in section II, see Henry Schechter, *The Residential Mortgage Financing Problem*, Subcommittee on Housing of the Committee on Banking and Currency, House of Representatives, September 1971; and William E. Gibson, "Protecting Homebuilding from Restrictive Credit Conditions," *Brookings Papers on Economic Activity*, No. 3, 1973.

[30]Anyone who is upset by the "unrealism" of this assumption may prefer to assume some other target (M_1, for example), and that each value of the assumed target implies a unique value for total credit.

strictive than maximum terms, so that liberalization accomplishes nothing. Of course, demand can be increased in other ways—for example, through Federal subsidy programs. Given other Federal expenditures and taxes, however, a rise in subsidies implies a corresponding rise in Government borrowing. Assuming total credit is fixed, this will be effective only to the degree that the additional credit raised to pay the subsidies comes at the expense of credit extended to other sectors. The problem is that (for reasons indicated below) much of the diverted credit is likely to come from the nonsubsidized part of the residential sector.

3. *Shift Credit from the Federal Government.* Government credit demands are absolutely inelastic and cannot be displaced in the market by other demands. Only if the Government voluntarily reduces its demands by curtailing expenditures and/or raising taxes can credit be shifted to other sectors. As noted earlier, this is in fact the preferred solution to the problem but for various reasons the solution is not generally available. Fiscal policy must be taken as a given.

4. *Shift Credit from the Corporate Business Sector.* The next best solution is to shift credit from the corporate business sector. There are several reasons why this is a preferred solution. First, corporate investment is generally given the lowest social priority in the short run.[31] Second, withdrawing funds from the corporate sector is supported by notions of "distributive justice"—that is, since the nonfinancial corporate business sector is mainly responsible for the reduced supply of funds available for residential construction during a period of monetary restraint, it is only fair that the business sector be restrained.

... the dynamic impetus to economic fluctuations is provided by the corporations... when corporate investment demands increase, the associated demands on the capital markets raise interest rates and tighten credit, but the rebound effect of this tightening on the corporations themselves is slight. Potential home buyers, on the other hand, faced with the need to pay higher rates and to make larger down payments, are forced to curtail their expenditures on housing and

---

[31]There may be some important exceptions to this, however, such as investment related to defense or pollution.

their mortgage borrowing. Putting the matter crudely the volume of mortgage credit is a sort of residual, in that home buyers can obtain only that volume of credit which remains after the more volatile and persistent demands of corporations have been satisfied.[32]

Unfortunately, the inelasticity of corporate credit demands alluded to in the quotation above makes it very difficult to shift funds away from corporations through the market—that is, by increasing other demands.[33] This is why the Fed staff studies, quite justifiably, shifted attention to various possible selective control devices that might be used to curtail corporate demands.

5. *Shift Credit from Other Sectors.* Credit can be diverted to the residential sector from other (noncorporate) sectors with a weak position in credit markets akin to that of the residential sector. Either they are subject to nonrate credit rationing, as in the case of many small and particularly new businesses, or they are sensitive to changes in rate levels, as in the case of many states and municipalities. In general, those sectors from which credit might be diverted have high social priorities of their own, which rival that of housing. Only consumer credit is viewed as having a low priority and unfortunately consumer credit demands are similar to corporate business demands in being relatively inelastic.

Although the above analysis is admittedly brief and superficial, it does illustrate the difficulty of ameliorating the effects of monetary restraint on the residential sector, without undercutting the effectiveness of monetary policy generally and without resorting to selective controls.

This point can be sharpened by comparing the effect of an increase in mortgage purchases by FNMA with the effect of an equivalent decline in corporate credit demands resulting from selective controls. The FNMA purchases can be partitioned into the following categories.

---

[32]Jack M. Guttentag, "The Short Cycle in Residential Construction," op. cit., p. 292.
[33]Gramley notes that " . . . only recently have econometric studies been able to isolate even a relatively weak influence of credit variables on business investment." (Gramley, op. cit., p. 34).

(a) To some degree, total credit may rise—that is, the Federal Reserve may be forced to create more credit than it would prefer. This would be the case, for example, if FNMA purchases mortgages with funds raised through sale of debentures to commercial banks, and the Fed is unable to force the liquidation of a like amount of other bank assets as an offset for fear of generating market disorder. The result is that monetary policy has been weakened.

(b) To some degree ownership of newly created mortgages is simply shifted, at higher interest rates, from private investors to FNMA. This would occur if FNMA financed its purchases through the sale of securities to investors who otherwise would have purchased mortgages, or to households which reduce their claims against savings institutions. There are, of course, many more roundabout channels that lead to the same end result.[34] Because the residential sector is very large and rate elastic, it is likely that this type of "leakage" is substantial.[35]

(c) To some degree credit will be shifted to the residential sector from other "weak competitors," such as states and municipalities. Such diversion could occur, for example, if FNMA outbid a school district authority in placing securities with a pension fund or insurance company. Whether this is desirable is highly questionable.

(d) Credit diversion from low-priority sectors, which really is the ultimate objective of the operation, will no doubt comprise a small portion of the total. Yet interest rates will be raised for all borrowers.

Selective controls on the corporate business sector, in con-

---

[34]For example, FNMA securities may be purchased by a pension fund that otherwise would have purchased corporate bonds. The potential issuer of the bonds might sell commercial paper instead, and the paper might be purchased by banks that otherwise would have purchased mortgages.

[35]Grebler suggests that for every $100 of securities sold by FNMA and the FHLB System during 1966 and 1969, $20 or so was drained from savings accounts. He concludes that FNMA's and the FHLB System's net contributions to the residential mortgage market in those years was about 80 percent of their gross contributions. (See "Broadening the Sources of Funds for Residential Mortgages," Federal Reserve Staff Study. *Ways to Moderate Fluctuations in Housing Construction*, p. 186.) This is a non sequitur, however, since there are many other channels through which securities sales by the agencies drained funds from the residential market.

trast, divert credit from the sector from which society wishes credit diverted. The amount so diverted would become available to other sectors, and since the residential sector is the largest and its elasticity is high, it will obtain a large share. The remainder will go largely to other high-priority sectors. The reallocation will occur at lower rather than higher interest rates, and with no danger of an inflationary rise in total credit.

VI. SELECTIVE CONTROLS TO MAINTAIN SECTORAL BALANCE

The third possible objective of selective controls is to maintain structural stability in the economy in the face of unusually disruptive shifts in demand. This case can be distinguished from those in sections IV and V as follows. The one in section IV refers to a situation of excessive aggregate demand in all sectors, that in section V refers to a situation of excessive (or deficient) demand in the residential sector only, and that in section VI refers to a situation where there is excess demand in one or more sectors and deficient demand in others. These are somewhat fine distinctions and the case in section VI perhaps does not warrant separate notice except that the Eckstein report gave it considerable attention[36] and it is closely related to current thinking about resource allocation. Warren L. Smith's essay on monetary policy in the Eckstein report, which presents a case for an array of selective controls to replace general controls, is based on the situation in the section VI case.[37] The major relevant points of Smith's argument are as follows.

1. General credit controls are highly selective in their effect, bearing most heavily on residential construction and least heavily on those sectors "—including fixed investment, consumer durables, and inventories—which are subject to the greatest fluctuations and are the most serious generators of instability."[38]

---

[36]U. S., Congress, Joint Economic Committee, *Staff Report on Employment, Growth, and Price Levels*, 86th Cong., 1st sess., 24 December 1959.
[37]Ibid., pp. 315-429.
[38]Ibid., p. 394.

2. In an economy characterized by flexible prices and mobile resources, the shift in demand resulting from the uneven impact of monetary policy would result in relative price adjustments and resource flows, and no serious problems would result.

3. Where prices are rigid and labor immobile in the short run, however, as is the case in the United States today, such demand shifts can cause inflation and unemployment without excessive aggregate demand.[39]

4. Hence, an array of selective controls is needed to maintain a balance between demand and capacity in each major sector of the economy.

Having presented this case Smith then backs off by pointing out such controls would have to be

so quick-acting and selective as to be completely unrealistic; moreover, if such instruments were available, their use would tend to immobilize the machinery for reallocating resources to keep pace with changing needs and tastes.[40]

Smith's argument can be expressed in terms of the allocation problem. In the short run nonfixed factors (labor and materials) should be allocated in proportion to fixed capacity, while in the long run when all factors are variable they should be allocated in line with demand. The problem, as Smith sees it, is that demand shifts in the short run distort the proper balance between fixed and nonfixed factors, and the machinery of selective controls needed to prevent this will distort the long-run response of the system to demand.[41] He also assumes that selective controls would be credit-demand controls, along the lines of the United States experience with controls on residential mortgages and consumer credit. He does not, however, consider the characteristics of a *system* of selective controls of this type.

---

[39]This will be recognized as the "Schultze theory of inflation," which appeared in another of the staff studies prepared as part of the Eckstein report.

[40]Ibid., p. 403.

[41]He does not consider the possibility that society may wish long-run allocation to deviate from the pattern dictated by demand.

Under such a system, presumably the Fed would maintain selective controls on all major uses of funds and would provide sufficient funds to the market so that the supply of loanable funds available to all sectors would exceed the demand at the posted maximum terms. General monetary policy would have no function other than to maintain a surplus of loanable funds in the financial system at all times. This generalized excess supply of funds would be necessary to assure that the selective controls in each sector were policy-symmetrical. The controls would be the effective constraint on loan volume in every sector. Then by manipulating the maximum terms on this sector and that one, the Fed (in principle) could control resource allocation as well as aggregate demand. Smith's despair that such a system could not work probably reflects an implicit assumption that the costly and cumbersome administrative machinery employed in the United States to implement Regulations X and W would have to be replicated for each major use of funds.

It is not obvious that this assumption is justified. A comprehensive system of controls could be imposed on the *supply* of credit that might be much more manageable and flexible. Such controls might employ differential taxes, subsidies, reserve requirements, credit quotas or ceilings which could be applied to various types of financial instruments or institutions. In this type of system selective controls would not absorb the system of general controls, and the Federal Reserve would continue to run a general monetary policy.

The actual systems used in France and England seem to be a complex mixture of the two approaches. While the overall supply of loanable funds tends to be excessive in both cases, specific restraints are imposed more on the supply side than on the demand side. The following from Donald R. Hodgman regarding France illustrates the point.

One fact is central to an understanding of the varied approaches of the *Banque de France* to the regulation of the French money supply. At no time since the end of the second world war has the rediscount rate (or more properly, the array of rediscount rates) charged by the *Banque de France* been high enough to prevent the demand for credit in the economy from causing too rapid an expansion in the money supply for reasonable stability in the general price level. Deprived of the interest rate as an adequate price-rationing device for control of the money supply, the *Banque de France* has had to rely on a variety of expedients. . . .

These include control of deposit and lending rates set by banks and other financial firms, regulation of interest rates on government securities, annual and month-by-month controls on the maximum permissible rate of expansion in bank credit, direct administrative review of bank discounts and loans for large borrowers, control of security issues of borrowers in the capital market, control of instalment credit terms and of maximum loan-to-capital ratios for instalment lenders, a variety of controls on international capital movements, and general price controls. In addition, the public and semi-public financial intermediaries . . . are subject to direct administrative control with respect to their lending, discounting, and endorsement policies.[42]

Both the specific types of selective controls employed and the underlying reason for their imposition are somewhat different in France than in England. In France, following Hodgman, selective controls are designed to implement rather detailed allocational priorities, as well as to dampen aggregate demand in the face of a commitment to generally low interest rate levels. In England, imposition of controls has mainly reflected the unwillingness of the Bank of England to use the traditional general instruments of monetary control to restrain aggregate demand.[43] In both countries the system of controls seems to be rather jerry-built and ad hoc, and in neither case have controls been able to curb aggregate demand adequately.

The United States seems to be moving toward selective controls because of the increasing demand that resource allocation be controlled.[44] The Federal Reserve not only has expressed its serious concern over the problem (as evidenced, for example, in the staff studies on ways to dampen the residential construction cycle), but in 1966 used the selective measures available to it,

---

[42]"The French System of Monetary and Credit Controls," *Quarterly Review* of the Banca Nazionale del Lavoro, No. 99 (1971), pp. 334, 340-41.

[43]See Donald R. Hodgman, "British Techniques of Monetary Policy: A Critical Review," *Journal of Money, Credit and Banking* 3 (1971): 760-69.

[44]See David P. Eastburn, "Federal Reserve Policy and Social Priorities," *Business Review* of the Federal Reserve Bank of Philadelphia, November 1970, pp. 2-18.

not very good ones, in a deliberate effort to dampen the shift of resources from the residential to the business sector.[45]

It would be unfortunate if, in response to immediate pressures as they arise, we go the way of the British and French by drifting piecemeal and without forethought into an ad hoc system of selective controls that becomes increasingly complex over time. Perhaps it is inherent in the nature of the beast that only a very complex system can work, but it is not obvious that this is so. It is possible that a system can be devised that employs a limited number of specific tools, that will permit effective control over allocation and aggregate demand, and yet not require extensive and costly administrative interference in financial markets and the management of financial institutions. This is an issue deserving extensive research.

VII. INCREASING THE FLOW OF RESOURCES INTO HOUSING

Selective controls can also be used to increase the share of resources channeled into housing. This is essentially a long-run objective, involving "one-way" changes (toward liberalization). One might interpret the secular liberalization of terms on residential mortgages that has in fact occurred since the 1930s in this light—in part at least. In part, secular liberalization of terms also reflects the objective of equalizing the distribution of housing (discussed below).

Liberalization of lending terms is, of course, only one possible method of accomplishing the stated objective, and one pos-

---

[45]"The measures taken were designed to check the expansion of business loans by commercial banks which had not responded (except perhaps, perversely) to the general monetary tightness. In July, and again in September, reserve requirements were raised against large denomination certificates of deposit, and when interest rates on money-market instruments in September rose above the maximum rate allowable on CDs under Regulation Q, the Fed took no action to raise the ceiling. These measures were designed to impose additional pressures on the large money-market banks, which were in the forefront of the business loan expansion. Also in September, the System temporarily changed the basic ground rules surrounding member bank borrowing at the discount window. Banks were told in effect, that if they expected to borrow from their Federal Reserve Bank, they had better curtail the rate at which they were increasing their business loans." (See Guttentag, "The Federal Reserve and the Mortgage Market," p. 404.) It is doubtful that anyone in the Fed fooled himself about the effectiveness of such measures. Only one source of business credit was directly affected, which meant that the overall impact probably was quite small and was heavily concentrated on smaller firms without access to capital markets.

sible research project would be to examine the advantages and disadvantages of this approach relative to other approaches. Longer maturities can be viewed, for example, as an alternative to interest rate subsidies, while 110 or 120 percent loan-value ratios might be viewed as an alternative to lump-sum housing payments or even to public housing.

Crucial to such evaluation would be an analysis of the influence of mortgage terms on long-run housing demand. The existing literature on this problem is thin. Some econometric studies that aim to explain quarterly or annual fluctuations in construction, use credit terms as one of the arguments.[46] Such studies, to the extent that they succeed in measuring the effect of credit terms on housing demand, capture some mix of short- and long-run effects, with the former probably dominating. Clearly, changes in credit terms affect the timing of many house purchase decisions, but the long-run effect on demand is something else. Several microstudies have developed hypothetical estimates of the response of housing demand to changes in mortgage terms on the assumption that households always purchase the largest amount of house that existing terms allow.[47] However, they have provided no indications of the extent to which this assumption is valid.[48]

VIII. EQUALIZING THE DISTRIBUTION OF HOUSING

The objective of equalizing the distribution of housing considerably overlaps the objective of expanding the total volume of resources going into housing. Without doubt, elasticity of

---

[46]On econometric-type studies explaining the demand for new construction, where loan terms are explicitly included, see David S. Huang, "Effect of Different Credit Policies on Housing Demand," *Study of the Savings and Loan Industry* 3: 1211-41, and the sources cited there.

[47]See Jack E. Gelfand, "The Credit Elasticity of Lower-Middle Income Housing Demand," *Land Economics* 42 (1966): 464-72; Jack E. Gelfand, "Mortgage Credit and Lower-Middle Income Housing Demand," *Land Economics* 42 (1970): 163-70; and Ramsay Wood, "Credit Terms and Demand for Residential Construction," in U. S., Congress, Senate, Committee on Banking and Currency, Subcommittee on Housing, *Study of Mortgage Credit*, 85th Cong., 2d sess., 22 December 1958, pp. 87-120.

[48]In a study of this question as it applies to consumer loans, F. Thomas Juster and Robert P. Shay state that the majority of consumers are constrained by loan terms. See *Consumer Sensitivity to Finance Rates: An Empirical and Analytical Investigation*, Occasional Paper 88 (New York: National Bureau of Economic Research, 1964).

demand with respect to (nonrate) credit terms is highest among low-income households, so that for practical purposes, one objective implies the other. The secular easing of terms in the United States furthermore has been accompanied by preference accorded to lower-income households. Under the FHA program, this preference takes the form of higher loan-value ratios and longer maturities at low property values, as well as a maximum loan amount. In addition, there are income limits for eligibility to various special FHA programs. Under the VA program, a maximum guarantee amount causes private lenders to require higher down payments on more expensive houses.

There has been considerable discussion in recent years of various ways to increase the house-buying power of low-income families, and a major program of interest rate subsidies (FHA Section 235) has reached large dimensions while encountering very serious difficulties.[49] At the present time, experimentation is going forward on a new housing allowance approach. As far as this writer knows, no consideration has been given to the possibility of further liberalizing credit terms, the assumption being that we have gone about as far as we can or should go in that direction. Perhaps this assumption is justified, perhaps not. In any case, a research effort in this area would have to consider a range of alternatives, including interest rate subsidies. The basic problems of the interest-rate subsidy programs, as opposed to their myriad symptoms, are not yet clearly understood.

IX. CONCLUDING COMMENTS

From this exploration of selective controls on residential mortgages, we summarize the main conclusions bearing on research possibilities.

Broadly, there are two promising avenues of research. The first would focus on a question posed earlier: namely, is it possible to devise a system of selective controls that would

---

[49]See U. S., Congress, House, Committee on Banking and Currency, *Interim Report on HUD Investigation of Low- and Moderate-Income Housing Programs*, 92d Cong., 1st sess., 31 March 1971.

employ a limited number of specific tools, that will permit effective control over allocation and aggregate demand, and yet not require extensive administrative interference into financial markets and the management of financial institutions? This question would have to be explored within the framework of some assumptions regarding the extent of allocational concern. If the problem, for example, involves only allocation between the residential and corporate business sectors, controls on the latter probably would suffice. This was the assumption underlying the Board staff studies, which have made a very substantial contribution to the problem of applying selective controls to the business sector. Yet, this viewpoint seems too narrow. There already is considerable concern regarding allocation to the state and local sectors as well as to small (generally unincorporated) business. Hence, the study should consider a system of selective controls covering a number of broad sectors of the economy. It may be assumed that there is no need to consider allocation on the kind of very detailed basis that is employed in France, where there are separate controls (or control parameters) for many narrowly defined subcategories, in some cases extending to individual firms.

Another study might focus on the long-run allocation of resources to the residential sector. Credit term liberalization would be compared to other methods of increasing and equalizing the allocation of resources to the housing sector, such as interest rate subsidies or housing allowances. A principal focus of such a study would be the influence of mortgage terms on long-run housing demand.

RUDOLPH G. PENNER serves in the Office
of Management and Budget as Assistant to
the Director for Economic Policy and as
Deputy Associate Director for Economic
Policy. He holds a Ph.D. from Johns Hop-
kins University. Deputy Assistant Secretary
for Economic Affairs at the Department of
Housing and Urban Development from 1973
to 1975, and a senior staff economist for the
President's Council of Economic Advisers
during 1970-71, he has served as Professor
of Economics at the University of Rochester
and as economic consultant to the governments of Canada, Liberia, Tanzania, as well
as to various agencies of the U. S. Government. His writings include co-authorship of
Public Claims on U. S. Output and other
books and articles in professional journals
on public policy issues, primarily taxation
and government spending.

Taxation and the Allocation of Credit

RUDOLPH G. PENNER

I. INTRODUCTION

Tax laws greatly affect the supply and allocation of credit in an economy. In some cases they have been purposely designed to direct credit toward or away from certain economic activities. For example, the United States has imposed an interest equalization tax to discourage American investment abroad. In other cases, the effect on credit flows is simply a by-product of tax laws designed primarily to achieve certain redistributive goals or of compromises in tax legislation necessary to make the law easy to administer. This study focuses primarily on tax legislation purposely aimed at redirecting credit flows but, before analyzing particular tax techniques, it is necessary to put the problem in perspective by comparing the tax approach to other policy instruments which can be used to achieve the same end.

Presumably, any attempt to redirect credit away from or toward certain activities is based on the notion that privately motivated credit flows result in a misallocation of resources because they do not consider positive or negative externalities associated with particular activities, or that there are other imperfections in private markets which cause certain credit flows to depart from socially optimal levels. This study, then, is concerned with the efficiency of various policy techniques in achieving certain goals.

II. SOME GENERAL PRINCIPLES

Manipulation of credit flows represents a highly indirect approach to the fundamental goal of altering the pattern of economic activity. By altering the cost of credit, we are altering the cost of only one productive input, capital. Since producers are able to substitute capital for other factors of production, a subsidy or tax, resulting in a given percentage increase or decrease in the use of capital in an activity, typically results in a lower percentage increase or decrease in output. Thus, linkage of the subsidy or tax and output is weakened with the strength of the relationship depending on the production function's elasticity of substitution.

A more direct and perhaps more desirable approach to resource allocation is subsidizing or taxing output or all inputs to the activity that government hopes to alter. The results of the direct approach are probably more predictable. Furthermore, they are more efficient in that the producer's choice of an input combination is not distorted and is more likely to reflect true social costs. An exception occurs when credit markets are imperfect in that interest rates do not reflect the true opportunity cost of credit. Then, interference in credit markets can be justified but, since many credit programs seem to be designed to affect output patterns, this study shall continue to focus on this problem.

The link between the cost of credit and the activity to be encouraged or discouraged is also weakened by the fact that most investors engage in activities in addition to those the Federal Government wishes to affect. This leads to the following problem. Suppose that the Government wishes to stimulate home ownership by lowering the mortgage interest rate. Potential home buyers may take the opportunity to raise the debt-equity ratio associated with the house purchase in order to reduce the amount of instalment debt which they must assume in order to buy consumer durables. In other words, home buyers can substitute mortgage credit for other forms of credit and, consequently, the increase in mortgage credit outstanding will not be matched by a comparable increase in home purchases.

Now that some of the weak links between the cost of credit and real economic activity have been outlined, the effects of taxes on the pattern of credit flows may be analyzed. As a first step, it is necessary to examine the real investment decision briefly in order to catalog the ways in which tax laws affect that decision. To abstract from the problem raised in the previous paragraph, it should be assumed that we are considering an investor who is engaged solely in the activity which the government is trying to affect.

III. THE REAL INVESTMENT DECISION

Initially, we shall assume a world of perfect certainty and perfect markets for all products and factors of production including credit. Later these assumptions will be relaxed to some extent although consideration of all the complicated ramifications of introducing uncertainty into the model will be impossible.

Following Dale Jorgenson,[1] it can be assumed that the investor devises his investment strategy with the goal of maximizing the value of his firm. We shall also adopt Jorgenson's highly restrictive assumption that the firm manager assumes that sales, tax laws, and interest rates will remain constant. Under these circumstances, the investor will add units of capital to the point where the per-period, after-tax marginal revenue product of the last unit of capital installed equals the after-tax cost of using a unit of capital for one period. Abstracting from tax legislation, the cost of using a unit of capital equals

---

[1] "Capital Theory and Investment Behavior," Papers and proceedings of the Seventy-fifth Annual Meeting of the American Economic Association, *American Economic Review* 53 (May 1963): 247-59.

the value of the portion that wears out in each time period plus the opportunity cost of the funds invested in the capital good. Present tax law provides two direct subsidies for the purchase of the good. First, the investment tax credit reduces tax liabilities by 7 percent of the value of long-lived equipment investment and, thus, amounts to a 7-percent reduction in the price of the capital good if the investor has sufficient tax liabilities to offset the credit. Second, the law allows the investor to charge a depreciation allowance against taxable income and, in some situations, the value of the resulting tax reduction is also equivalent to a reduction in the price of the capital good. In addition, the annual cost of using a unit of capital is reduced by the fact that interest on borrowed funds can be deducted from taxable income. Therefore, when taxes are considered, the value of the firm is maximized when

(1) $(1 - t)MRP = q(d + r - atr) (1 - y - tz)$

where: t is the profit tax rate;

q is the price of a unit of capital;

d is the proportion of capital which really wears out every time period;

r is the opportunity cost of capital;

a is the proportion of the opportunity cost which can be written off against taxable income. (Under present law this equals the proportion of the investment financed by debt issues.);

y is the investment tax credit;

z is the present value of the depreciation deduction used for tax purposes.

The formula becomes somewhat more complicated if the investor expects capital gains or losses on the capital good.

From (1), the before-tax marginal revenue product is equated to:

(2) $$\frac{q(d + r - atr) (1 - y - tz)}{(1 - t)}$$

This expression is referred to as the cost of capital (c).

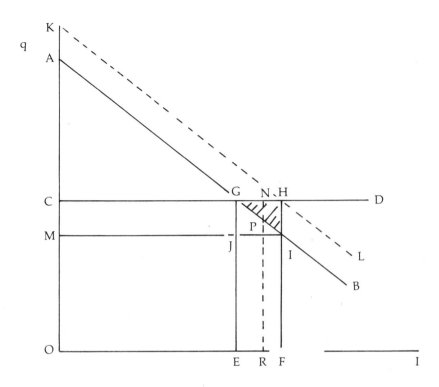

The pattern of credit flows will, of course, be affected first by the tax laws which directly apply to the investor thus influencing the demand for credit. These are the laws affecting t, a, y, and z. Second, credit flows will be affected by those laws which work indirectly on the supplies of credit and determine r, the opportunity cost of funds. In our perfect world this will be equivalent to the interest rate on debt.

Before providing a detailed analysis of particular tax changes, it is useful to compare the effectiveness of tax changes in general with other means of stimulating investment in particular sectors of the economy. For concreteness, assume that we wish to stimulate investment in a depressed area of the nation.

Before any change in policy, the demand for investment

goods at various capital good prices (q) and for given tax laws and interest rates is shown by the solid line AB in the adjacent Figure. It is assumed that the supply of capital goods is perfectly elastic to this area at price OC. Before any policy change, the equilibrium level of investment is OE. Now suppose that in order to encourage investment the Government offers the investor an explicit subsidy equivalent to AK per unit of installed capital goods. The equilibrium level of investment is increased to OF at a cost to Government of CHIM. Note that of this cost, CGJM represents a windfall to investors who would have made capital expenditures in the depressed area even in absence of any subsidy program.

The budget cost of the program could clearly be reduced significantly if the same increase in investment could be induced without making this transfer. Theoretically, this could be achieved in the following way. The Government would announce that it was making x dollars available to subsidize investments in depressed areas. It would then invite investors to bid for these dollars which would be auctioned off in, say, thousand-dollar lots. If bidding were competitive, the price would, of course, be $1000 for investment "lots" until total investment reaches E since no marginal subsidy is required to induce investment. For investments to the right of E, firms would be willing to pay an amount equal to the marginal revenue product of the investment goods which could be purchased for $1000. For example, suppose that one unit of capital cost $1000 = OC = RN. Once total investment reaches OR the price of a thousand-dollar grant would be bid up to RP and the net cost to government would be PN. Similarly, at OF investment the top bid would fall to FI and the net cost to government of the marginal unit would be IH. In other words, if the scheme worked properly, EF extra investment could be induced at a net budget cost of the shaded area GHI as opposed to the cost of CHIM for a straight subsidy scheme. Consequently, the bidding procedure seems like a far superior approach to inducing extra investment in particular sectors of the economy.[2]

---

[2]Here this procedure was applied to a grant scheme, but theoretically one could have firms bid for tax advantages worth equivalent amounts of money. However, there is no special reason for doing this, and it may be more difficult to administer.

Despite the bidding approach's advantages, it has probably never been implemented. Its novelty seems to provoke hostility, and it is often argued that it gives large firms an advantage because they have a greater supply of resources to finance their bids. Given perfect credit markets and perfect knowledge, this charge would be completely false, if the lots were sufficiently small, because all firms should be willing to bid the MRP of the capital which they can buy with the grant. If big firms outbid small firms, it is only because they are more efficient and then they should be the recipients of the grants. However, large firms would have an unwarranted advantage if credit markets are imperfect in that there is discrimination against small firms. In addition, a firm can never be certain of the MRP associated with a given investment and it may be true that large firms are better able to bear the risk of making a certain bid—that is, they would demand a lower-risk premium. Despite these possible disadvantages, the potential saving associated with bidding procedures should be tried.[3]

Since it is probably unrealistic to assume that a bidding scheme could be implemented, let us proceed to compare straight subsidy schemes to various tax measures—for example, a subsidy and a tax concession, both of which impose an equal cost on the Government and move the market demand curve for capital goods from AB to KL.

Stanley Surrey has vigorously argued that tax concessions are an inferior way of reallocating resources because they lead to inefficient management of Government policies.[4] He contends that once concessions are established, they are seldom reexamined and tend to outlast their usefulness. In contrast, explicit subsidies must be reexamined every year as part of the regular budget review process. In addition, they appear in the budget, and expenditures can be determined by interested parties. Tax concessions are hidden and revenue losses are often difficult to estimate. Even where it is easy to estimate losses, it is

---

[3]Probably the real reason that the idea is politically unpopular as compared to subsidies is that investors will lobby vigorously to avoid losing the windfall equivalent to CGJM.

[4]"Tax Subsidies as a Device for Implementing Government Policy: A Comparison with Direct Government Expenditures," in U. S., Congress, Joint Economic Committee, *The Economics of Federal Subsidy Programs*, 92d Cong., 2d sess., 8 May 1972, Part 1, pp. 74-105.

not done regularly. Of course, the matter is not completely one-sided. Political pressures make eliminating any subsidy exceedingly difficult, whereas we have seen that the investment tax credit has been constantly reexamined and has varied much more than the typical subsidy scheme.

Proponents of tax concessions argue that they are relatively easy to administer. Once established they work more or less automatically and do not have to be constantly monitored. In contrast, subsidies usually involve application procedures and constant surveillance. While this view may have some merit in relation to broadly based tax concessions such as the investment tax credit and the tax exemption on state and local bonds, narrowly based tax concessions tend to involve the same administrative complexities as explicit subsidies. For example, if a special tax credit were established for investments in depressed areas, it would probably be administered by a special board which is given the responsibility of certifying that the taxpayer actually made an investment in an eligible area. We, therefore, concur with Surrey in favoring explicit subsidies over narrowly based tax concessions.

However, tax concessions will remain popular politically, perhaps for the very reason that they are not scrutinized on a regular basis. Therefore, it is useful to analyze them more carefully, weighing the advantages and disadvantages of various tax measures resulting in the same outward shift in the demand curve for capital goods shown in Figure on page 71. The analysis will be organized as follows: First, the tax measures directly affecting the cost of capital (c) will be briefly compared. As noted previously, these are the investment-tax credit, depreciation allowances, the amount of the interest deduction allowed against taxable profits, and the tax rate. Second, current opinion on the impact of changing c on the investment decision will be reviewed. Third, the question of changing c will be reconsidered, but through the indirect approach of using tax concessions or penalties to change the cost of credit to the firm. Although it might have been more pleasing logically to consider the direct and indirect methods of changing c together, the latter is so complex that it was convenient to do it separately. Moreover, a more detailed analysis is necessary, since the indi-

74

rect approach is of greater interest to the sponsors of this contribution.

IV. DIRECT TAX POLICIES

1. Investment Tax Credit. The investment tax credit (ITC) is the tax measure most resembling a straight subsidy for the purchase of capital goods. Like a direct subsidy, a given ITC has a greater impact on the percentage cost of capital of short-lived investments than of longer-lived ones, because the present value of the depreciation allowance—z in formula (2)—is higher for short-lived investments. In current law, we crudely correct for this distortion by lowering the tax credit allowed on investments expected to last less than eight years and by eliminating it altogether for investments lasting less than three years.

It should be noted that tax credits and subsidies are, in a sense, more valuable to people in higher tax brackets. This can be seen from formula (2) which has $1 - t$ in the denominator. Put another way, a tax-free payment in the form of a subsidy or tax credit is equivalent to a greater addition to taxable income the higher the recipient's tax bracket. This effect can be neutralized by considering the subsidy or tax credit as part of taxable income, but this is not done in the case of our current tax credit.

The major difference between a subsidy and tax credit is that the recipient must have tax liabilities in order to take advantage of the latter. Generous carry-forward provisions in current law imply that most investors are able to take advantage of the tax credit eventually, but to the extent that is delayed, its value must be discounted.

2. Depreciation Allowances. For a constant value of t, anything which raises the present value of the depreciation deduction (z), lowers the cost of capital. The value of z can be raised either by shortening the life of the equipment assumed for tax purposes or by allowing a higher proportion of the total depreciation deduction to be taken early in the life of the equipment. If t is expected to go up significantly in the future, then it may be possible that it is to the taxpayer's advantage to postpone the depreciation deduction either by assuming a long life for his investment or by choosing a technique, like straight-line depreciation, which lowers the proportion of the total deduction occurring early in the life of the investment. The Asset Depreciation Range adopted in 1971 allows taxpayers to assume lives either longer or shorter than guideline lives and hence is a double-edge incentive. Presumably, longer lives would be chosen by private investors and small corporations expecting higher incomes and marginal tax rates in the future. However, this assumes that the higher tax deduction in the future outweighs the fact that future benefits must be discounted and for most taxpayers this will not occur. Hence, most will choose shorter tax lives for their investments.

Because tax credits result in a permanent reduction of tax liabilities while more generous depreciation allowances only postpone tax liabilities, it is sometimes alleged that the latter provide a cheaper way of encouraging investment. However, this is true only if Government has a much lower rate of discount than the investor. It can be shown that if both investors and Government apply the same rate of discount, investment tax credits cost less than changes in depreciation allowances providing the same reduction in c.[5] Moreover, the value of more lenient depreciation allowances rises more rapidly than the value of an investment tax credit as the tax bracket of the investor rises. For both these reasons, most observers favor investment tax credits as a means of stimulating investment.

3. *Deduction of Interest from Taxable Income.* In formula (2), a denotes the proportion of the opportunity cost of capital deductible against taxable income. There are two ways in which a could be increased beyond its level in current law. First, a deductible interest charge could be imputed for equity invested in real capital. Second, more than 100 percent of interest paid on debt could be deductible. Neither of these approaches has much appeal as compared to the investment tax credit. In both, the advantage gained by the investor depends more heavily on his tax bracket. In the first approach, the imputation of an interest

---

[5]See E. William Dinkelacker, "Alternative Tax Incentives for Investment," *Journal of Political Economy* 72 (1964): 184-88.

rate could only be an approximation and would therefore discriminate between investors. In the second approach, it would be virtually impossible to determine whether the debt issues were necessary to finance some other activity of the taxpayer.

A more controversial interest deduction is that for mortgages on owner-occupied houses. The controversy arises because the owner pays no taxes on the imputed rent earned on the house and, therefore, the deduction of interest must be regarded as an extra subsidy to home ownership. With no tax rate on the imputed return, and no tax deduction for depreciation, the cost of capital invested in a house (ch) becomes:

$$ch = (d + r - atr).$$

The formula clearly indicates the capricious nature of the subsidy, because it is strongly affected by a, the ratio of debt to total value, and t, the tax bracket of the owner.

Henry Aaron has carefully studied the implications of this subsidy, using a comprehensive file of individual tax returns for 1966.[6] In that year, the subsidy cost $1.6 billion in foregone tax revenues, and together with the property tax deduction lowered the cost of home ownership from 10 to 15 percent. Various empirical studies estimate that the elasticity of demand for housing is between 1.0 and 1.5, and this implies that the two deductions increase the demand for housing by at least 10 percent and perhaps by more than 20 percent. Unfortunately, Aaron's methods make separation of the effects of the interest deduction from the property tax deduction difficult because the situation is complicated by the taxpayer's option of taking the standard deduction which has become much more generous since 1966. Recent estimates suggest that the interest deduction alone is responsible for slightly more than half the combined effect.

The reason for the interest deduction subsidy has never been made very explicit. If its goal is to increase home ownership because of some positive externality, then a direct subsidy for all of the costs of a home would be both more efficient and more equitable, although it may be more difficult to administer. An investment tax credit for new housing may be more readily

---

[6]See his "Income Taxes and Housing," *American Economic Review* 60 (1970): 789-806.

administered and it would also be superior to the interest deduction.

If the goal of the deduction is to counter imperfections in mortgage markets, it is somewhat more defensible although it still is a crude instrument. The deduction is most valuable to those in the highest brackets who are least likely to be affected by market imperfections. A straight interest subsidy is more equitable and can be focused on areas of the market with the most serious imperfections. However, given all of the Government's guarantee, insurance, and secondary-market programs, it is hard to believe that imperfections remain.

4. *Changing the Income Tax Rate*. Since most taxpayers are engaged in a variety of activities and may already have old investments in the socially desirable activity, it would often take a complicated cost accounting job to identify the return on new investment in the socially desirable activity. Therefore, an income tax concession on the return to eligible investments only is not a very practical approach. Moreover, the same degree of encouragement to particular investments can more readily be gained by adjusting tax credits or depreciation allowances. For example, if we allow an investor to expense his capital expenditures, we obtain a result equivalent to the elimination of profit taxes on that investment. To see this, assume that an investor buys a machine for $100 and earns a return of 10 percent after adjusting for real depreciation. Now apply a 50-percent tax to his return, but allow him to expense the machine. The after-tax cost of his machine is now $50 on which he earns $5 after tax. In other words, his rate of return is still 10 percent, and in this sense the expensing of the machine has neutralized the imposition of the tax. By allowing varying initial allowances, any implicit tax rate can be obtained; so there is no need to engage in the complicated matter of providing tax rate concessions on particular investments.

In conclusion, tax credits seem the most desirable of the direct tax concessions. Depreciation allowance adjustments would come second, and changing the nature of the interest deduction or the income tax rate would rank far behind.

V. THE IMPACT OF CHANGING THE COST OF CAPITAL

We have been examining various approaches to changing c, the cost of capital. Now we must ask how changes in c affect the investment decision and there is little agreement on this point with regard to business investment. Yet, there is general agreement that housing investment is sensitive to r and, therefore by implication, to c.

At one extreme of the business investment studies is Dale Jorgenson who believes that changes in c have a very powerful impact.[7] He reaches this conclusion after fitting a "neoclassical investment" model which assumes that the elasticity of substitution between labor and capital equals 1. Believing that his model fits as well as any of its competitors, he cites considerable independent evidence that the elasticity of substitution is in fact close to 1.

At the other extreme are Robert Eisner and M. I. Nadiri.[8] Although they would presumably admit that changes in c would have a potent effect in a certain world with a high elasticity of substitution, they believe that in our uncertain world, the typical change in c is small relative to changes in sales, another important determinant of investment, even in Jorgenson's model. Consequently, businessmen concentrate their limited decision-making resources on predicting sales, and in doing this, they are strongly influenced by past changes in sales. In substantiating their view, Eisner and Nadiri fit an accelerator model with independent tests of the importance of c and conclude that changes in the latter are quite insignificant.

Charles W. Bishoff has studied both models and reaches a middle-ground position.[9] His results indicate that changes in c are significant, but not quite as important as Jorgenson indi-

---

[7]Jorgenson, op. cit.

[8]See their "Neoclassical Theory of Investment Behavior: A Comment," *Review of Economics and Statistics* 52 (1970): 216-22.

[9]See his "Hypothesis Testing and the Demand for Capital Goods," *Review of Economics and Statistics* 51 (1969): 354-68.

cates. Moreover, they influence the investment decision with a longer time-lag than do sales.[10]

The models discussed so far attempt to explain aggregate investment in broadly defined sectors of the economy.[11] Even if Eisner and Nadiri are right in believing that changes in c have little effect on aggregate investment, a differential reduction of c for a narrowly defined type of socially desirable investment may have an impact on the investor, particularly if he believes that the returns to all types of business investment tend to be positively correlated over the business cycle. In other words, a tax concession reducing c for investments in a depressed area has a large impact on investment in that area although a reduction in c to the whole economy has little impact.

However, the nature of the impact on the depressed area must be carefully examined to see if the rise in investment helps to meet social goals. A reduction in c will attract investment to the depressed area for two reasons. First, some firms will relocate in order to take advantage of the tax concession. Second, firms, which would have located in the depressed area anyway, will have an incentive to substitute capital for labor. If the social goal is to increase employment in a depressed area, then the first effect will be in the right direction, whereas the second effect will work against it in the long run. Consequently, the net effect can be positive or negative depending on the substitutability of capital for labor. This indicates that if increased employment is the goal, application of our tax incentive directly to the employment of labor rather than to investment would have yielded more effective results. Similarly, if we wish to maximize certain types of output, direct subsidies are more effective. Repeating the point made earlier, tax concessions aimed at reducing c only make sense if more investment is desired for its own sake, because of positive externalities associated with the investment itself or because of constraints imposed by imperfections in the market for capital goods or credit.

---

[10]In Jorgenson's model the time-lags for both variables are constrained to be equal.

[11]Other researchers have experimented with cash flow and stock market variables. But rightly or wrongly, these approaches will not be discussed in this study, largely because they are passé. However, for more detailed information on these models, see Jorgenson's "Econometric Studies of Investment Behavior: A Survey," *Journal of Economic Literature* 9 (1971): 1111-47.

VI. AFFECTING C BY AFFECTING THE RATE OF INTEREST PAID BY BORROWERS

An examination of the formula denoting the cost of capital indicates that c is quite sensitive to changes in the interest rate. Speaking roughly, a one-third fall in r would be equivalent to the provision of a 7-percent investment-tax credit for the typical equipment investment lasting about ten years. However, a caveat is in order. The theory of the real investment decision underlying formula (2) was based on the assumption of a perfectly certain, perfectly competitive world in which the opportunity cost of capital would equal the interest rate on borrowing which would, in turn, be equal for all firms. While this very unrealistic assumption may be an adequate approximation when studying the real investment decision as a whole, it may be misleading when the borrowing practices of firms are analyzed. When lending practices are analyzed, it becomes essential to consider an uncertain world, because lenders are mainly concerned with minimizing the risk that must be absorbed in reaching an expected rate of return.

Looking first at the borrowing practices of firms, the issue is greatly complicated by tax law. If there were no taxes and no transactions costs on credit markets, Franco Modigliani and Merton Miller have shown that the financial practices of firms would be irrelevant to their value, because investors could always gain any degree of leverage that they desire by manipulating their own equity-debt ratio independently of the debt-equity ratios chosen by particular firms.[12] In the real world the shareholder must bear transactions costs in attempting to neutralize the firm's financial policies. Consequently, the corporation has greater incentive to be solicitous of its shareholders' needs in formulating its borrowing policies. In turn, one of the primary determinants of the wishes of shareholders will be their own tax situation. Joseph E. Stiglitz has shown that if a corporation's shares and bonds are held by individuals significantly below the top personal income-tax bracket, the total tax bill on the income stream generated by the corporation will

---

[12]"The Cost of Capital, Corporation Finance, and the Theory of Investment," *American Economic Review* 48 (1958): 261-97.

be lowered by maximizing borrowing.[13] However, extremely wealthy shareholders would wish the corporation to minimize borrowing. Yet, generalizing is difficult because small differences in the tax status of shareholders may alter their wishes. For example, the fact that capital gains are not taxable at death implies that shareholders with a strong bequest motive will have different desires than those who plan a consumption binge before their death. However, Stiglitz has shown that for wealthy shareholders (those with personal tax rates above the corporate rate), the total tax bill is fairly insensitive to a firm's financial policies. This implies that fairly significant tax changes might be necessary to get significant changes in the relative supplies of debt and equity issues. Therefore, instead of exploring the effect of taxes on the supply of securities, their effects on the composition of demand should be considered. To analyze this problem, it is necessary to explain briefly the current theory regarding the ways in which an investor compiles his portfolio of real and financial investments.

Although the theory of portfolio choice is highly developed, the theory of the effects of taxation on that choice is still in a primitive state. The classic article in the field is that of Joseph Stiglitz,[14] and we shall first summarize that article and then discuss the empirical and theoretical problems which remain unresolved.

The theory of portfolio choice assumes that investors handle the problem of uncertainty by attaching a probability distribution of returns to each asset. If the distribution is normal it can be completely described by its mean and variance, but if it is more complicated, it is necessary to calculate higher moments of the distribution in order to provide an adequate description.

Given a probability distribution of returns for each individual asset and a budget constraint, the investor can achieve a

---

[13]See his *Taxation, Risk-Taking, and the Allocation of Investment in a Competitive Economy* (New Haven, Conn: Cowles Foundation for Research in Economics at Yale University, 1970).

[14]See his "Effects of Wealth, Income, and Capital Gains Taxation on Risk-Taking," *Quarterly Journal of Economics* 83 (1969): 263-83. Many scholars have studied the problem in a similar way. Among the more recent are Jan Mossin, "Taxation and Risk-Taking: An Expected Utility Approach," *Economica* 35 (1968): 74-82; and Martin S. Feldstein, "The Effects of Taxation on Risk-Taking," *Journal of Political Economy* 77 (1969): 755-64.

wide variety of probability distributions of returns for his portfolio by combining various assets in different proportions. The final choice will depend crucially on the shape of the investor's utility function.[15] If the investor is subject to diminishing marginal utility, the difference between the amount of utility derived from an outcome x dollars above the mean and the utility derived from the mean will be less than the utility difference between the mean and an outcome x dollars below the mean. In other words, the expected utility derived from a probability distribution of returns will be less than the level of utility which would be derived from receiving the mean of the distribution with certainty. This shortfall varies directly with the variance of the distribution. Therefore, given a choice between two distributions with the same mean an investor with diminishing marginal utility will always select the one with lower variance and for that reason is known as a risk-averter. Similarly, an investor with increasing marginal utility of wealth likes variance[16] and is known as a risk-lover. However, since it is generally believed that risk-averting behavior predominates in business and in society, in general, the rest of this analysis will assume that all investors are risk-averters.

When a proportional income tax with perfect loss offset is applied to the probability distribution of returns of a given portfolio, it has two opposite effects on the desirability of that portfolio. The tax, of course, lowers the expected value of the distribution, thus making it less desirable. At the same time, the after-tax distribution has a lower variance than the before-tax distribution, making it more desirable to the investor. Whether the portfolios that are riskier before-tax rise (or fall) in the investor's preference ordering hinges on the rate at which his marginal utility diminishes.

Two measures of this rate have developed. The first, known as a measure of absolute risk aversion, is defined as the ratio of the second derivative of utility with respect to wealth to margi-

---

[15]Portfolio theory assumes that utility can be measured cardinally, and therefore an expected utility level from any probability distribution of returns can be found.

[16]This statement is somewhat oversimplified. It is possible to characterize a risk-lover with a cubic-utility function in which case, he still dislikes variance, but likes positive skewness.

nal utility, $-\frac{U''(W)}{U'(W)}$. This measure is referred to as A(W). The second, evaluating something known as relative risk aversion, is defined as the elasticity of marginal utility with respect to wealth, $-\frac{W \cdot U''(W)}{U'(W)}$. This measure is denoted as R(W).

On the one hand, if A(W) is increasing, the investor will put fewer dollars in risky ventures as his wealth increases. On the other hand, if R(W) is increasing, the individual will also invest less in risky ventures as his wealth increases.

The quadratic, one of the more popular utility functions in theoretical analysis, implies that both A(W) and R(W) are increasing. The exponential implies that A(W) is constant while R(W) is increasing. And the logarithmic assumes A(W) is decreasing while R(W) is constant. A major issue in this field is what behavior of A(W) and R(W) best characterizes investor-utility functions. Virtually everyone agrees that A(W) must be decreasing, because it seems totally unrealistic to assume that individuals invest absolutely less in risky enterprises as they become richer. Therefore, the quadratic-utility function must be rejected. However, there is little agreement about the proper assumption for R(W). Kenneth Arrow believes that R(W) must be increasing. He bases this view on both theoretical and empirical considerations.[17] Theoretically, for reasons too complex to be described here, the utility function must be bounded from above. Mathematically, this implies that R(W) must be increasing over a considerable range of W. Empirically, Arrow refers to time-series data which indicate that the proportion of assets held in cash has been increasing as the economy has become wealthier. Stiglitz questions this view.[18] The fact that R(W) must be increasing over some range of the utility function does not necessarily imply that it must be increasing over the range of W relevant to most investors. Secondly, cross-section data on wealthier individuals shows that the portion of their portfolio held in cash and bonds decreases as wealth increases.

---

[17]*Aspects of the Theory of Risk Bearing*, Yrjö Jahnsson Lectures (Helsinki: Yrjö Jahnsson Saatio, 1965).

[18]Stiglitz, Effects of Wealth, Income and Capital Gains Taxation on Risk-Taking," pp. 263-83.

As we shall see, resolution of this issue is crucial for understanding the effects of income taxation on portfolio choice, and further research is clearly warranted.[19]

Stiglitz's analysis applies only to the choice between a safe and a risky asset. If we accept Arrow's view that R(W) is increasing and A(W) is decreasing, Stiglitz shows that a proportional income tax with perfect loss offset will increase the demand for the risky asset. Consequently, the relative rate of return on such assets should fall. The same result follows if R(W) is constant or decreasing slightly. However, if R(W) decreases at a more rapid rate, the tax will reduce the demand for the risky asset.

The conclusions are altered significantly if the perfect-loss offset assumption is eliminated. First and most obvious, the demand for the risky asset will always be less, given a tax with less than perfect loss offset, than under the same tax rate with perfect loss offset. In addition, Stiglitz is able to prove a number of propositions under the assumption that the rate of return on the safe asset is zero, but it is not clear how the conclusions are affected if a positive rate of return applies to the safe asset. The major propositions are as follows:

1. In comparison with zero tax rate, a no-loss-offset income tax decreases the demand for the risky asset if $R(W) \leq 1$. It can be noted that $R(W) = 1$ for a logarithmic function, sometimes called the Bernoulli function. It should be emphasized that this is sufficient but not a necessary condition—that is, the same conclusion can hold over some range when $R(W) > 1$.
2. A no-loss-offset tax reduces private risk-taking if A(W) decreases. This means only that the after-tax variance of the portfolio is lower. Under some conditions the before-tax variance can rise.

The success of any attempt to divert credit flows toward certain activities by using differential tax rates also depends crucially on the behavior of A(W) and R(W). If only the safe asset is taxed, demand for the risky asset will be increased if A(W) is constant or increasing. We noted before that this condition on

---

[19]To this writer's knowledge, very little research has been done on this issue. Some data on the portfolios of wealthier individuals do exist and probably more can be acquired from estate tax returns.

A(W) seems unrealistic, but also note that it is a sufficient, but not a necessary condition. Demand for the risky asset will also be increased if $R(W) \leq 1$. If A(W) decreases and $R(W) > 1$, it is quite possible that a tax on the safe asset alone will lead to less rather than more risk-taking. If we compare a tax on the safe asset alone to one on both assets which imposes the same expected utility loss on the investor, it is not certain that the former leads to more risk-taking than the latter.

In conclusion, Stiglitz's analysis reveals that knowing more about the appropriate form of R(W) is vital, before trying to predict the effect of income taxes on the choice between risky and safe assets. While his article is an intellectual achievement, some theoretical issues remain unresolved. First, it is not clear how the results are altered if the investor must choose between two risky assets rather than between a risky and a safe asset. Under Stiglitz's assumption, an increase in the demand for the risky asset always implies that the before-tax risk attached to the whole portfolio rises. When there are two risky assets this simple relationship no longer holds, and under certain conditions an increase in the demand for the riskier of two risky assets may reduce the risk attached to the portfolio because of the power of diversification. Second, the analysis is greatly simplified by the assumption that the investor must choose between two assets. It is not clear whether the results hold if many assets are considered.

Despite the many theoretical and empirical uncertainties which emerge from the above analysis, one conclusion stands out: The loss offset provisions of the tax laws are extremely important because they reduce the negative portion of the probability distribution of returns for which the marginal utility of income is relatively high. Consequently, if Government wishes to enhance demand for particular securities, it should first be certain that loss offset is perfect. This will, of course, have a more powerful impact, the riskier the security.

In current tax law, loss offsets come very close to perfection. Capital losses of individuals can first be deducted against realized capital gains. Where capital losses exceed capital gains, total short-term losses and half of long-term losses can be deducted against regular income up to a limit of $1000. When losses exceed this limit, they can be carried forward indefinitely. As a result of these provisions, most losses are offset eventually. However, offsets are imperfect to the extent that the taxpayer may have to wait in order to take advantage of them. Yet, the loss-offset provision overcompensates the taxpayer if he is able to offset long-run losses against the short-run gains, since only half the long-run gains would be subject to tax. Before the Tax Reform Act of 1969 the probability of overcompensation was even greater, because long-term losses could be fully offset against regular income up to the limit of $1000.

Because current loss offsets are quite generous, there is not too much scope for being even more lenient with favored securities. However, certain minor steps could be taken. The income deduction limit could be waived and refunds could be paid where other income was not sufficient to cover losses. This would avoid the waiting period and ensure that the taxpayer would be able to recover the tax benefits of all losses. One could go further and overcompensate by allowing all long-run losses to be offset against regular income. The problem is that this greatly favors high-bracket taxpayers.

Because these are minor steps, their impact would be fairly insignificant, but they should be quite powerful relative to the trivial tax revenue losses which they would imply. If the Government wishes to go further in the direction of reducing risk on particular securities, it should move toward a loan guarantee or insurance program rather than using the relatively awkward device of tax offsets to overcompensate for losses. Loan guarantees can have a large impact relative to their budget cost. George Break has substantiated this point regarding insurance programs applied to mortgages.[20]

While portfolio selection theory implies that loss offsets are vital, it casts considerable doubt on the effectiveness of tax concessions applied to the rate of return on particular securities. To repeat Stiglitz's conclusion: Eliminating the tax on the risky security may actually reduce the demand for it if $R(W) > 1$. However, this outcome is not intuitively appealing, and casual

---

[20]*The Economic Impact of Federal Loan Insurance* (Washington: National Planning Association, 1961).

observation suggests that the tax exemption on state and local bonds has been highly effective in driving down the rate of return, while tax penalties implied by the interest equalization tax have apparently been effective in reducing capital flows into foreign securities, although this point has not been as carefully substantiated. There are ways of reconciling the theoretical uncertainty regarding the effectiveness of tax concessions with the casual observation that such concessions are highly effective. First, the special tax provisions noted above may apply only to relatively safe securities, in which case the theory would suggest that they would be more potent. Undoubtedly, state and local bonds are relatively safe securities, but the same may not be true for foreign securities. Second, R(W) may, in fact, be less than one for most investors. Third, and most important, Stiglitz's analysis may be greatly limited by the fact that only two securities are considered. When large numbers of securities are considered, groups of securities with similar rates of return and risk characteristics can be found. If, in addition, there is a high positive covariance among the rates of return on these securities, they will become excellent substitutes for one another in the portfolios of investors. (Therefore, a tax concession applied to only one set of securities will greatly increase the demand for it. For example, state and local bonds and Federal bonds are probably highly substitutable in the portfolios of investors. Consequently, a tax concession affecting only state and local bonds has a very powerful impact.

For this reason, we can be confident that a tax concession can be effective if it is aimed at a narrowly defined set of securities, although we should withhold judgment on the effect of broadly based tax concessions such as those applied to all capital gains.

Although this writer believes that a tax exemption on part or on all of the return to a certain security can be an effective method of lowering the rate of interest to a borrower, it is not a very desirable approach. The basic problem is that an exemption is worth very much more to a high tax-bracket investor than to a low-bracket one. Moreover, there are so few individuals in the highest bracket that it is unlikely that the return will be bid down sufficiently so that they are indifferent between holding the favored security and other securities. Thus, the point of indifference is likely to come lower in the tax scale. Anyone in a higher bracket will receive a windfall which is not matched by any benefit to the borrower. For example, suppose that a certain security originally paying 10 percent interest is given an exemption and as a result the return falls to 4 percent. Investors in the 60-percent bracket will be indifferent between a tax-exempt 4 percent and a taxable 10 percent, while those in the 70-percent bracket will receive a one-percentage point windfall. Thus a straight 60-percent subsidy would have been of the same benefit to the borrower but cheaper for the Government.

A straight percentage subsidy could be obtained by using an interest tax credit, but of course identical effects result only where the investor has other current tax liabilities against which to deduct the credit. Remember that tax credits or subsidies are relatively more valuable to the high-bracket taxpayer unless the subsidy or credit is itself taxed. However, the degree of discrimination is very much less than in the case of an exemption. Hence, for these and other reasons discussed in relation to the real investment decision, this writer ranks a straight subsidy first in order of desirability, with a tax credit second, and a tax exemption a poor third.

If, despite these objections, a tax-exemption approach is chosen, it should be noted that there are various ways of granting a given exemption. Instead of a partial exemption lasting the life of the security, a larger exemption could be granted for the first part of the life—for example, a tax holiday could be granted for the first year. If the investor has a larger discount rate than the Government, the tax holiday approach will have a larger impact for the same present value of the Government's tax loss. However, the tax holiday approach may be slightly more difficult to administer.

VII. INTEREST EXEMPTION FOR STATE AND LOCAL BONDS

In fiscal 1968, the tax exemption for the interest on state and local bonds resulted in a revenue loss to the Treasury of $1.8

billion, most of which benefited very high bracket taxpayers.[21] In the previous discussion, it was suggested that this tax loss far exceeded the interest saving to states and localities, and, while this is undoubtedly true, the issue is extremely complex. It is even theoretically possible for the interest saving to exceed the tax loss, but empirical studies of the problem suggest that this is a highly unlikely outcome.[22]

The problem is complex because it is not known exactly how individuals in different tax brackets would shift their portfolios if the tax exemptions were removed and how relative yields would adjust as a result of the portfolio change.

Elimination of the tax exemption would result in two basic shifts. First, current holders of state and local bonds would shift toward other investments and in particular they would seek other tax shelters. Second, the before-tax interest rate on state and locals would rise, attracting present holders of taxable investments. Since there would be a greater demand for remaining tax shelters, the relative rate of return would fall, inducing some previous holders of these investments to shift to other taxable securities including state and local bonds.

Taking account of these changes, David Ott and Allan Meltzer estimate the following outcome for 1960 assuming that the exemption were removed only from new issues and, somewhat unrealistically, that the volume of all security issues remained unchanged.[23] First, interest costs to state and local governments would rise between 30.7 and 53.5 percent. After taking account of the shifts outlined above, this implies that the average marginal tax rate of those buying municipals before the change would have to be between 23.5 and 34.9 percent in order for new tax revenues to be equal to the increased interest cost. In fact, they estimate that the marginal rate is 41 to 43 percent, indicating new tax revenues far in excess of extra interest costs.

---

[21]For a detailed discussion of the distribution of the tax benefit, see Susan Ackerman and David Ott, "An Analysis of the Revenue Effects of Proposed Substitutes for Tax Exemption of State and Local Bonds," *National Tax Journal* 23 (1970): 397-406.

[22]Detailed studies of the problem can be found in David Ott and Allan H. Meltzer, *Federal Tax Treatment of State and Local Securities* (Washington: Brookings Institution, 1963); and Harvey Galper and John Petersen, "An Analysis of the Subsidy Plans to State and Local Borrowing," *National Tax Journal* 24 (1971): 205-34.

[23]Ott and Meltzer, op. cit.

In addition, certain other budgetary effects must be considered. On the one hand, relative interest costs on the Federal debt would probably rise because of shifts of lower-bracket investors into state and local issues. On the other hand, state and local governments would probably be allowed to tax Federal interest as a quid pro quo. The geographic distributional effects of the latter change would be quite uneven because they would depend on Federal bond holding in each state and locality and the relative importance of income taxes in those jurisdictions.

In a somewhat different approach to the problem Harvey Galper and John Petersen[24] look at the effect of substituting a 50-percent interest subsidy for the present exemption on municipal bonds only. Their study, based on regression estimates of the supply and demand for municipal bonds, concludes that the net cost to the U. S. Treasury would be $20 to $60 million after taking account of increased tax revenues. The interest saving would be $46 million under the assumptions leading to the cost of $20 million and $105 million under the assumptions leading to the cost of $60 million. In the former case, total borrowing would increase $1.2 billion and in the latter, $0.5 billion. All of these estimates suggest that a tax exemption on interest is a very ineffective way of diverting funds to particular activities as compared to a straight subsidy.

VIII. TAX LAWS AFFECTING FINANCIAL INTERMEDIARIES

In closing, it is necessary to examine briefly a highly indirect approach to lowering interest costs for particular borrowers. The Government has attempted to increase the demand for mortgages by restricting the portfolios of savings and loan institutions and mutual savings banks to this instrument and to various Government and Government-agency securities. Presumably, similar restrictions could be imposed to increase the demand for any security that the Government wishes to favor.

---

[24]Galper and Peterson, op. cit.

The problem is that restrictions reduce the competitive power of the restricted institution and, without complementary policies, the restricted institutions would shrink in size and, perhaps, disappear altogether. Therefore, various regulations and subsidies have been implemented to enhance the competitive power of such institutions. In the past some of these subsidies took the form of tax concessions. Financial institutions gained two important advantages: (1) they were able to deduct for the accumulation of bad debt reserves far in excess of those required; (2) they were allowed to deduct capital losses on bond holdings from regular income, although gains were subject to the more favorable capital gains tax. The Tax Reform Act of 1969 removed the second advantage by forcing institutions to consider capital gains on bonds as regular income. The first advantage was also reduced greatly, but still such institutions receive generous bad debt allowances.

Clearly, this is an indirect approach toward the enhancing of certain types of credit flows. On the one hand, the restrictions are usually crude and generate much waste. On the other hand, the complementary policies which reduce competition imply that a large portion of the cost of diverting credit flows falls on the depositors in the restricted institutions who, for various reasons, do not have suitable investment alternatives and who, therefore, must accept lower, regulated, interest rates. Perhaps the portfolio restriction plus tax advantage approach to diverting credit flows is the least desirable of all of the approaches considered so far.

IX. SUMMARY AND CONCLUSIONS

Although tax concessions and penalties have often been used to influence the pattern of credit flows, they cannot be considered as very effective means of affecting output patterns in the economy. Two factors undermine their effect on output. First, tax changes altering the cost of capital will induce producers to alter the ratio of capital to labor inputs, and, consequently, the resulting changes in the pattern of investment will exceed the changes in the pattern of outputs. Second, changes in taxes lowering the cost of debt will encourage a higher debt-equity ratio, and, therefore, changes in credit patterns will exceed changes in investment patterns. Moreover, the fact that investors are typically engaged in numerous activities makes it difficult to ensure that tax concessions for particular types of borrowing have an effect on the real activity that the Government wishes to favor. Investors may simply substitute favored borrowing for other sources of credit in activities far removed from those which the Government wishes to influence. Therefore, if changes in output patterns are desired, it is much more effective to subsidize or penalize the output directly or to subsidize or penalize all inputs in particular activities.

If tax concessions or penalties are aimed at imperfections in credit markets rather than at output patterns, they become easier to justify. However, interest subsidies or penalties are generally more equitable and efficient. Subsidies are also more desirable administratively, because, being a budget outlay, they are regularly scrutinized. In contrast, tax concessions are not reexamined regularly, and they are likely to outlive their usefulness. If, despite these deficiencies, the tax approach is chosen, tax credits are generally more desirable than other types of concessions, because they discriminate less between taxpayers in different tax brackets and generally cost less for a given impact.

WILLIAM L. SILBER is Professor of Economics and Finance at the Graduate School of Business Administration at New York University. He holds a Ph.D. from Princeton University, specializing in monetary policy, fiscal policy, and financial institutions. A former consultant to the Federal Reserve Board and the Federal Home Loan Bank Board, he served as a senior staff economist on the President's Council of Economic Advisers during 1970-71. He currently serves as an Associate Editor of the *Journal of Finance* and the *Review of Economics and Statistics*. Author of *Portfolio Behavior of Financial Institutions* and coauthor of *Principles of Money, Banking and Financial Markets*, he has contributed to the *American Economic Review*, the *Review of Economics and Statistics*, and the *Quarterly Journal of Economics*.

The author is grateful to Allan H. Meltzer for his helpful comments. The views expressed therein are the author's and do not necessarily reflect those of Mr. Meltzer.

94

Selective Credit Policies: A Survey

WILLIAM L. SILBER

I. INTRODUCTION

The increased attention paid to reordering national priorities in recent years has been paralleled by renewed interest in selective credit controls or, in more general terms, selective credit policies (policies and controls will be used interchangeably throughout the paper). In the United States, the Congress has launched an investigation into the activities of foreign central banks aimed at promoting social welfare programs, members of the Board of Governors of the Federal Reserve System have discussed the use of specific tools to direct credit to specific social purposes, and other Government-sponsored agencies have expressed renewed determination to aim their policies toward social goals.[1] Academic economists have also directed

---

[1] U. S., Congress, House, Committee on Banking and Currency, *Activities of Various Central Banks to Promote Economic and Social Welfare Programs: A Staff Report*, 91st Cong., 2d sess., December 1970; Andrew F. Brimmer, "The Banking Structure and Monetary Management," Remarks before the San Francisco Bond Club, 1 April 1970; Sherman J. Maisel, "Credit Allocation and the Federal Reserve," Remarks before a lecture sponsored by the Banking Research Center at Northwestern University, April 1971; and Preston Martin, "New Credit Policies for the 1970's: A Discussion of FHLBB Objectives," *Journal of the Federal Home Loan Bank Board*, December 1970, pp. 1-5, 30-31.

their efforts to analyzing selective credit policies. At least one general survey paper has been written,[2] and a number of analytical works have been presented defining and explaining the conditions under which selective credit policies work, such as the papers by Richard Davis,[3] by D. C. Rao and Ira Kaminow,[4] and by Rudolph Penner and William L. Silber.[5] Finally, a number of empirical studies have been conducted which bear directly on the issue of whether selective credit policies have an impact either in the aggregate or on various sectors of the economy, such as the studies by Paul Anderson,[6] Leonall Andersen,[7] Jacob Cohen,[8] David Huang,[9] Dwight Jaffee,[10] Francisco Arcelus and Allan Meltzer[11] and Ray Fair and Jaffee.[12]

This survey is directed at reviewing both the theoretical and empirical literature on selective credit policies. The major concern with most of the researchers in this area has been the range of conditions under which selective policies are effective. Our

---

[2]Donald R. Hodgman, "Selective Credit Controls," *Journal of Money, Credit and Banking* 4 (1972): 342-59.

[3]Richard G. Davis, "An Analysis of Quantitative Credit Controls and Related Devices," *Brookings Papers on Economic Activity*, No. 1 (1971): 65-97.

[4]D. C. Rao and Ira Kaminow, "Selective Credit Controls and the Real Investment Mix: A General Equilibrium Approach," *Journal of Finance* 28 (1973): 1103-18. Reprinted in this volume on pp. 173-95.

[5]Rudolph G. Penner and William L. Silber, "The Interaction between Federal Credit Programs and the Impact on the Allocation of Credit," *American Economic Review* 63 (1973): 838-52.

[6]Paul S. Anderson, "Monetary Velocity in Empirical Analysis," *Controlling Monetary Aggregates*, Conference Series No. 1 (Federal Reserve Bank of Boston, 1969), pp. 52-56.

[7]Leonall C. Andersen, "Discussion," ibid., pp. 37-51.

[8]Jacob Cohen, "Integrating the Real and Financial via the Linkage of Financial Flow," *Journal of Finance* 23 (1968): 1-27; and "Direct versus Indirect Controls as Instruments of Monetary Policy," *Quarterly Review of Economics and Business*, No. 3 (1970): 25-35.

[9]David S. Huang, "Further Analysis of Residential Mortgage Credit Flows," Paper presented at the Western Economic Association Meeting, Vancouver, B. C., Canada, 1971.

[10]Dwight M. Jaffee, "An Econometric Model of the Mortgage Market," Edward Gramlich and Dwight M. Jaffee, eds., *Savings Deposits, Mortgages, and Housing* (Lexington, Mass.: D. C. Heath and Company, Lexington Books, 1972), pp. 139-208.

[11]Francisco Arcelus and Allan H. Meltzer, "The Markets for Housing and Housing Services," *Journal of Money, Credit and Banking* 5 (1973): 78-99.

[12]Ray C. Fair and Dwight M. Jaffee, "The Implications of the Proposals of the Hunt Commission for the Mortgage and Housing Markets," *Policies for a More Competitive Financial System: A Review of the Report of the President's Commission on Financial Structure and Regulation*, Conference Series No. 8 (Federal Reserve Bank of Boston, 1972), pp. 99-148.

objective will be, in part, to determine where in this spectrum the real world fits. Before examining that question below, two other issues will be discussed, namely, what are selective credit policies and the real versus financial effects of such policies. A section on the costs, efficiency and equity of credit controls will conclude the paper. The institutional structure of the United States is used throughout.

II. WHAT ARE SELECTIVE CREDIT POLICIES?

Selective credit policies usually refer to one of two things: (a) The attempt to influence general credit conditions by a policy tool other than changes in the magnitude of claims against the central bank;[13] (b) The use of a policy tool to channel credit into a particular financial market, hence (although, not necessarily) into a particular real market.[14] Many tools are classified as selective according to both definitions, such as the real estate and consumer credit controls of the Korean War. On the other hand, there are differences in the practical application of each definition. For example, varying the maximum rate payable on savings accounts at bank and nonbank financial institutions would clearly be a selective policy according to definition (a) but not necessarily according to definition (b). In particular, if varying (or failure to vary) the ceiling rates were undertaken primarily for their possible aggregative effects (as might be said of 1966) then this would not qualify as a selective credit policy.

The first issue is, therefore, what one means or should mean by the term selective credit policies. Definition (a) is probably the implicit definition most often used when economists talk of selective credit policies. The reason for this is that changes in the liabilities of the central bank (changes in high-powered money) are considered neutral, i.e., not explicitly favoring one use of credit or real resources over some other use. Thomas Mayer has pointed out, however, that what noneconomists frequently mean by neutrality is proportionality, i.e., each type of credit or real resource is expanded or contracted proportion-

---

[13]Hodgman, op. cit., pp. 342-59.
[14]Rao and Kaminow, op. cit., pp. 1003-18.

ately by expansionary or contractionary monetary policy.[15] By this definition, varying the claims against the central bank does not possess the quality of neutrality. Most economists recognize that there are differential or selective impacts of changes in monetary policy, such as the evidence presented by Sherman J. Maisel.[16] The problem is to establish a normative standard by which to judge the impact of a contracyclical stabilization policy. There does not seem to be any such standard.

It is tempting to argue that, since changes in high-powered money have a stable and predictable impact on what we conventionally define as money,[17] and since money presumably has a stable and predictable impact on the gross national product,[18] the appropriate standard is, in fact, changes in high-powered money. Such an argument clearly begs the question, namely, what makes changes in money, however defined, neutral in the sense of producing the appropriate incidence of a contracyclical stabilization program? We will return to this topic, i.e., the normative aspects of stabilization policy, and monetary policy in particular, in the last section of the paper.

A possible reconciliation of definitions (a) and (b) can be developed along the lines of aggregate effects versus differential (or selective) effects of a particular policy. In the absence of a normative standard against which to judge selective versus general credit policies, all that may be possible is a ranking of different policies according to their relative aggregate versus selective impacts. For each policy one would calculate the impact on some economic aggregate, say, GNP, and one would also calculate its impact on the redistribution of real resources (or funds) into different sectors. The ratio of aggregate effects to redistribution effects would be the basis on which to rank a policy as primarily a selective credit policy or primarily a gen-

---

[15]Thomas Mayer, "Financial Guidelines and Credit Controls," *Journal of Money, Credit and Banking* 4 (1972): 360-74.

[16]"The Effects of Monetary Policy on Expenditures in Specific Sectors of the Economy," *Journal of Political Economy* 76 (1968): 796-814.

[17]Karl Brunner, "The Role of Money and Monetary Policy," *Review* of the Federal Reserve Bank of St. Louis, July 1968, pp. 9-24.

[18]Michael J. Hamburger, "Indicators of Monetary Policy: The Arguments and the Evidence," *American Economic Review*, Papers and proceedings of the Eighty-second Annual Meeting of the American Economic Association, 60 (May 1970): 32-39.

eral credit policy. This measure varies between zero and infinity and the larger the number the more general (as opposed to selective) is the particular credit policy. For example, a change in high-powered money which produces a significant change in GNP but produces only a small redistribution of GNP among different sectors would have a high ratio, while controls over real estate credit, which might have an impact on the proportion of GNP going to housing but only negligible aggregate effects, would have a very low ratio. Regulation Q could be ranked by the same criterion. It would then be possible to see if Regulation Q is more like a general credit policy or resembles more closely a selective credit policy.

The measure just suggested for identifying selective versus general credit policies requires at least one theoretical clarification before it can have empirical relevance. While the aggregate impact of a policy can be defined in a relatively straightforward manner, the selective impact is more difficult to isolate. A key problem is whether the ultimate objective of a selective credit policy is the redistribution of real resources or financial flows. The next section discusses these alternative impacts of general and selective credit policies.

It must also be recognized that it is not possible to measure aggregate and selective impacts of policies without a macroeconometric model with a highly detailed financial sector. We can, however, identify the factors which determine the rankings of different policies according to whether the aggregate or selective impacts dominate. This requires an analysis of the conditions which determine the effectiveness of selective credit policies. This will be presented in a subsequent section.

III. "FINANCIAL" VERSUS "REAL" EFFECTS OF SELECTIVE CREDIT CONTROLS

Current discussion of selective credit policies has centered about their potential usefulness in redirecting the allocation of real resources in the economy. If selective credit controls are to reallocate the uses of real resources, a clear prerequisite is that they also have a redistribution effect on credit flows and hence (before any real sector reaction) on relative rates of interest on various financial instruments. The changed flows of funds may be either to different financial institutions and/or changed flows of funds in different financial instruments.

Selective credit policies need not and, indeed, have not been used exclusively to implement resource reallocation objectives in the real sector of the economy. The objective of some selective credit policies stops with the impact on financial markets. A good example is margin requirements in the stock market which seeks to prevent "unhealthy" speculation in the market. It is probably true that unhealthy speculation in the stock market is considered worth preventing because of the dangers that financial crises pose for the real sector. Hyman Minsky, John Culbertson, and Allan Meltzer have all discussed the use of selective credit controls to implement financial market objectives because of the potential dangers of financial market irregularities for the real sector.[19] Other examples of such use of selective credit policies are compulsory deposit insurance for banks and other deposit-type intermediaries and the differential application of ceilings on deposit rates (which seeks to shelter some financial institutions from completely free competition).

We can now turn our attention to the conditions which determine the effectiveness of selective credit controls and the related empirical evidence. A list of the major types of selective policies used in the United States and the general categories into which they fall will also be presented.

IV. DETERMINANTS OF THE EFFECTIVENESS OF SELECTIVE CREDIT POLICIES: THE THEORY

A simple classification of selective credit policies can be developed along the same lines as that of taxation. In particular, policies can be classified according to the initial incidence of the credit policy, much in the same way as we classify taxes into

[19]Hyman P. Minsky, "Can 'It' Happen Again?" and John M. Culbertson, "Government Financial Policy in the Effective Market Economy," in Deane Carson, ed., *Banking and Monetary Studies* (Homewood, Ill.: Richard D. Irwin, 1963), pp. 101-11 and 151-70; and Allan H. Meltzer, "Major Issues in the Regulation of Financial Institutions," *Journal of Political Economy*, Supplement, 75 (1967): 482-501.

Classifying Credit Policies

Classifications	Examples
I. *On Lenders*	
a. Portfolio restrictions	Ia. Savings and loan association can hold only Governments and mortgages
b. Differential reserve requirements	Ib. Not in use
c. Other subsidies to lenders who make certain types of loans	Ic. September 1966 "letter" of Federal Reserve System
II. *On Borrowers*	
a. Interest rate subsidy	IIa. HUD 235 and 236 mortgage interest subsidies
b. Capital issuing committee	IIb. Not in use
III. *On Instruments*	
a. Interest rate ceilings and controls over other terms of credit	IIIa. Regulation Q; FHA-VA ceilings; usury laws; minimum down payment requirements
b. Policies aimed at changing certain characteristics of an instrument	IIIb. FHA-VA insurance; operating a secondary market, e.g., FNMA

direct and indirect groups. This, of course, leads directly to the key question of shifting and incidence of credit controls just as one analyzes shifting and incidence of taxes. Credit policies can, therefore, be categorized as being imposed on the lender, the borrower, or on a particular financial market instrument. The Table provides such a listing. It is meant to be illustrative rather than exhaustive.

While most of the examples are self-explanatory, some require further elaboration. Item Ib lists differential reserve requirements for different categories of assets held by financial institutions (banks in particular), as has been proposed by Andrew Brimmer.[20] Entry Ic is a general category of subsidies to lenders who make (or refrain from making) certain types of loans. In this context the word subsidy is to be considered in its broadest sense. An extreme example is the September 1, 1966

---

[20]Brimmer, "The Banking Structure and Monetary Management."

"letter" from the Federal Reserve indicating that favorable treatment at the discount window (read: subsidy) would be accorded to those banks that refrained from excessive expansion in business loans.[21] Item IIb is a capital issuing committee which has the power to approve or disapprove new corporate stock or bond issues. While no such institution operates in the United States, certain foreign countries, such as Sweden, have a capital committee.[22] Item IIIa includes controls on interest rates and other terms of credit, such as minimum down payment, that are levied on a particular financial instrument rather than on borrowers or lenders. While Regulation Q or other time-deposit ceilings are often thought of as being imposed on institutions, such is not the case, since other types of liabilities can be (and are) issued by these institutions without being subject to ceilings. Item IIIb is another catch-all category which incorporates all policies aimed at altering the characteristics of a financial market instrument, thereby making it more desirable from either the lender's standpoint and/or the borrower's.

The effectiveness of each type of selective credit policy depends, of course, on its objectives, e.g., a reallocation of financial market flows from one institution to another or real resource reallocation. There is a common characteristic which determines whether a credit policy can impinge on real resource allocation or redirect financial flows. The common characteristic is the degree of substitutability between financial market instruments by borrowers and lenders. The degree of substitutability between securities determines the shifting and incidence of the credit policy much in the same way as the shifting and incidence of taxes is determined by the elasticities of the supply and demand curves.

The clearest formal statement of the substitutability conditions determining the effectiveness of selective credit policies is contained in Rao and Kaminow.[23] Cohen, Davis, Hodgman, and Penner and Silber also discuss the general substitutability

---

[21]*Monthly Review* of the Federal Reserve Bank of New York, September 1966, p. 209.
[22]See Gunnar Elliasson, *The Credit Market, Investment Planning, and Monetary Policy—An Econometric Study of Manufacturing Industries* (Stockholm: Almquist and Wiksell, 1969).
[23]Rao and Kaminow, "Selective Credit Controls and the Real Investment Mix," pp. 1103-18.

conditions influencing the efficacy of selective credit policies.[24] Most of the authors have restricted their analysis to type I selective controls, i.e., those imposed on lenders. It turns out that in order for type I selective controls to have an impact on relative interest rates, lenders must view the different categories of securities as poor substitutes for each other. A simple example is sufficient to demonstrate this point. If a particular group of lenders, say one category of financial institutions, is forced to hold only one asset, say mortgages, and, therefore, must sell the other assets, say corporates, from its pre-constrained diversified portfolio, then the decline in yield on mortgages relative to corporates will be larger the less responsive is the demand for securities (in lender portfolios) to changes in relative rates, i.e., the poorer is the degree of substitutability between mortgages and corporates. In the extreme case, if mortgages and corporates were perfect substitutes for each other then as the demand for mortgages rises (due to the portfolio restriction) driving mortgage rates down relative to the yield on corporates, other institutions will respond by increasing their demand for corporates and decreasing their demand for mortgages until the relative yield between the two instruments is restored to its original level.

In order for type I controls to have an impact on real resource allocation, in addition to imperfect substitutability in lender portfolios, borrowers (the final spenders) must view different categories of securities as poor substitutes for any particular type of expenditure. For example, in order to finance the purchase of a home, borrowers must be unable to substitute freely between mortgage credit and, say, bank loans, consumer credit or security credit. To the extent that borrowers can easily finance real expenditures with different types of credit, the change in relative rates of interest on securities (induced by selective credit policies) will result only in changes in the type of funds borrowed, with little or no effect on the composition of real spending. This ability to substitute one type of credit for another in making a particular real expenditure, need not be

---

[24]Cohen, "Integrating the Real and Financial via the Linking of Financial Flow," pp. 1-27; Davis, "An Analysis of Quantitative Credit Flows and Related Devices," pp. 65-97; and Penner and Silber, "The Interaction Between Federal Credit Programs . . . ," pp. 838-52.

true for everyone. As long as it is true for a significant number of marginal investors there might be no impact on real spending.

Type I selective credit policies can have an impact on aggregate economic activity if all the conditions heretofore set forth are satisfied plus the additional condition that the interest elasticities of different categories of expenditure be different. For example, a selective policy which raises the mortgage rate and lowers the corporate bond rate will lower GNP if the interest elasticity of corporate investment spending is less than the interest elasticity of residential construction.

Before turning to the conditions determining the effectiveness of the other types of credit policies and the related empirical evidence, it is important to note that our analysis until now suggests quite clearly that the larger the set of lenders affected by selective controls the greater the impact of such policies. As Franco Cotula and Tommaso Padoa-Schioppa argue, this follows from the fact that under such circumstances there is less of an offset to the direct effects of the selective control.[25] Two related points should also be noted: (1) While extending selective controls to all lenders increases their effectiveness, this also implies an increase in the administrative costs of selective policies, a subject to which we will return later in the paper. (2) Even if selective credit controls were extended to all institutionalized lenders this would still leave direct lending between surplus and deficit units as a potential offset to controls. This leads directly to a consideration of controls over borrowers, as say, via a capital-issuing committee (IIb).

The conditions determining the effectiveness of type II selective controls, i.e., those imposed on borrowers, are quite different from those determining the efficacy of type I controls. In fact, it has been shown by Penner and Silber that an interest subsidy (type IIa) is more effective in reallocating financial flows (and real resources under the conditions spelled out above) if there is a high degree of substitutability between securities in lender portfolios.[26] This is clear once it is recognized that an interest-rate subsidy produces an increased demand for that category of funds. If the elasticity of supply is

[25]"Direct Credit Controls as a Monetary Policy Tool,"*Quarterly Review* of the Banca Nazionale del Lavaro No. 98 (1971): 203-14.
[26]Penner and Silber, op. cit., pp. 838-52.

great (i.e., if the elasticity of substitution on the part of lenders is large) then the increased demand for funds elicits a large increase in supply and a large decline in the rate charged to the borrower (the upper limit occurs where the supply of funds is infinitely elastic so that the decline in the rate is equal to the subsidy).

The effectiveness of the capital-issuing committee in changing the flows of funds to different firms and hence altering the allocation of resources depends on the elasticity of substitution between different sources of funds in borrower portfolios. For example, if control over long-term bond issues by the committee leads to complete and easy substitution of trade credit or bank loans in the financing of real resources, then the impact of the control will be very small. Once again, the greater the number of sectors covered, i.e., the number of financial instruments requiring committee approval, the less is the offset to the direct control. Furthermore, the capital committee will be more effective in the presence of type I controls, since under such circumstances replacing capital issues with bank loans could also be circumscribed.

Type III selective policies refer to controls or policies directed at particular financial market instruments. The two sub-categories under type III policies are quite different, both in terms of the determinants of their effectiveness and their objectives. Controls over the interest rate on particular financial instruments (type IIIa) have been among the most popular types of selective credit controls. Regulation Q as applied to commercial bank time deposits and the FHA-VA ceiling on mortgage rates are the two best-known examples. Each of these controls represents a different form of ceiling on an interest rate: the FHA-VA ceiling applies to a primary security, i.e., issued by a deficit unit, while Regulation Q applies to an indirect security, i.e., issued by a financial intermediary. Accordingly, each control has different objectives.

Robert Lindsay, in an interesting study, has applied the analysis of the price control literature to determine the effects of Regulation Q ceilings and FHA-VA ceilings.[27] The objective of usury laws, of which FHA-VA ceilings are but one example, is

---

[27]*The Economics of Interest Rate Ceilings* (New York: Institute of Finance, New York University, 1970).

to lower the rate charged to borrowers. If such ceilings are imposed on one security, then the ability of lenders to substitute away from that security will make the ceiling counterproductive. In the extreme case, if the elasticity of supply of that security were infinite the imposition of a ceiling below the market equilibrium rate results in a decline of funds flowing to that market to zero. The greater the elasticity of supply the greater is the reduction in the flow of funds. Hence, while the ceiling may indeed reduce the rate charged to a subset of borrowers, there will be a decrease in supply to such favored borrowers. If these borrowers are driven to other markets (in this case to the market for conventional mortgages) the rate charged to borrowers in the uncontrolled market rises. The total supply of funds (mortgages to the controlled and uncontrolled market) will, under certain conditions, be greater than in the absence of ceilings.[28]

Ceilings on deposit rates, such as Regulation Q, have a less straightforward justification. Holding down rates paid to depositors is not an objective in and of itself, especially if it is assumed that the small unsophisticated saver is most adversely affected. The use of Regulation Q before 1966 is best explained in terms of its favorable implications for the position of nonbank financial institutions, especially savings and loan associations (S & Ls), in the competition for savers' deposits. In some sense, Regulation Q shifted the burden of the portfolio restriction on S & Ls from the owners (in the case of stock companies) to commercial bank depositors.[29] Regulation Q tried to prevent the restricted industry, S & Ls, from losing deposits to banks, in order to prevent a loss in mortgage funds. Here is a perfect example of a selective credit policy whose primary objective is a redirection of financial flows.

Once again, the condition of substitutability between securities is a determinant of the effectiveness of such policies. If the primary source of competition for deposits at nonbank financial institutions comes from commercial bank time deposits, then a ceiling on the rate of interest paid on such deposits will

---

[28]Ibid., p. 12.
[29]Penner and Silber, op. cit., pp. 838-52.

prevent the loss of funds. On the other hand, if open market securities are also good substitutes for such deposits, then the ceiling on rates paid by deposit-type institutions will divert credit directly into the capital markets rather than through financial institutions.

The aggregate impact of Regulation Q has been analyzed in numerous articles, including Robert Lindsay and James Tobin.[30] It has been shown that an increase in the ceiling rate is likely to be marginally expansionary since it encourages intermediation,[31] and given the lower reserve requirement on time deposits compared with demand deposits it also releases reserves within the banking system.

The last category of selective credit policies is type IIIb, policies aimed at changing certain characteristics of a financial market instrument, such as FHA-VA mortgage insurance and the operation of a secondary market in mortgages by the Federal National Mortgage Association (FNMA) and the Federal Home Loan Mortgage Corporation (FHLMC). The objective of such policies is to increase the demand for these securities by lenders, increasing the flow of funds to that market and lowering the yields to borrowers. It has been shown by Penner and Siber[32] that the effectiveness of such policies is independent of the degree of substitutability between securities. It is also interesting to note that the implementation of such policies alters the degree of substitutability between securities and hence changes the relative effectiveness of different credit policies. The magnitude of type IIIb selective policies is determined by the impact of changes in risk on the demands for securities by lenders. If lenders are very sensitive to slight changes in the underlying risks of securities then type IIIb policies will have a significant impact on flows of funds and interest rates.

We can now turn to the empirical work done on the various elasticities of substitution and elasticities of supply. This will help in evaluating the real world effectiveness of selective credit policies.

---

[30]Lindsay, op. cit.; James Tobin, "Deposit Interest Ceilings as a Monetary Control," *Journal of Money, Credit and Banking* 2 (1970): 4-14.

[31]Tobin, op. cit., p. 6.

[32]Penner and Silber, op. cit., pp. 838-52.

V. THE EFFECTIVENESS OF SELECTIVE
CREDIT POLICIES: EMPIRICAL EVIDENCE

The empirical work bearing on the effectiveness of selective credit policies can be divided into a number of categories. One group of studies has examined the degree of substitutability between securities in lender portfolios, such as Huang, Jaffee and Silber.[33] These studies have implications for selective credit policies of type Ia, b, c, IIa, and IIIa. Some of these authors—Jaffee, Silber, Fair and Jaffee and others such as Dalip Swamy—have gone one step further and analyzed the impact of very specific selective policies (Regulation Q, Federal Home Loan Bank advances, FNMA mortgage purchases) by calculating the impact multipliers of such policies within the context of econometric models of the financial sector.[34] Direct estimates of reduced forms or semi-reduced forms have also been set forth with similar objectives in mind.[35]

Substitutability on the part of borrowers has received much less attention. Barry Bosworth has estimated equations for corporate financing decisions but he was not particularly concerned with the questions of selective credit policies.[36] Cohen, in a more grandiose effort, was directly concerned with the efficacy of selective credit policies.[37] He examined the linkages between particular credit flows and various categories of real expenditures. There have also been a number of crude attempts

---

[33]Huang, "Further Analysis of Residential Mortgage Credit Flows," Jaffee, "An Econometric Model of the Mortgage Market," pp. 139-208; and William L. Silber, *Portfolio Behavior of Financial Institutions: An Empirical Study with Implications for Monetary Policy, Interest-Rate Determination and Financial Model-Building* (New York: Holt, Rinehart, and Winston, 1970).

[34]See Jaffee, "An Econometric Model of the Mortgage Market," Silber, *Portfolio Behavior of Financial Institutions;* Fair and Jaffee, "The Implications of the Proposals of the Hunt Commission for the Mortgage and Housing Markets"; and Dalip Singh Swamy, "An Econometric Study of the United States Financial Markets," Ph.D. dissertation, University of Pennsylvania, 1970.

[35]For example, David S. Huang, "Effect of Different Credit Policies on Housing Demand," *Study of the Savings and Loan Industry* (Washington: Federal Home Loan Bank Board, 1969), 3: 1211-41; Arcelus and Meltzer, "The Markets for Housing and Housing Services," pp. 78-99.

[36]"Patterns of Corporate External Financing," *Brookings Papers on Economic Activity,* No. 2 (1971) 253-79.

[37]Cohen, "Integrating the Real and Financial via the Linkage of Financial Flow" and "Direct versus Indirect Controls as Instruments of Monetary Policy."

at examining the aggregate effects of changes in portfolio composition by banks, such as Paul Anderson, Leonall Andersen, and Silber.[38]

Before presenting a more detailed review of these studies, there is one general conclusion that emerges. All of the studies examining the degree of substitutability between securities in lender portfolios, e.g., Silber, Swamy, have found that the short-run elasticities are significantly smaller than long-run elasticities.[39] This follows from the familiar stock adjustment models which have been applied to portfolio behavior. This suggests that the initial impact of a selective credit policy will be larger than the long-run impact. The short-run response to a sudden change in relative interest rates brought on by the imposition of a selective control is muted by institutional rigidities and other transaction costs. In the long run, institutional portfolios respond in greater magnitude to rate differentials, thereby partially offsetting the initial impact.

This type of portfolio behavior, together with the more casual observation that the free market responds to constraints in one area by creating new instruments or institutions to circumvent the restrictions, suggests that selective credit policies have their greatest potential usefulness within a cyclical context rather than secularly. Once a selective credit policy is implemented, time tends to erode the impact of such policies by providing an opportunity for extensive portfolio adjustments and the creation of means for evading the controls.

We can now turn to a more detailed examination of some of the empirical studies listed above. The studies by Silber and Swamy present structural models of the portfolio behavior of financial institutions. The equations estimated for security demands by individual institutions suggest rather small cross-elasticities of demand.

The elasticity of substitution for the market as a whole must take into account at least two other factors, namely, the reaction of other participants in the securities markets not formally incorporated in the models and the portfolio adjustment of the

---

[38]Anderson, op. cit.; Andersen, op. cit.; and William L. Silber, "Velocity and Bank Portfolio Composition," *Southern Economic Journal* 36 (1969): 147-52.
[39]Silber, *Portfolio Behavior*; Swamy, op. cit.

public, especially with respect to the allocation of funds among different institutions and the securities market. Simulations or impact multipliers are reported by both authors and these do take into account the impact of the latter on the market's cross-elasticities of demand. Silber reports the impact of changes in Regulation Q and changes in the FHLB rate on the endogenous variables of the model and Swamy provides simulations of changes in Regulation Q. As far as Regulation Q is concerned, the impact on relative rates of interest of a one percent increase in the maximum time deposit rate is negligible and the impact on different categories of real investment is also negligible. On the other hand, there are significant impacts on flows of deposits between S & Ls and commercial banks. According to Swamy, one year after a 1-percent increase in Regulation Q, deposits at S & Ls decline by $.71 billion and commercial bank time deposits increase by $1.2 billion. According to Silber, one year after a 1-percent increase in Regulation Q, total commercial bank deposits rise by $4.4 billion while S & L deposits decline by $1.5 billion.

The simulations of the FMP model of Fair and Jaffee were carried out with a view toward evaluating the impact of the "Hunt Commission" proposals on the financial sector and housing.[40] With this in mind, they distinguish between the effects of removing deposit ceilings that constrain just commercial banks versus the effect of removing ceilings that have constrained both banks and other thrift institutions. If only commercial banks were constrained, then removal of Regulation Q seems to have a significant impact on financial flows, the mortgage rate and housing investment. If all thrift institutions were constrained, the impact of removing Q is negligible on all of these variables. Fair and Jaffee argue that their results suggest a very modest effect of changes in Regulation Q.

The impact of an increase in the lending rate at the Federal Home Loan Bank System is also rather small, at least as reported by Silber.[41] A 1-percent increase in the rate charged on advances raises the mortgage rate by nearly five basis points after

---

[40]Fair and Jaffee, op. cit.

[41]Silber, op. cit., pp. 82-89.

one quarter and then declines to an increase of three basis points after one year. Jaffee, using a detailed model of the mortgage market, found a significant impact of changes in the FHLB lending rate on mortgage flows.[42] An increase of 1 percent lowers S & L holdings of mortgages by $2 billion after one year with little or no offset from other mortgage lenders even after 32 quarters of simulation. Jaffee finds similar results for an exogenous increase in FHLB advances. On the other hand, he finds that an exogenous purchase by FNMA raises mortgage demand initially, but after seven quarters other participants in the market have fully offset the impact on mortgage flows (but not on the mortgage rate). This asymmetry in response to FHLB and FNMA policy is puzzling to Jaffee, and he provides no justification.

There are a number of problems common to all of these structural models which limit their usefulness and, perhaps, credibility in evaluating the impact of selective credit policies. None of these models fully articulates the linkages between real and financial markets, hence the impact of such policies on the real sector cannot be properly measured by the reported simulations. Second, all of the models leave out sectors and market interrelationships that would affect the overall elasticities of substitution between different securities. Hence, while Silber,[43] for example, reports very significant initial impacts of exogenous changes in the demand for particular categories of securities (mortgages and corporates) on relative rates of interest, this must be taken with considerable reservation.

In an attempt at circumventing the problem of "omitted sectors," Huang estimated the elasticity of substitution between different categories of mortgages and corporate bonds directly, i.e., via a reduced form approach.[44] In general, he finds rather high elasticities of substitution between Government-insured mortgages and corporate bonds and very little substitutability between conventional mortgages and corporates. Huang also estimates aggregate supply and demand equations for

---

[42]Jaffee, "An Econometric Model of the Mortgage Market," Gramlich and Jaffee, op. cit., pp. 139-208.

[43]Silber, *Portfolio Behavior of Financial Institutions*, table VII, p. 108.

[44]Huang, "Further Analysis of Residential Mortgage Credit Flows."

mortgages. The supply equation includes both FHLB advances and FNMA purchases. The impact of FHLB advances is quite large while FNMA's effect seems to be zero. This asymmetry appears once again in Huang's estimates of the impact of FNMA and FHLB activity on residential construction[45] (others, such as Brady and Fair produced similar results).[46] However, until these reduced form equations take explicit account of the endogenous countercyclical behavior of these government-sponsored agencies these results cannot be accepted at face value.

A related empirical question is raised by Jene Kwon and Richard Thornton.[47] They show that the financing side of FHLB advances, i.e., the issuance of FHLB bonds, produces a direct offset to the impact of FHLB advances on mortgages since there seems to be a high degree of substitutability between FHLB securities and S & L deposits. While their explicit test of substitutability is plagued by multicollinearity among interest rates (which they seek to avoid by using only one rate at a time to see which produces the highest R^2—a doubtful procedure at best) their empirical findings cast further doubt on the asymmetrical response of the mortgage market to FHLB and FNMA activity.

The question of whether mortgage credit in general (not just FHLB or FNMA credit) affects housing expenditure was tested by Arcelus and Meltzer.[48] They estimated demand equations for housing services and new houses and included mortgage credit as an explanatory variable. Their regression equations show that the stock of mortgages is negatively related to housing demand. They also argue that the flow of mortgage credit is not an appropriate variable in the estimated equations. Rather

[45]"Effect of Different Credit Policies on Housing Demand."

[46]Eugene Brady, *An Econometric Analysis of the U. S. Residential Mortgage Market*, Working Paper No. 11 (Washington: Federal Home Loan Bank Board, 1970); and Ray C. Fair, *A Short-Run Forecasting Model of the United States Economy* (Lexington, Mass.: D. C. Heath and Company, Lexington Books, 1971), pp. 73-88.

[47]See their "An Evaluation of the Competitive Effect of FHLB Open Market Operations on Savings Inflows at Savings and Loan Associations," *Journal of Finance* 26 (1971): 699-712; and "The Federal Home Loan Bank and Savings and Loan Associations: An Examination of the Financing of Federal Home Loan Bank Advances," *Review of Economics and Statistics* 54 (1972): 97-100.

[48]Arcelus and Meltzer, "The Markets for Housing and Housing Services," pp. 78-99.

than evaluating their surprising findings here, you can judge for yourself by reading a comment by Swan and a reply by Arcelus and Meltzer which summarize the pluses and minuses of the Arcelus-Meltzer findings.[49]

The most comprehensive grandiose attempt at an empirical test of the potential usefulness of selective credit policies is by Jacob Cohen.[50] Cohen's model was constructed with the explicit objective of integrating financial flows and real resource allocation. Evaluating the potential effectiveness of selective credit policies was a key objective. It is not surprising, therefore, that his model bears most closely on the efficacy of selective policies. Had some of the formal structural models of the financial sector discussed above been constructed with similar objective, the results would have been of greater use.

Cohen uses regression analysis to see if there is a more significant relationship between different categories of real expenditures (e.g., residential construction, consumer durable expenditures, corporate plant and equipment expenditures and inventories) and particular categories of financial flows (e.g., mortgage flows, consumer credit, corporate stock, and corporate bonds) or whether aggregate financial flows do as well as specific categories. This is a crude procedure but certainly gets at the issue at hand: namely, is there a significant relationship between particular financial market flows and specific real expenditures? Cohen finds that except for consumer durable expenditures there is a stronger relationship between a narrowly defined financial flow and a specific category of expenditure, e.g., residential construction and mortgage flows than between the real expenditure and a broader category of financial flow, e.g., total financial liabilities. Cohen concludes that his results make a reasonable case for the efficacy of selective credit policies.

As with all empirical studies, Cohen's approach and empirical tests are subject to qualification. While Cohen argues in favor of measuring substitutability by using credit flows rather

---

[49]Craig Swan, "Comment on the Markets for Housing and Housing Services"; Arcelus and Meltzer, reply, *Journal of Money, Credit and Banking* 5 (1973): 960-72; 973-78.
[50]Cohen, "Integrating the Real and Financial via the Linkage of Financial Flow."

113

than interest rates, his confrontation between these two groups of variables is extremely oversimplified. Substitutability is best measured from a theoretical standpoint by responses to relative interest rates, not different financial flows (unless credit rationing is dominant and interest rates have no relevance). Furthermore, Cohen does not include the many other variables that ought to enter expenditure equations in addition to financial flows. Hence the *ceteris paribus* conditions are not satisfied and the true partial effects of altering credit flows has not been captured. Finally, no attempt is made at incorporating lagged variables in the estimated equations to test for the existence of offsetting effects over time, as discussed above. Despite these criticisms, however, Cohen's attempt at an empirical evaluation of the effectiveness of selective credit controls is a step in the right direction. Additional effort along these lines, in light of the criticisms set forth here would be worthwhile.

The last group of empirical studies bearing on the issue of the efficacy of selective policies is the work by Paul Anderson, Leonall Andersen and Silber on the importance of bank portfolio composition in the determination of GNP or money velocity.[51] This bears directly on the question of whether there is an aggregate impact of different types of financial flows. Regression equations reported by Anderson and Silber show that changes in the money supply associated with bank loans (on the asset side) have a larger impact on GNP (hence a larger velocity) than changes in the money supply associated with other asset acquisitions by commercial banks. In a comment on Paul Anderson, Leonall Andersen produces results suggesting that such differences between "loan money" and "bill money" last for only one quarter. Such an amendment is consistent with the arguments set forth above regarding the offsetting effects brought on after credit flows have their initial impact. On the other hand, the one quarter reversal found by Andersen seems rather arbitrary and requires further investigation, especially by trying more gradual distributed lagged relationships.

---

[51]Anderson, "Monetary Velocity in Empirical Analysis," Andersen, "Discussion," and Silber, "Velocity and Bank Portfolio Composition."

VI. SELECTIVE CREDIT POLICIES: COSTS, EFFICIENCY AND EQUITY

In the section above entitled "What are Selective Credit Controls?" we raised the issue of the appropriateness of an offset to the incidence of monetary policy via selective credit policies. We deferred such a discussion until this point so that this question of the equity or normative aspects of selective credit policies could be examined along with an analysis of costs and efficiency.

It was noted above that some economists, such as Mayer, have used the neutrality of money (in the sense of no explicitly designed favoritism to any particular sector of the economy) as an argument against the use of selective credit controls.[52] This assumes that the incidence of stabilization policy is optimal when implemented by monetary policy. There is little justification for such a position. D. C. Rao argues rather convincingly as follows:

Since different stabilization policies which would have the same impact on aggregate output would have different sectoral impacts, it is not possible even for an ardent purist [noninterventionist] to avoid having to make a judgment about the relative merits of the allocational effects of alternative stabilization measures.[53]

The only possible argument for the optimality of the allocational impacts of monetary policy lies along the following lines: Since the problem of eliminating inflation or recession can be reduced to one of altering the timing of expenditures, i.e., postponing expenditures in the case of inflation and moving to the present future expenditures in the case of recession, and since the interest rate is the variable which influences the intertemporal allocation of resources, this suggests that stabilizing expenditures over time by using monetary policy to influence the interest rate has the advantage of operating through the market's intertemporal allocation mechanism. While this

---

[52]Mayer, "Financial Guidelines and Credit Controls."
[53]"Selective Credit Policy: Is It Justified and Can It Work?" *Journal of Finance* 27 (1972): 474.

approach is appealing it seems that one must explain more rigorously the reasons for needing countercyclical stabilization policy in any particular situation before concluding that, in general, monetary policy is optimal from an equity standpoint. Furthermore, taxation can also be used to influence the intertemporal allocation of resources so that the case presented for the incidence of monetary policy, even in this context, is far from definitive.

The more fundamental economic justification for selective credit policies aimed at real resource reallocation rests on the existence of externalities in particular types of expenditures; hence the free market would either underinvest (where there are social benefits) or overinvest (in the presence of social costs) if there were no government intervention. Given the need for government intervention to direct resources to a particular sector, the case for using selective credit policies must be made on the grounds that credit policies accomplish the objective more efficiently, i.e., they cost less or the benefits per unit cost are higher, than other means of reallocating real resources. The simplest alternative to selective credit policies is a system of taxes and subsidies favoring certain categories of expenditures. Note also that within the category of selective credit policies there are different types of policies which also must be evaluated along similar lines.

In this context, a strong case against selective credit policies has been made by a number of economists. Meltzer, for example, argues that if there are externalities then the appropriate method of subsidization is direct subsidies rather than credit-type subsidies since the latter subsidize only one of the inputs, i.e., credit, while the former subsidizes all inputs equally.[54] In other words, credit policies impose welfare costs by distorting the use of inputs in the production process, i.e., favoring credit. This assumes that the credit markets are efficient. If there are imperfections in the capital market, then subsidization of output X via selective credit policies would be extremely efficient; it would offset the imperfections in the capital market as well as subsidizing output X in light of the externalities involved. Gov-

---

[54]"Aggregative Consequence of Removing Restrictions," prepared for the President's Commission on Financial Structure and Regulation, Mimeograph, February 1971.

ernment subsidies to stimulate housing are almost completely of the credit policy variety. One justification for such an approach[55] is the existence of imperfections in the mortgage market.

Measuring the costs of selective credit policies and comparing them with the costs of direct subsidies is quite difficult. A recent study by the Joint Economic Committee as well as the supporting paper by Weidenbaum are the first steps in that direction.[56] One trap to be avoided is the use of budget costs as recorded by the Federal budget. Many selective credit policies, e.g., portfolio restrictions, interest ceilings, etc., have no budget costs, while direct subsidies or tax benefits clearly have budget costs. Using just budget costs ignores the social costs of selective credit policies. While the ability to keep the costs of selective credit policies outside the budget may have strong political advantages, an economist cannot ignore the true costs of such policies, which clearly include nonbudget social costs. There is one real cost, however, that is, in fact, avoided by keeping down the budget costs of a policy, namely, one avoids the excess burden associated with the imposition of taxes to finance the budget expenditure.

The budget cost of direct subsidies, i.e., the amount of money the Government pays out as a subsidy has been referred to as the net income transfer cost.[57] This is not a cost to society, but rather a transfer of funds from one sector (taxpayers) to another group (recipients of the subsidy). While credit controls do not give rise to such transfer costs within the budget, they do produce such transfers outside the budget. The case of portfolio restrictions is a perfect example. Portfolio restrictions produce a subsidy to mortgage borrowers and home buyers under conditions outlined above. The cost of such restrictions is the reduced return per unit of risk to those institutions subjected to restrictions.[58] This cost is also shifted to the depositors of such institu-

---

[55]As pointed out by Penner and Silber, op. cit., 838-52.

[56]U. S., Congress, Joint Economic Committee, *The Economics of Federal Subsidy Programs*, 92d Cong., 2d sess., 8 May 1972; and Murray L. Weidenbaum, "Subsidies in Federal Credit Programs," ibid.

[57]Carl S. Shoup, "The Economic Theory of Subsidy Payments," *The Economics of Federal Subsidy Programs*.

[58]See Penner and Silber, op. cit., 838-52.

tions in the form of lower returns (interest rates) on their deposits, (or, in the case of Regulation Q, the cost is shifted to the deposits of other institutions).[59] The main point is that such income transfers occur in all selective credit policies, only in some cases they occur within the budget and in others outside the budget. While there is an advantage in terms of excess burden of taxation in keeping them outside the budget, the uncertainty of the incidence of the cost of such selective credit policies may itself be a drawback.

The real social costs imposed by selective credit policies include: (a) administrative costs of the regulatory agency charged with implementing the credit policy and supervising compliance, (b) costs to be regulated in complying with the credit controls, (c) resources of the private sector devoted to evading credit controls, and (d) welfare costs associated with the inefficiencies imposed by the selective credit policy. We will examine each category of costs from two aspects: whether there is a counterpart to such costs in direct subsidies and the method of measuring such costs, if that is possible.

The administrative costs of the regulating agency is the simplest to analyze. There is a straightforward measure of costs, i.e., the actual costs of the agency charged with administrating the program or the controls. There is also a counterpart in direct subsidies, namely the cost of the agency running the program. There is no reason to expect one type of program to be more costly to administer than the other.

The costs to the regulated, in terms of record-keeping, etc., is not as easy to measure. It should be possible to get at such numbers by asking the affected institutions for the man hours, etc., devoted to such tasks. There is also a counterpart to such costs in direct subsidies as long as criteria are established by the Government defining eligibility for particular subsidies.

These first two categories of costs are not usually stressed by those presenting the drawbacks of selective credit policies. Rather, the latter two categories, cost of evasion and the welfare costs, (in terms of capital market efficiency) are seen as the major problems with selective credit policies. Allan Meltzer and

---

[59]See ibid., for a full discussion of such complementary cost-shifting policies.

Milton Friedman, for example, are most concerned with these aspects of the cost of selective controls.[60] Both authors cite under costs of evasion the structural readjustments imposed on financial institutions in an effort to evade selective credit controls. Key examples are the emergence of the Eurodollar market and the payment of interest-in-kind (free deposit service, gifts, and other promotional gimmicks) in response to ceilings on deposit rates. While there is no estimate of such costs it is quite possible that they are nonnegligible.

Are there analogous costs in the case of direct subsidies? As long as there are criteria for eligibility for direct subsidies the counterpart to costs of evasion are the costs associated with feigning eligibility. A direct subsidy to homebuyers, for example, to replace the myriad of selective housing credit policies may very well generate a very active secondary market in houses—e.g., "I buy yours and you buy mine"—in order to qualify for the subsidy.

Interference with the efficiency of the capital market is viewed as a major cost of selective credit policies by Meltzer, Friedman, and others. Capital mobility is impaired by portfolio restrictions and the regulation of interest rates eliminates their usefulness in the intertemporal allocation of resources. Such welfare costs of these regulation-type selective credit policies do have a counterpart in the excess burdens associated with all types of subsidies (credit and noncredit) that are financed via taxation. Aside from that, the only justification for such market interference lies in the existence of imperfections in the capital market which these selective controls are correcting. In addition, applying the second-best criterion,[61] if some regulations must be imposed for other reasons, e.g., deposit insurance or reserve requirements for financial market stability, then reallocating resources via selective credit policies might be optimal given the existence of these and other types of interference (monopolies, imperfections) in the capital market.

---

[60]Meltzer, "Aggregative Consequences of Removing Restrictions," and Milton Friedman, "Controls on Interest Rates Paid by Banks" *Journal of Money, Credit and Banking* 2 (1970): 15-32.

[61]R. G. Lipsey and Kelvin Lancaster, "The General Theory of Second Best," *Review of Economic Studies*, No. 2324 (1956-57): 11-32.

One general conclusion that emerges with respect to the relative welfare costs of different types of selective credit policies is that control over interest rates directly is less efficient than other types of selective credit policies. It seems that it is better to let the market determine the interest rate (price) so that it retains its value as an allocator of funds subject to the constraint imposed by Government credit policies. As long as the ultimate objective is quantity of resources in a particular use, it is best to retain price as determined by the market (both in the input and output market) so that consumers and producers and borrowers and lenders are using funds and resources efficiently once the externalities and imperfections have been taken into account by Government subsidy.

VII. FUTURE RESEARCH

This survey of the literature on selective credit policies points to at least three areas needing major research efforts. The need for a normative theory of the incidence of stabilization policy is an obvious requirement. Unless such an analysis is available, policymakers will have no standard by which to judge whether the incidence of countercyclical policy should or should not be offset by selective policies of one type or another.

On the empirical front, two topics require major additional work. An econometric model integrating the structural approach to financial institution portfolio behavior with a model of real resource utilization[62] is a prerequisite for an accurate evaluation of selective credit policies. Accepting the results of existing models, not especially designed for evaluating the efficacy of selective credit policies simply will not do. Finally, additional effort along the lines of the Joint Economic Committee's approach to measuring the costs of Federal subsidies[63] as well as an evaluation of the benefits per unit of cost of each subsidy is a prerequisite for formal policy recommendations.

---

[62]Along the lines of Cohen, "Integrating the Real and Financial via the Linkage of Financial Flow."

[63]U.S., Congress, Joint Economic Committee, *The Economics of Federal Subsidy Programs.*

PAUL F. SMITH is Professor of Finance at the University of Pennsylvania. He holds a Ph.D. from American University and specializes in financial institutions and consumer credit. From 1949 to 1960 he served as an Economist at the Federal Reserve Board, with responsibility for statistical and analytical work in consumer credit. He has served as a consultant on consumer credit to the American Bankers Association, the Federal Reserve Board, the National Commission on Consumer Finance, and other public and private groups. He is the author of *Consumer Credit Costs, 1949-59, Economics of Financial Institutions and Markets* and of numerous articles and studies.

A Review of the Theoretical and Administrative History Of Consumer Credit Controls

PAUL F. SMITH

I. INTRODUCTION

Consumer credit controls were first used in the early 1930s to encourage expenditures for the improvement and repair of residential buildings and to stimulate the use of electrical appliances. They were used during World War II to discourage expenditures on consumer durables and the diversion of war materiel into consumer channels. On both of those occasions, they were designed to affect special types of consumption expenditures and their success has to be judged in terms of those specific objectives.

After World War II, consumer credit controls were cast in a broader role. As one of a set of selective credit controls, they were used as supplements to general monetary controls in attempting to achieve the goals of full employment and price stability. Judgments about their effectiveness in this broader role depend on a number of controversial theoretical and empirical considerations.

123

First, judgments about the potential importance of selective controls on consumer credit require an understanding of the role of consumer credit as an economic force. Some economists argue that consumer credit is a force for instability that accentuates business fluctuations. Others regard it as a passive variable dependent upon more fundamental pressures.

Second, decisions to use selective controls require knowledge of the effectiveness of various methods of controlling consumer credit. Some economists argue that it can be controlled by general monetary controls. Others contend that it is not responsive to general monetary controls and can only be controlled by selective measures.

Third, decisions to use selective controls require judgments about the advantages and disadvantages on different approaches to the problem of controlling the level of economic activity.

The first four sections of this study examine the theoretical and empirical work on the central issues regarding the use of selective credit controls. The next two sections concern experience with selective controls in the United States. The concluding section considers the implications of the analysis for further research.

II. ECONOMIC ROLE OF CONSUMER CREDIT

Since the question of credit controls usually arises in connection with cyclical problems, the role of consumer credit in the business cycle is an important issue in the controversy about the use of selective controls. The central issue is whether or not the consumer credit sector has inherent cyclical features.

A. Potential Instability in the Consumer Credit Sector. One potential source of instability in the consumer credit sector can be traced to the durability of the goods purchased on credit. Some economists argue that the consumer sector has become an important source of economic variability in recent years as a result of the growing importance of expenditures for expensive durable goods and of the use of credit to finance them. George Katona outlines this position as follows.

124

First, there has been what some analysts have called an income revolution. We now have broad middle- and upper-middle-income groups rather than masses of poor and a few very rich ones. ... American consumers today have a larger amount of reserve funds than ever before. ... Next there is the fact that buying on credit is today a generally accepted and widely practiced form of behavior. ... Still another significant change in consumer spending over the past fifty years is the importance attached to durable and nonperishable goods by consumers. ... Finally it is important for any consideration of the greater influence of the consumer on the economy to note that the economic intelligence of the American people has increased.[1]

These arguments imply greater flexibility in the timing of consumption decisions and set the stage for cyclical behavior. Since the flow of services for durable goods is related to the stock of these goods, changes in the demand for these services will result in a proportionally greater change in the demand for durable goods. The resultant "accelerator effect" resembles that associated with investment in producers' durable goods. The durable nature of the goods accentuates any variations from the stable pattern of the demand for the services of durables. These variations, in turn, create waves of replacement cycles that are keyed to the life of the items. Thus, arguments have been developed for an inherent cyclical pattern in consumer expenditures on durable goods similar to that studied in business investment.

Since consumer durable goods are frequently purchased with credit, any cycle in expenditures for durable goods is reflected in extensions of instalment credit. This generates another cyclical pattern that arises from the nature of money flows on instalment contracts. Each contract involves a large loan amount at the time of the purchase and a subsequent series of smaller repayments, the size of which depends upon the maturity of the contract. If extensions of credit continue at a constant rate from month to month, the amount of extensions and the amount of repayments will approach equality. When equality is attained, the outstanding level of credit will remain unchanged despite the continuous stream of activity. If, however, irregularities

---

[1] *The Powerful Consumer* (New York: McGraw-Hill Book Company, 1960), pp. 11-13.

appear in extensions of credit, repayments will reflect only a fraction of the change in extensions and only after some time-lag. Consequently, any cyclical pattern in extensions of credit is reproduced in a lagged and dampened form in repayments. These two cycles, in turn, produce a third cycle in outstanding credit with related, but different timing.[2]

The lagged repayment pattern associated with instalment credit leads to what Paul McCracken and his coauthors refer to as the "burden" theory of business fluctuations.

According to this theory, business depression has its cause in the overexpansion of credit which inevitably occurs in a boom. When the consumers have finally burdened themselves to the limit with debts and repayments, further credit expansion must cease, and this is considered enough to set off a slump in consumer durable goods industries and in the economy as a whole.[3]

This view considers instalment credit as a stimulus to the potential volatility of the demand for durable goods which produces first strong expansionary pressure and then, through the feedback of the lagged repayments, a subsequent contraction.

Most observers agree that some cyclical patterns are inherent in the use of consumer credit. However, there is considerable disagreement about the role of these events in the overall problem of economic stability. Some view them as passive; others view them as causal in nature. However, final judgment on this issue depends upon the nature of the interaction between consumer credit and other cyclical forces.

B. *Consumer Credit as a Cyclical Force*. Perhaps the easiest way of narrowing discussion of the complex interaction between consumer credit and other sectors of the economy is to define consumer credit as an endogenous component of a model

---

[2]Paul A. Samuelson outlined the mathematics of these relationships in Appendix B, "A Mathematical Analysis of the Relationship of New Credits, Outstanding and Net Credit Change," in Gottfried Haberler, *Consumer Instalment Credit and Economic Fluctuations*, Financial Research Program No. 9, Studies in Consumer Instalment Financing (New York: National Bureau of Economic Research, 1942), pp. 197-205.

[3]Paul W. McCracken, James C. Mao, and Cedric V. Fricke, *Consumer Instalment Credit and Public Policy*, Michigan Business Studies (Vol. 27, No. 1), Graduate School of Business Administration (Ann Arbor: University of Michigan, 1965), p. 41.

of the economy that is affected by other variables in the system and, in turn, affects other variables. When consumer credit is viewed as a dependent variable, some of the independent variables that belong in the structural demand and supply equations can be identified.[4] The close ties between expenditures for durable consumer goods and the use of credit suggest that the demand and supply equations for these goods should be considered in conjunction with those for consumer credit. Once the independent variables in these equations are identified and the nature of the relationships established, the role of consumer credit as an independent variable can be examined.

The list of variables in the structural equations for extensions of consumer credit and the demand for consumer durable goods would include personal income (or perhaps the more refined concept of discretionary income), changes in income, various confidence measures that would affect consumers' willingness to incur debts, and variables affecting the supply of credit and credit terms. It would also include the variables affecting the demand and supply of durable goods such as the age and stock of consumer durables, prices, and demographic factors.

Since many variables on this list have cyclical characteristics or are related to cyclical forces, a close relationship between the cycles in consumer credit and those of general economic activity can be expected. Numerous studies of the problem have confirmed the general correspondence between consumer credit and measures of general business activity. These studies show measures of outstanding consumer credit as coincident with or lagging business cycle turning points and extensions of credit, and the net change in credit as leading or coincident with the turning points.[5]

The general correspondence between the movement of consumer credit and measure of general business activity and the role of numerous cyclical variables in the structural equations for consumer credit has led to the widely accepted conclusion that "movements in consumer instalment credit do result in

[4]Avram Kisselgoff, *Factors Affecting the Demand for Consumer Instalment Sales Credit*, Technical Paper No. 7 (New York: National Bureau of Economic Research, 1952).

[5]Philip A. Klein, *The Cyclical Timing of Consumer Credit, 1920-1967*, Occasional Paper 113 (New York: National Bureau of Economic Research, 1971), pp. 13, 26.

somewhat wider cyclical swings in business activity."[6] This view regards consumer credit and the demand for durable goods as responding to changes in business conditions in a way that tends to accentuate the underlying cyclical forces. Consumer durable goods and consumer credit cycles are in this way superimposed on other cyclical events.

The correct measure of the role of consumer credit as an independent variable in the structural equations for the other sectors of the economy is a matter of some controversy. The traditional approach looks to changes in outstanding credit as an exogenous source of funds that plays a role similar to an increase in investment or government outlays in generating the familiar multiplier effects. Under this approach the expansion of outstanding credit is viewed as the exogenous event initiating a multiplier effect.[7]

The new approach argues that the analysis should be based on the separate examination of new extensions of credit and repayments on old contracts. Under this approach, a change in the level of new extensions initiates the multiplier effect in much the same way as a change in investments or government expenditures. A change in the level of repayments also produces a multiplier effect that requires an approach similar to that used in analyzing the tax multiplier. Some economists argue that the net impact of these separate forces provides a better measure of the role of consumer credit.[8] Since the net of changes in extensions and repayments of credit is equal to the change of outstanding credit (second difference), this approach reveals an error in the analysis of the older approach. It indicates that the correct measure of the potential multiplier effect of consumer credit should be based on the rate of change in outstanding credit rather than on the simple change in outstanding credit.

---

[6]McCracken et al., op. cit., p. 56.

[7]Haberler, op. cit., pp. 140-41; F. R. Oliver, *The Control of Hire-Purchase* (London: George Allen and Unwin Limited, 1969), p. 126.

[8]Paul F. Smith, "Multiplier Effects of Hire-Purchase," *Economica* 31 (1964): 190; Klein, op. cit., pp. 33-35; Board of Governors of the Federal Reserve System, *Consumer Instalment Credit: Growth and Import*, 2 vols. (Washington: Government Printing Office, 1957), 1: 20 (hereafter cited as *Consumer Instalment Credit*).

The error in the older approach arises from a confusion between stock and flow concepts. The nature of the conceptual differences can be illustrated by a comparison of the measures of consumer credit with those used to analyze the role of investment.

	Investment	Consumer Credit
Stock (asset) concept	C	O
Flow concept	ΔC or I	$\Delta O = E - R$
Source of multiplier effect	$\Delta^2 C$ or ΔI	$\Delta^2 O = \Delta E - \Delta R$

Where: C = Capital E = Extension of new credit

       I = Investment R = Repayment

       O = Outstanding credit

The use of the change in outstanding credit as the measure of the potential multiplier impact is analogous to applying the investment multiplier to the level of investment.

These two views result in different interpretations of the impact of consumer credit on the overall level of economic activity. The traditional view regards outstanding credit as an indication of the timing of the impact. The newer view looks at the net change in outstanding credit as the relevant indicator. As was pointed out earlier, outstanding credit usually lags the business cycle's turning point but the net change series tends to lead. In the traditional view, consumer credit exerts an expansionary force throughout the expansionary phase of the business cycle that continues after other factors have been turned down. In the newer view, the expansionary role of consumer credit occurs early in the general business expansion but generally slows and is usually exerting a restraining effect by the time the peak in general activity is reached.

These two views quite clearly lead to very different attitudes toward the need for selective credit controls. Under the traditional view, the consumer credit sector appears to exert pressure for instability that persists after other forces have been dampened and after general attempts to control the expansion have been used. The newer position leads to a much less doctrinaire

129

attitude toward the consumer sector and permits the view that the consumer credit sector may be subject to changing forces during an expansion that may lead to a dampening of credit expansion. Thus, the possibility exists that the slowdown in consumer credit may come early enough to depress overall expansionary forces.

A recent study of the cyclical patterns of consumer credit advances evidence that the newer measures of consumer credit impact show a leading role in 11 out of 14 business cycle turning points and a lead-time of several months.[9] Statistical evidence of this type, when interpreted by current theories, suggests that consumer credit has tended to dampen cyclical movements.

III. IMPACT OF SELECTIVE CONSUMER CREDIT CONTROLS

A considerable amount of direct and indirect evidence is available on the impact of selective credit controls on specific types of consumption expenditures. Two types of evidence can be brought to bear on this question.

First, studies of the effects of credit terms on the demand for automobiles and other durable goods provide indirect evidence of the potential effectiveness of selective controls. One early econometric study found evidence of a relationship between credit terms and the demand for credit.[10] Other studies of the demand for automobiles and other durable goods have found evidence of the role of credit terms.[11] Specific studies of the dramatic developments in the automobile market in the mid-1950s provided evidence of the role of credit terms.[12] A national survey of new car purchasers for 1954-55 underscored

---

[9]Klein, op. cit., p. 26.

[10]Kisselgoff, op. cit.

[11]L. Jay Atkinson, "Consumer Markets for Durable Goods," *Survey of Current Business,* April 1952, pp. 19-25; C. F. Roos and V. von Szeliski, "Factors Governing Changes in Domestic Automobile Demand," *The Dynamics of Automobile Demand* (New York: General Motors Corporation, 1939), pp. 73-81.

[12]See Thomas R. Dyckman, Appendix A: "Instalment Credit in the 1955 Auto Sales Year: A Case Study," in McCracken et al., op. cit., pp. 181-240.

the importance of credit terms in the demand for automobiles.[13]

Second, examination of the impact of selective credit controls in the United States provides direct evidence of the relationship between controls and specific types of consumption expenditures.[14] The analysis of the specific relationship between demand and selective controls in the postwar years was complicated by the pent-up demand for durables, but observable changes in the sales of automobiles and other durables could be traced to the changes in controls.[15]

The question of impact of selective controls on the overall level of aggregate demand is much more complex. Since the imposition of selective controls does not alter the total supply of funds available for expenditures, funds may merely be diverted from one type of expenditure to another without affecting the total.

The extreme positions on this question illustrate the nature of the problem. Proponents of selective controls often seem to assume that any reduction in the use of funds for consumer credit will reduce consumption expenditures and therefore total expenditures by an equal amount. This position ignores the possibility that savings that do not flow into consumer credit may be diverted to other uses. Opponents of selective controls contend that the funds that do not flow into consumer credit are merely diverted to other channels, so that the selective controls merely change the composition of expenditures, not the level.

The best statement on this question appears in a study by Paul W. McCracken, James Mao, and Cedric Fricke. The authors conclude:

1. In a period of acutely active demand for credit generally, the effect of an increase in consumer credit outstanding is largely a diversion of credit from other uses, with little effect on total demand. Conversely, in a recession an increase in consumer credit outstanding is almost dollar for dollar an increase in total demand for output. Of course, the economy is usually in a position between these two extremes. At such

---

[13]Board of Governors of the Federal Reserve System, *Financing New Car Purchases* (Washington: Government Printing Office, 1957).

[14]*Consumer Instalment Credit*, 1: 132-39.

[15]McCracken et al., op. cit., pp. 143-55; *Consumer Instalment Credit*, 1: 119-48, 164-81.

times an increase in consumer credit outstanding results in some enlargement of total demand for output, and a decline means some reduction in total demand. The magnitude of the change would depend on how close to full employment the economy was operating.

2. Consumer instalment credit outstanding varies directly with the level of business activity. The conclusion therefore is that consumer instalment credit tends to reinforce business fluctuations. Its effect is least, however, when the economy is operating at capacity; changes in one type of credit are largely neutralized by offsetting changes in other types. The impact is greatest in slack periods when changes in one type of credit demand do not force offsetting changes elsewhere.[16]

These conclusions suggest that selective controls on consumer credit will be effective in altering the aggregate demand under some economic conditions, but not under others. They suggest that the controls will be least effective in periods of strong expansionary pressures when the need for policy action is the greatest and most effective when the adjustments in consumer credit are not offset by compensating changes in other sectors of the economy.

The McCracken conclusions have not been tested empirically, and it may be impossible to develop conclusive evidence on this question. But the answer is critical to judgments about the effectiveness of selective controls.

Theory, empirical evidence, and marketing folklore all support the judgment that selective controls on consumer credit can effectively influence the level of expenditures for automobiles and other items purchased on credit. Neither evidence nor theory provides a good basis for a judgment about the impact of selective controls on the total level of expenditures. If the McCracken position is accepted, selective controls on consumer credit would presumably be of very little value in directly controlling the level of income and employment. During periods of strong expansionary pressures, selective controls on consumer credit would merely alter the composition of the expenditure pattern. During periods when the restraints on consumption

---

[16]McCracken et al., op. cit., p. 27.

expenditures might be effective in altering the total level of expenditures, controls are unnecessary.

IV. IMPACT OF GENERAL CREDIT CONTROLS ON CONSUMER CREDIT

A germane question in the debate on selective controls is the extent to which consumer credit is responsive to general monetary controls. If consumer credit is found to be insensitive to general monetary controls, selective controls may be the only alternative for those who believe the control of consumer credit is essential.

Those who argue that consumer credit is not responsive to general controls claim that it has a preferred position because (1) it is an important sales tool and retailers, wholesalers, and manufacturers will make whatever concessions are necessary to maintain the flow of credit to support their sales and (2) the consumer's demand for credit is inelastic to interest rates and therefore will not be dampened by high rates designed to curtail credit demand.

Those who claim that consumer credit is responsive to general credit controls argue that even though the demand for consumer credit is inelastic to interest rate changes, it is restrained by credit rationing and other nonprice devices. They argue that banks and other financial institutions do not merely supply credit to the highest bidder but that they ration the funds in a number of ways.

Two types of studies have been used to develop information on the impact of general monetary conditions on consumer credit. One has involved an examination of the market adjustment that occurs during periods of tight money. Studies of this type have looked for evidence of credit rationing or nonprice adjustments that would affect the flow of funds into consumer credit. An impressive array of evidence of various types of credit rationing and nonprice restraint was developed by a committee set up by the Federal Reserve System to study the problem.[17]

---

[17]*Consumer Instalment Credit*, 1:257-85; 2:43-140.

The other type of study has involved the direct examination of the allocation of funds by banks during periods of tight money to find evidence of the treatment of consumer credit demands relative to other loan demands. These studies have failed to support the argument that consumer credit is immune from tight money-market conditions. In general, they show that banks faced with the problem of restricting their lending tend to cut back on all types of lending activities rather than exempt any particular type of credit. The pattern may differ from bank to bank, but there appears to be no evidence that consumer credit has a preferred position in these adjustments.[18]

These studies in general seem to indicate some responsiveness on the part of consumer credit to general monetary conditions. They provide enough evidence to refute the position that consumer credit is insensitive to general monetary controls. Achieving the exact response of consumer credit to general monetary controls is part of the broader problem of determining the precise impact of general monetary controls.

V. CHOICE OF CONTROL TECHNIQUES

The techniques for achieving various control objectives range from the exclusive use of general controls through various combinations of selective and general controls to the exclusive use of selective techniques. The choice among these alternatives depends upon a complex of judgments about the impact of the controls and value judgments about the expected results and related effects.

The choice between general and selective controls may be influenced by the decision-maker's attitude toward the role of the market mechanism in the economic process. Many of the arguments for selective controls reflect specific economic or social objectives and imply that the market cannot be trusted for one reason or another to achieve these objectives. This type of argument is particularly common regarding selective controls

---

[18]G. L. Bach and C. J. Huizenga, "The Differential Effects of Tight Money," *American Economic Review* 51 (1961): 52-80; Paul F. Smith, "Response of Consumer Loans to General Credit Conditions," *American Economic Review* 48 (1958): 649-55.

134

on consumer credit. It may reflect a lack of confidence in the "typical" consumer to make wise decisions about his debt obligations, or it may arise from the view that funds used by consumers to accumulate automobiles and other expensive durables might be better spent on more socially desirable goals. During periods of strong inflationary pressures, it may be argued that the demand for consumer durables should be restricted because it diverts resources from the production of industrial capacity that could be used to relieve the inflationary pressures by expanding supply. Or some may argue for selective controls to prevent unfair competition in the form of easier credit terms. All of these arguments have a common denominator—they seek an objective through a direct approach.

Opponents of selective controls reject them on the grounds that they interfere with free-market adjustments and allocations. While arguing that the controls result in discrimination, inefficiency, and the substitution of bureaucratic decisions for individual choice, they also cite the administrative difficulties and the interference with the decision-making process.

VI. EARLY EXPERIMENTS WITH SELECTIVE CONTROLS

The first attempt to use selective controls on consumer credit in the United States came in the mid-1930s. The early proposals were part of a broad governmental program designed to stimulate business activity. Among the plethora of New Deal programs were two for using consumer credit to stimulate consumer spending. The Federal Housing Administration (under Title 1 of the National Housing Act) was given the responsibility of supplying free insurance to private lending institutions against losses on loans for the repair and modernization of residential properties. The Electric Home and Farm Authority was to provide financing for retail purchases of electrical appliances.[19]

---

[19]Joseph D. Coppock, *Governmental Agencies of Consumer Instalment Credit*, Financial Research Program No. 5., Studies in Consumer Instalment Finance (New York: National Bureau of Economic Research, 1950).

These programs involved governmental agencies in the direct participation and support of the consumer credit process. They were designed to subsidize and participate in the lending process rather than merely regulate private activities. Both programs used credit terms to stimulate the use of credit. Both made provisions for extending maturities beyond the customary limits and for reducing down payments and in this way made use of the principal tools of selective controls. Moreover, they provided for lower rates and promotional activity.

In a memorandum to the Senate Committee on Banking and Currency, the National Emergency Council justified the modernization loan program to help in

... relieving the unemployment situation ... facilitate the flow of money from its present sources to the point of need without an excessive use of Government financing ... and to reduce the costs of this type of financing.[20]

The original FHA modernization loan program provided for the insuring of any reliable financial institution against losses up to 20 percent of the total amount of the net proceeds advanced to borrowers. The insurance applied to the aggregate loans of the institution and not the loan of a specific borrower. Insured loans were limited to $2000 and could only be used for the improvement of residential property owned by the borrower. A 9.7-percent ceiling was established on the finance charge and a five-year contract was permitted. No charge was made for the insurance, and the lending agency could file a claim with the FHA for the unpaid balance of defaulted loans plus interest. This plan was continued for about three years with only minor modifications.

The Electric Home and Farm Authority was a Government sales finance company created by Executive Order of the President of the United States in December 1933. It was originally chartered as a Delaware corporation and was managed by the directors of the Tennessee Valley Authority. It was concerned with stimulating the use of electricity and acted to provide low-cost, long-term financing to consumers for electrical

---

[20]Ibid., p. 3.

appliances. The EHFA bought contracts from retailers. The contracts provided for a minimum down payment of 5 percent, 36-month maturities, and finance charges of slightly less than 10 percent. The Authority bought 74,000 contracts during the four years of its existence. The average contract was about $138.

Both of these programs were initiated as part of a broader range of policies designed to stimulate the business recovery. Both were justified in selective terms as stimulating consumption expenditures of a type deemed to be socially desirable. It is doubtful that the specific objectives of these programs would have been sufficient to lead to their adoption without the overall demand for action of any type that might help the general business situation. They were conceived as part of a solution to the general economic problem.

Their contributions to the solution of the general economic problem can be judged as favorable but of very minor importance. The combined volume of credit extended under these programs was less than $600 million over a period of about three years.[21] Even if it is assumed that all of the expenditures generated by this credit were exogenous and that the general impact could be measured as some multiple of the full amount, the total impact would have been of a magnitude of less than a half of 1 percent of the gross national product. Commentaries on the contribution of the FHA program in the 1930s seem to regard its principal achievement as educational rather than economic. Some observers felt that it may have helped to reduce the cost of credit to consumers and that it introduced commercial banks to the business potential of small amortized loans to consumers.[22]

Selective programs for insuring or otherwise encouraging consumer loans for specific objectives appeared later in the 1930s and after World War II. The insurance program for repair and modernization loans became a permanent feature of the consumer credit market. Various programs to subsidize loans to veterans, and later student loans, were adopted. However, these programs had specific social objectives and were not significantly related to economic and credit controls.

---

[21]Ibid., pp. 6-18.
[22]Ibid., pp. 4-5.

VII. REGULATION OF TERMS ON CONSUMER CREDIT

Selective controls on the terms of consumer credit contracts have been imposed on three separate occasions in the United States—the first was before and during World War II, the second during the immediate postwar boom, and the third at the outbreak of the Korean War. Events during these periods provide some insights into the operations of selective controls. Unfortunately, however, all three periods were unusual in some respect so that the range of experience is limited to abnormal conditions.

During World War II and the Korean War, controls were used primarily to curtail consumer spending for automobiles and other durables and to relieve pressures on raw materials and other resources that were needed for defense production. Some reduction in the overall demand may have been a derived benefit, but the controls were not regarded as a solution to broader economic problems except in 1948-49. In the immediate postwar period, the need for restricting the demand for durable goods arose from the pent-up demands developed during the war which existing productive facilities could not meet.[23]

In all three periods selective controls on consumer credit were justified as solutions to specific allocational problems that general controls would not handle. It is not clear whether they had any implications for the overall level of economic activity. Output and employment were close to maximum levels in all three periods. The controls shaped the composition of output, rather than affecting the level. Proponents of the controls clearly hoped or expected that they would reduce some of the inflationary pressures as well.

During all three periods, the monetary authorities were limited in the use they could make of general controls. During World War II they were faced with the problems of financing defense expenditures and the necessary productive facilities. In

---

[23]The pent-up demand that led to the postwar controls was one of the original justifications for imposition of controls in 1941. The executive order creating the controls contained the following statement: "to aid in creating a backlog of demand for consumers' durable goods." *Code of Federal Regulations*, Cumulative Supplement 2.1 (Washington, 1943), p. 977.

the two postwar periods, they were limited by their commitment to support Government bond prices. The difficult question about the role of selective controls during these periods is whether they reduced the need for general controls and in this way served as a substitute for the general controls or whether they only shaped the nature of the demand. This question can only be answered within the context of a complete economic model that provides for the substitution effects of the use of the total supply of credit for different purposes. All of the discussions of this question are couched in a partial equilibrium framework where the assumptions in effect determine the conclusions.

A. *Regulations during World War II.* The President's Executive Order 8843 authorizing the regulation of consumer credit provided a detailed statement of the objectives.

Whereas the public interest requires control of the use of instalment credit for financing and refinancing purchases of consumers' durable goods the production of which absorbs resources needed for national defense, in order (a) to facilitate the transfer of productive resources to defense industries, (b) to assist in curbing unwarranted price advances and profiteering which tend to result when the supply of such goods is curtailed without corresponding curtailment of demand, (c) to assist in restraining general inflationary tendencies, to support or supplement taxation imposed to restrain such tendencies, and to promote the accumulation of savings available for financing the defense program, (d) to aid in creating a backlog of demand for consumers' durable goods, and (e) to restrain the development of a consumer debt structure that would repress effective demand for goods and services in the post-defense period. . . .[24]

In implementing the order, Marriner S. Eccles, Chairman of the Federal Reserve Board, made it clear that the primary purpose of the regulation was to check the demand for durable goods.

Civilian demand for goods must be adjusted as closely as possible to supplies available for consumption. Regulation of instalment credit is a necessary measure to this end.[25]

---

[24]Reprinted in *Federal Reserve Bulletin* 27 (September 1941): 837.
[25]Ibid., p. 826.

The initial provisions of the regulation were directed at purchases of durable goods. Down payment and maturity limits were imposed on a schedule of "listed articles." The initial provisions, made effective on September 1, 1941, were generally "in line with existing trade standards."[26] It was recognized that they could be tightened as the need arose.

Within a very short time the need to tighten the requirements arose. In March 1942 the regulation was expanded considerably by an increase in the number of listed articles and the terms on major articles were tightened. As the war progressed, the regulation was extended to all types of consumer credit, including single payment loans and charge accounts, and the "list" was expanded to include soft goods as well as durables. Toward the end of the war the "list" was again reduced and maturities on some items were increased. The regulation was terminated in 1947 by legislation specifying that no consumer credit controls should be imposed after August 8 of that year, except in a case of a national emergency declared by the President.

The World War II experience with regulation provides a good insight into some of the practical and administrative problems associated with selective controls. But it sheds little light on the theoretical issues at stake in the debate on peacetime controls. The administrative adjustments in the regulation that were required during the war provide evidence of the strong forces for the substitution of unregulated types of credit for regulated types and in this way provides indirect evidence of the difficulties involved in trying to control the total amount of credit by selective techniques.

B. Regulations in 1948-49. Soaring prices after the removal of wartime regulations created national concern over the dangers of inflation. The basic pressures were arising from the pent-up demand, from the demobilization of savings and from the expansion of bank loans, as banks shifted their funds from Government securities into loans. The rapid growth of consumer credit attracted special attention and in the President's message to Congress on November 17, 1947, the restoration of consumer credit controls appeared as the first item on a list of

---

[26]*Consumer Instalment Credit,* 1: 291.

proposals for controlling the inflation. The President's request came only 17 days after the authorization had expired, but Congressional action did not permit the regulation to become effective until September 20, 1948.

The President's message emphasized the overall problem of the use of credit but the only specific recommendation dealt with consumer credit.

... At a time when the economy is already producing at capacity, a further expansion of credit simply gives people more dollars to use in bidding up the prices of goods.

Consumer credit is increasing at a disturbing rate. The amount outstanding has risen from 6½ billion dollars in 1945 to 11 billion dollars today. Even more expansion is under way now, because the controls on consumer credit exercised by the Federal Reserve System expired November 1. These controls should be restored. Also, some restraint should be placed on inflationary bank credit.[27]

This statement implies the expectation that a curtailment of consumer credit would lead to a curtailment of the overall use of credit. This expectation is inconsistent with theoretical arguments presented earlier in this study.

In a period of acutely active demand for credit generally, the effect of an increase in consumer credit outstanding is largely a diversion of credit from other uses, with little effect on total demand.[28]

These two positions highlight one of the most difficult questions about the impact of consumer credit controls. The President's message suggested that they could be used as a partial substitute for general controls. This problem lies at the heart of their use during peacetime. If they can be used this way, they become an alternative to general controls or at least a device for reducing the need for general controls.

Congress passed a joint resolution authorizing the reimposition of consumer credit controls which were made effective September 20, 1948. The scope of the regulation was essentially

---

[27]*Congressional Record*, 81st Congress, 2nd Session.
[28]McCracken et al., op. cit., p. 27.

the same as before the controls were lifted. Some decline in sales of automobiles and other listed items was observed in the weeks after the regulation became effective.[29] It was not clear whether this decline resulted from the regulation or reflected a drop from artificially high demand induced by anticipation of the regulation. In either event, some signs of a softening in the level of economic activity in early 1949 led to relaxation of credit terms under the regulation. By the time that the regulation expired in June 1949, the terms of the regulation seemed to be as liberal as the market would accept.[30] This brief period of regulation provided a unique opportunity for a case study of the use of consumer credit controls. Numerous studies and discussions of the specific events have resulted, but no thorough study of the controls within the context of overall economic developments of the period has been made. The superficial evidence suggests that the regulation was effective as a substitution for restrictive monetary action, but a much more careful analysis is required.

C. *Regulations during the Korean War.* Consumer credit controls were reimposed in 1950, as part of the response to the outbreak of the Korean War. The authorization was included in the Defense Production Act of 1950 and the controls were approved only on an emergency basis. These actions were taken within the background of the World War II controls and were clearly designed as preparatory to problems that might arise. As the title of the act implies, the primary concern was with the mobilization of defense production.

In a statement supporting the Defense Production Act of 1950, the Federal Reserve System stressed the role of selective credit controls in the allocation of resources.

It would help to make materials and manpower more readily available for the national defense and military effort, including the materials and manpower necessary to expand our total productive capacity.[31]

Regulations issued on September 18, 1950 were only "moder-

---

[29]*Consumer Instalment Credit*, 1: 298.

[30]"A Study of Instalment Credit Terms," *Federal Reserve Bulletin* 35 (December 1949): 1447.

[31]*Federal Reserve Bulletin* 36 (August 1950): 944.

142

ately restrictive in relation to practices generally prevailing in the instalment financing trade."[32] Provisions of the regulations were tightened substantially in October 1950. Later in 1951 the terms were eased so that by the termination of the regulations, they were not much different than the trade was willing to offer without regulation.

VIII. IMPLICATIONS FOR FURTHER RESEARCH

Experience with the use of selective controls on consumer credit and the debate that accompanied this experience makes it possible to identify the major issues that remain controversial and those on which there is substantial agreement.

A. *Specific Impact of Controls on Maturities and Down Payments*. Empirical and theoretical arguments all seem to support the position that selective credit controls are effective in influencing the amount of credit used for expensive consumer durables, the level of expenditures, and the sales and output of these durables. However, the effects are limited to a fairly narrow range of commodities and do not extend to commodities not purchased on credit. Further research might be productive in refining and clarifying earlier studies. The techniques for research of this type are suggested by the earlier studies of the demand for durable goods and studies of the impact of changes in credit terms.

B. *Cyclical Role of Consumer Instalment Credit*. The issues in the debate on this problem have been specified and two clear-cut positions can be identified. However, the justifications for these positions are almost entirely theoretical. The theoretical arguments of the new approach that uses the rate of change in outstanding credit as the relevant measure of the impact of consumer credit seem persuasive to me. This generally leads to the conclusion that consumer credit does not create a unique cyclical problem. But the work on this question is expository rather than empirical. Statistical evidence on this debate will probably be very hard to obtain. The problem can only be approached within the context of a complete economic model

---

[32]*Consumer Instalment Credit*, 1: 300.

that attempts to measure the interaction between consumer credit and the relevant durable goods sectors on the one hand and the credit markets and other expenditures sectors on the other.

C. *Selective Controls as a Substitute for General Controls.* Many of the arguments for selective controls seem to imply in the simplest sense that curtailment of any part of credit represents curtailment of total credit. However, this ignores the possibility of the substitution of one type of credit for another with no impact at all on the total. Paul McCracken has suggested that the effectiveness of selective controls may depend upon conditions in the credit market as a whole. Views on this problem are based almost entirely on theoretical arguments. These depend to a considerable extent upon the proponent's attitude toward the effectiveness of credit markets in adjusting to changes and in arbitraging exogenous events. Tests for the existence of these substitution effects require market-interaction models that are designed to handle price and non-price effects. The two postwar periods of regulation provide potential test periods. Measurement of market substitutions between consumer credit and other types of credit under unregulated conditions might also give some insight into the problem.

D. *Impact of General Monetary Controls on Consumer Credit.* The problem of the impact of general monetary controls resembles the previous one in that it involves interaction among markets for different types of credit. However, more work has been done on this question. Studies by Federal Reserve System committees and some of the studies of bank behavior suggest techniques can be used. The conclusions of these studies, however, are not universally accepted. The problem, like the preceding one, involves an understanding of the extent of the separation and independence of various credit markets and the ease with which impacts in one are felt by others.

PART 2

JOHN H. WOOD is Esmée Fairbairn Professor of Investment at the University of Birmingham (England). He holds a Ph.D. from Purdue University, specializing in monetary and fiscal policy. A staff economist to the Federal Reserve Board from 1962 to 1965, he has served from time to time as consultant and economist in residence at the Federal Reserve Bank of Philadelphia. He was Associate Professor of Finance at the University of Pennsylvania from 1967 to 1971. Author of *A Model of Commercial Bank Loan and Investment Behavior* and "A Model of Federal Reserve Behavior" in *Monetary Process and Policy: A Symposium* (edited by George Horwich), he has published in the *American Economic Review*, the *Journal of Political Economy*, and the Philadelphia Fed's *Business Review*.

The author is grateful for helpful comments by Ira Kaminow and James M. O'Brien and by F. M. Wilkes, R. M. Young, and other members of the University of Birmingham Workshop in Money and Finance.

Some Effects of Bank Credit Restrictions on the Short-Term Behavior of Large Firms

JOHN H. WOOD

There has been much concern in the United States about the unequal effects of monetary policy. Restrictive measures adopted by the Federal Reserve System to combat aggregate inflationary pressures are said to impinge most heavily on state and local governments, the building industry, and small firms. Large firms, however, may evade the more serious impacts of tight money because of the preferred status they enjoy at commercial banks, who seek to maintain continuous relationships with large depositors, and because of their ability to raise funds in the money and capital markets. This study is not concerned with the accuracy of these representations of the effects of tight money. Rather, it is assumed that the monetary authority believes the above description to be accurate, that it regards these effects as undesirable and that it takes steps to counter them, specifically, through directives or other means, by imposing ceilings on the amounts that may be borrowed by large firms from commercial banks. This study seeks to present the results of an examination of the effects of such bank credit ceilings on the decisions of a large, multiperiod optimizing firm that borrows short-term funds from banks and in the commercial paper market, borrows long-term funds in the capital markets, applies fixed and variable inputs to the production of a single output, holds cash, and carries inventories.

The importance of the imposition of a bank credit ceiling for the financial, production, and capital investment decisions of the firm will depend upon the elasticities of the supplies of funds to the firm in the bond and commercial paper markets, upon the costs of carrying inventories, and upon the technological relationships that determine the elasticity of supply of the firm's output. But the effects of such a restriction may also be affected by whether the imposition of the ceiling comes as a surprise. If the firm correctly predicts the timing and extent of a limitation on bank credit, we should in most cases expect the effects of such a restriction on the firm's decision variables to be smaller and spread more evenly over time than if the firm were surprised by the introduction of a credit ceiling. Although the probable effects of bank credit restrictions on prime business borrowers has been widely discussed, the distinction between the impacts of anticipated and unexpected controls is not often made. In discussing the effects of a reduction in bank lending to business, Richard G. Davis argued that

> ... nonfinancial units that formerly borrowed from banks are most unlikely to be willing or able to shift to nonbank sources of funds, dollar for dollar, at the existing interest rates. This reluctance is, indeed, the strongest single reason for believing that a bank credit ceiling would, on balance, depress aggregate demand.[1]

In this passage and elsewhere, Davis limits his analysis to contemporaneous asset-substitution possibilities. He implicitly assumes credit restrictions to be unanticipated. But James S. Duesenberry, commenting on Davis's paper, points out that

> If the regulations became a normal instrument of monetary restraint, the financial system would adapt to them.... For these reasons,

---

[1]Richard G. Davis, "An Analysis of Quantitative Credit Controls and Related Devices," *Brookings Papers on Economic Activity*, No. 1 (1971): 75.

quantitative restrictions must not be allowed to become anticipated; they must "sneak up" on the market quickly and unexpectedly to be effective.[2]

This paper develops the conditions under which Duesenberry's position is correct within the framework of what is perhaps the simplest model of a firm that is consistent with an analysis of the points at issue. The firm, which is described in sections I and II, is a perfect competitor in the factor and product markets. It may be an imperfect competitor in the financial markets and its managers, in planning current (first-period) and future input, output, inventory and financial decisions, seek to maximize the value of the firm at the end of the fourth period. This enables us to consider a series of decisions in which there is no credit rationing in the first or third periods but rationing is imposed in the second period. Within such a model, a firm that foresees the imposition of rationing will be able to reallocate borrowing and real resources between all periods while a firm that is taken by surprise will be limited in its reallocation possibilities to second- and third-period decisions. The case of surprise rationing will be considered in section III and anticipated rationing will be discussed in section IV. It will be seen that the effects of an unanticipated imposition or tightening of credit restrictions on the behavior of our simple firm will in most cases exceed the effects suffered when the restrictions are anticipated.[3] This is consistent with Duesenberry. But it will also be seen that in certain special cases, such as when the firm is a perfect competitor in the commercial paper market, the impacts of rationing in the two cases are identical. These special cases also tend to be situations in which rationing, foreseen or not, has little effect on the firm.

The discussion in sections I-IV is concerned solely with a microeconomic analysis of the response of a firm to credit ra-

---

[2]"Comment," *Brookings Papers on Economic Activity*, No. 1 (1971): 98-99.

[3]The problems considered here suggest the use of stochastic constraints. It is hoped to extend the study in such a direction, but the analysis of this paper is limited to the consideration of decisions taken under conditions of certainty—either the extreme situation in which the firm is certain (and correct) that bank credit will be restricted by a known amount or the opposite extreme in which the firm is certain (and wrong) that rationing will not be imposed or tightened.

tioning where the decisions of other economic units not in direct contact with the firm are assumed to be unaffected. But credit rationing has macroeconomic implications which may involve a substantial change in the environment within which the firm operates. Section V introduces these macroeconomic effects and considers their influence on the firm's decisions in the cases of anticipated and unanticipated rationing.

I. THE FIRM

The system presented below is a short-term model of a large manufacturing firm applicable only to the conditions usually prevailing around a business cycle peak. For example, interest rates are assumed to be high and sensitive to demands for financial assets. Furthermore, because the model is restricted to short-term decisions, certain of the firm's decision variables, which are in general subject to change, may for our purpose be taken as fixed—for example, dividends and equity finance.

Production. The firm pays for additions to plant and equipment, ΔK_t, at the date of delivery, paying k_t per unit of plant and equipment (capital). However, because we want the productive process to take time, and because it is reasonable to allow some time for the installation of capital, capital purchased in the $(t-1)^{th}$ period does not contribute to output until the tth period. Variable inputs purchased in the tth period, X_t, contribute to output, Z_t, in the same period.

(1) $$Z_t = Z(X_t, K_{t-1}) = Z(X_t, K_{t-2} + \Delta K_{t-1})$$

It should be noted that K_{t-1} is fixed for purposes of the production of Z_t but is variable in the longer run. The short-term nature of the model allows us to abstract from depreciation and obsolescence. A more restrictive assumption is that old and new capital are identical.

Inventories of output may be carried from one period to the next:

150

(2) $$I_t = I_{t-1} + Z_t - S_t$$

where I_t is the quantity of output carried over from the tth period and S_t is sales in the tth period. The handling, storage, and other costs of carrying inventories, $g(I_t)$, are incurred in the period during which inventories are accumulated.

Borrowing. The firm borrows one-period funds from banks, B_t, and in the commercial paper market, C_t, at interest rates b_t and c_t, respectively, and may borrow longer-term funds, L_t, at an interest rate, ℓ_t. Since the firm's decision horizon will be limited to four periods, the longest maturity that can be handled within the framework of the model is three periods. Consequently, it is assumed that long-term borrowing, L_t, matures in the $(t + 3)^{th}$ period. There are no two-period securities. Marginal costs of borrowing are assumed to be increasing functions of the amounts borrowed, which is more likely to be the case during periods of tight money than when interest rates are low or falling. That is, $B_t'', C_t'', L_t'', > 0$

where

$$B_t'' = \frac{d^2[(1 + b_t)B_t]}{dB_t^2}, \quad C_t'' = \frac{d^2[(1 + c_t)C_t]}{dC_t^2},$$

$$L_t'' = \frac{d^2[(1 + \ell_t)^3 L_t]}{dL_t^2}$$

and

$$\frac{db_t}{dB_t}, \frac{dc_t}{dC_t}, \frac{d\ell_t}{dL_t} > 0.$$

The demand for cash balances will normally be an inverse function of market interest rates and will tend to be large when interest rates are low. But when interest rates are high, as assumed in the present study, desired cash balances will be the minimum level necessary to finance discrepancies between the timing of receipts and expenditures. However, the firm may be required by its banker or other creditors to hold more than this desired level as a condition for obtaining bank loans or finding

151

purchasers of its commercial paper. For example, "commercial-paper buyers require that issuers have open (unused) lines of credit with commercial banks to cover a significant fraction of outstandings. On these open lines, a compensating-balance requirement of at least 10 percent is required."[4] Under these conditions the firm's cash balances in the tth period will be

$$(3) \qquad R_t = R(B_t, C_t) = \max[R_B(B_t), R_C(C_t)]$$

where only one of the derivatives of R_t with respect to B_t and C_t is likely to be non-zero in any period. The firm's cash includes demand deposits and certificates of deposit and earns an average rate of return, r_t, which is assumed to be independent of R_t.

We abstract from equity issues, which provided only about 3 percent of the funds raised by American corporations during 1956-73 and consisted mainly of issues by smaller firms and by utilities and financial institutions. Dividends are assumed to be predetermined in our short-term analysis because dividend payments appear to adjust to variations in earnings only gradually over time.[5]

The inflow of funds in the tth period is the sum of revenue from current sales, $p_t S_t$ (where p_t is the price per unit of output), borrowing, $B_t + C_t + L_t$, and interest earnings on cash balances, $r_{t-1} R_{t-1}$. *Outflows of funds* result from payments for variable inputs, $w_t X_t$ (where w_t is the cost per unit of X_t), payments for additions to plant and equipment, $k_t \Delta K_t$, the cost of carrying inventories, $g(I_t)$, repayments of borrowings $(1 + b_{t-1}) B_{t-1} + (1 + c_{t-1})C_{t-1} + (1 + \ell_{t-1})^3 L_{t-1}$, and dividends, D_t. The excess of these receipts over these expenditures is equal to the increment in cash balances.

---

[4]Burton Gordon Malkiel, *The Term Structure of Interest Rates: Expectations and Behavior Patterns* (Princeton, N.J.: Princeton University Press, 1966), p. 130.

[5]On both of these points, see William L. White, "Debt Management and the Form of Business Financing," *Journal of Finance* 29 (1974): 565-77.

$$(4) \quad R_t - R_{t-1} = p_t S_t + B_t + C_t + L_t + r_{t-1} R_{t-1} - w_t X_t$$
$$- k_t \Delta K_t - g(I_t) - (1 + b_{t-1}) B_{t-1}$$
$$- (1 + c_{t-1}) C_{t-1} - (1 + \ell_{t-3})^3 L_{t-3} - D_t;$$
$$(t = 1, 2, 3)$$

The Objective Function. Assume that the firm wishes to maximize the funds available to the owners at the end of the fourth period (we ignore D_1, D_2, D_3, and D_4, which are pre-determined):

$$(5) \quad V_4 = P_4 S_4 + (1 + r_3) R_3 - w_4 X_4 - (1 + b_3) B_3$$
$$- (1 + c_3) C_3 - (1 + \ell_1)^3 L_1 + k_4 K_3$$

where no long-term securities are issued in the second or third periods ($L_2 = L_3 = 0$) and k_4 is the value of the firm's plant and equipment at the end of the terminal period.

Although the firm is an imperfect competitor in the markets for financial assets (except cash), we shall assume for reasons of simplicity that it is a perfect competitor in the factor and product markets—that is, p_t, k_t, and w_t are independent of Z_t, K_t, and X_t. This assumption will be relaxed from time to time in sections III-V.

II. THE OPTIMUM WHEN ACCESS TO CREDIT IS UNRESTRICTED

The firm maximizes (5) subject to (1)-(4) with respect to X_t, K_t, I_t, B_t, C_t ($t = 1, 2, 3$), L_1 and X_4. The necessary conditions for a maximum imply the following marginal relations:

$$(6) \quad \hat{C}'_t = \hat{B}'_t = \frac{p_{t+1}}{g'_t + p_t} = \frac{p_{t+1} Z^K_{t+1} + k_{t+1}}{k_t} \quad (t = 1, 2, 3);$$
$$p_t Z^x_t = w_t \ (t = 1, 2, 3, 4); \quad L'_1 = \hat{C}'_1 \, \hat{C}'_2 \, \hat{C}'_3$$

and, rearranging,

$$(7) \quad g'_t = \frac{p_{t+1}}{\hat{C}'_t} - p_t; \quad k_t = \frac{p_{t+1} Z^K_{t+1} + k_{t+1}}{\hat{C}'_t} \quad (t = 1, 2, 3)$$

153

where

$$C'_t = \frac{d[(1 + c_t)C_t]}{dC_t}; \quad B'_t = \frac{d[(1 + b_t)B_t]}{dB_t};$$

$$L'_t = \frac{d[(1 + \ell_t)^3 L_t]}{dL_t};$$

$$g'_t = \frac{dg(I_t)}{dg_t}; \quad Z^K_t = \frac{\partial Z(X_t, K_{t-1})}{\partial K_{t-1}}; \quad Z^x_t = \frac{\partial Z(X_t, K_{t-1})}{\partial X_t};$$

$$\hat{C}'_t = \frac{[C'_t - (1 + r_t)R^c_t]}{(1 - R^c_t)}; \quad \hat{B}'_t = \frac{[B'_t - (1 + r_t)R^b_t]}{(1 - R^b_t)};$$

$$R^c_t = \frac{\partial R(B_t, C_t)}{\partial C_t};$$

$$R^b_t = \frac{\partial R(B_t, C_t)}{\partial B_t}$$

Beginning with the definition of C'_t, the marginal cost of borrowing in the commercial paper market is the marginal payment of interest and principal per dollar of the paper issued, C'_t, less the marginal return from the proportion of the issue held in cash in order to maintain open lines of bank credit, $(1 + r_t)R^c_t$, as a proportion of the borrowings actually available for the purchase of inputs and the repayment of debts, $(1 - R^c_t)$. In the simple case in which c_t is fixed and R^c_t is the fixed (and binding) quantity of cash balances required as a proportion of commercial paper issues, we would have

$$\hat{C}'_t = \frac{(1 + c_t) - (1 + r_t)R^c_t}{1 - R^c_t}$$

The marginal cost of bank loans, B'_t, is similarly defined.

The first and last statements in (6) show that the firm borrows from available sources up to the points at which the marginal costs of borrowing are equated. The firm buys variable inputs up to the point at which the value of the marginal product, $p_t Z^x_t$, equals the cost per unit of the input, w_t. No discount factor is involved in this relation because variable inputs contribute to current output. The firm borrows to finance inventories up to

154

the point at which the marginal cost of carrying inventories is equal to the excess of the discounted value of next period's price over the current price. The firm borrows to finance capital investment up to the point at which the marginal cost of borrowing is equated to the discounted value of the capital equipment purchased (the discounted value of the marginal product of capital plus its resale value) as a proportion of its purchase price. The second equation in (7) expresses this result in another way: Capital is purchased up to the point at which the discounted value of the stream of returns from capital is equal to the price of capital.

The second-order conditions for a maximum are satisfied if

(8) $\qquad\qquad Z_t'', \; g_t'', \; \hat{B}_t'', \; \hat{C}_t'', \; L_1'' > 0; \text{ all } t$

where

$$Z_t'' = \frac{\partial^2 Z_t}{\partial X_t^2} \frac{\partial^2 Z_t}{\partial K_{t-1}^2} - \left(\frac{\partial^2 Z_t}{\partial X_t \partial K_{t-1}}\right)^2; \; g_t'' = \frac{dg_t'}{dI_t};$$

$$\hat{B}_t'' = \frac{d\hat{B}_t'}{dB_t}; \; \hat{C}_t'' = \frac{d\hat{C}_t'}{dC_t}.$$

The condition $Z_t'' > 0$ implies decreasing returns to scale and ensures that terminal value, V_4, would decline as a result of further applications of X and K. If g_t' were constant or a decreasing function of I_t, the firm would either store nothing or sell nothing each period. If $\hat{B}_t'$, $\hat{C}_t'$, and L_t' were constant or decreasing functions of the amounts borrowed, the firm would engage in only one form of borrowing. A zero value of one, but no more than one, of the three second derivatives $\hat{B}_t''$, $\hat{C}_t''$, L_t'' in each time period is consistent with the satisfaction of the second-order conditions; for example, if $\hat{C}_t'' = 0$ (t = 1, 2, 3), the firm would borrow in the three markets up to the point at which the rising marginal costs of bonds and bank loans were equated to the constant marginal cost of commercial paper. However, except in certain special cases to be discussed toward the ends of sections III and IV, it will be assumed that all of the statements in (8) hold.

155

III. A RESTRICTION ON BANK LOANS

If B is constrained such that $B_2 \leq \bar{B}_2$ and if $\bar{B}_2$ is less than the optimal B_2 so that the constraint is binding the firm will, if the restriction is anticipated, maximize V_4 subject to (1)-(4) and

$$(9) \qquad\qquad B_2 = \bar{B}_2.$$

It is assumed that B_1, B_3, and other sources of finance are unconstrained. That is, rationing will not be invoked until the second period and will be relaxed immediately thereafter. The marginal conditions for $t = 1, 3, 4$ in this case are identical to those for the unrestricted borrowing case shown in (6). But the first part of (6) is altered as follows for $t = 2$, where μ is the Lagrangian multiplier associated with (9):

$$(10) \quad \hat{C}'_2 = \hat{B}'_2 + \frac{\mu}{\hat{B}'_3(1 - R^b_2)} = \frac{p_3}{g'_3 + p_2} = \frac{p_3 Z^K_3 + k_3}{k_2}.$$

The penultimate equation in (6) is unchanged and the last statement may be extended as follows:

$$(11) \qquad L'_1 = \hat{C}'_1 \, \hat{C}'_2 \, \hat{C}'_3 = \hat{B}'_1 \left[\hat{B}'_2 + \frac{\mu}{\hat{B}'_3(1 - R^b_2)} \right] \hat{B}'_3.$$

The Lagrangian multiplier μ is the shadow price of the constraint $\bar{B}_2$ and is equal to

$$(12) \qquad\qquad \mu = (\hat{C}'_2 - \hat{B}'_2)(1 - R^b_2)\hat{C}'_3.$$

The cost of the credit restriction to the firm is positively related to the excess of the marginal cost of second-period commercial paper over second-period bank loans and the marginal cost of refinancing this excess in the third period. This cost is inversely related to the supply elasticities of credit sources alternative to second-period bank loans—namely, bank loans in the first and third periods and sources other than bank loans in all periods.

156

As a general pattern, one might expect the firm to adjust to a forced reduction in B_2 by increasing issues of other debt instruments, although by less in total than the decrease in B_2, and, because of resulting increases in the marginal costs of funds, to reduce inputs and therefore levels of output. This pattern is closely adhered to in the second, third, and fourth periods in the case of unforeseen rationing, where first-period responses are, of course, zero. But some important exceptions arise when rationing is anticipated. The remainder of this section is devoted to an examination of the surprise case while the anticipated case will be considered in section IV.

Equations (A.2)-(A.4) in Appendix A.2 show that

$$(dC_2/d\bar{B}_2)^S, \ (dC_3/d\bar{B}_2)^S, \ (dB_3/d\bar{B}_2)^S \ < \ 0$$

where the S superscripts indicate surprise rationing. That is, a reduction in $\bar{B}_2$—an imposition or tightening of the constraint—induces increases in alternative forms of borrowing, including an overall rise in third-period debt. However, total second-period borrowing will decline since C_2 will not rise sufficiently to offset the decline in B_2. The exception is when R_2^c is very large, where the amount of C_t required to finance inventories and capital purchases in any period is positively related to the proportion of commercial paper borrowings that must be held in the form of cash balances (if C_t rather than B_t is the binding constraint on the demand for cash). This result is shown in (A.7).

X_2 is independent of interest rates and is therefore unaffected in the surprise case. Z_2 is a function of X_2 and K_1 and is also unaffected. However, the expansions in C_2, C_3, and B_3 imply increased costs of financing capital and inventories with the result that I_2, I_3, K_2, and K_3 are reduced. The reductions in K_2 and K_3 cause declines in the marginal products of X_3 and X_4 and resulting decreases in purchases of variable inputs. The smaller K_2, K_3, X_3, and X_4 mean smaller Z_3 and Z_4. Second- and fourth-period sales are respectively increased and reduced, but the effect on S_3 is uncertain because of decreases in both Z_3 and I_3. These results are indicated in the lower portion of the

157

t	dL	dC	dB	dF	dX	dZ	dK	dI	dS	
1	+	−	−	+	o	o	+	+	−	
2		+	−	−	+	+	−	−	+	
3		?	?	?	−	−	?	?	?	A
4					?	?			?	
2		+	−	−	o	o	−	−	+	
3		+	+	+	−	−	−	−	?	S
4					−	−			−	

Responses to a Reduction in $\bar{B}_2$

Table, where the signs assume that R_t^b and R_t^c are not sufficiently large to dominate the direction of adjustment of F_t.

Our understanding of these adjustments and the interpretation of the statements in Appendix A.2 will be assisted by the consideration of certain extreme cases. For example, assume the firm to be a perfect competitor in the commercial paper market—that is, $\hat{C}_t'$ is constant and $\hat{C}_t'' = 0$. In this case, a forced reduction in B_2 will be offset by increases in C_2 and C_3 at constant marginal costs in such a way as to maintain the marginal conditions in (6) at unchanged levels of inputs, outputs, and inventories. Although real variables are unaffected, the credit restriction will nevertheless involve some cost to the firm. In the absence of rationing, the firm obtains bank loans up to the amount B_2^* shown in the Figure, where the rising marginal cost of loans, $\hat{B}_2'$, equals the constant marginal cost of commercial paper, $\hat{C}_2'$. Commercial paper borrowings amount to $F_2^* - B_2^*$. A reduction in B_2 to $\bar{B}_2$ forces a greater reliance on the

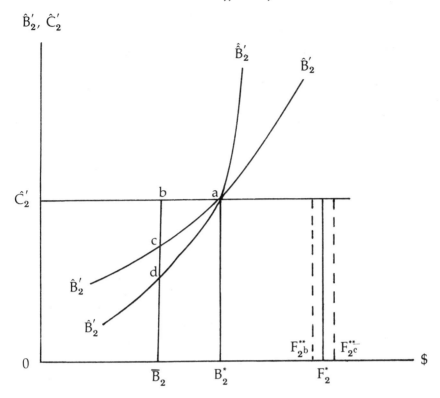

Responses of C_2 and F_2 when $\hat{C}_2'' = 0$

commercial paper market and an increased cost of borrowing amounting to the area abc between $\hat{C}_2'$ and $\hat{B}_2'$. The shadow price of the restriction, μ, indicated in (A.17) in Appendix A.3 is directly proportional to $\hat{B}_2''$, the slope of $\hat{B}_2'$. For example, if the marginal cost of bank loans is a steeply rising function of B_2, indicated by $\hat{B}_2'$ in the Figure, the reduction in the firm's terminal value will be proportional to the area abd (times the cost in the third period of refinancing the added cost of second-period borrowing). Additional third-period borrowing will be entirely in the form of commercial paper at the constant marginal cost $\hat{C}_3'$, where B_3 remains at the level such that the rising marginal cost of loans, $\hat{B}_3'$, equals $\hat{C}_3'$.

These results are subject to small adjustments for changes in required cash balances. In the present example, in which the

159

revenue from sales is unaffected and the amount of second-period funds available for the purchase of inputs, the repayment of maturing debt and holding inventories is unchanged, total second-period borrowing adjusts only in response to changes in cash. Therefore, if B_2^*, C_2^*, R_2^* and $\bar{B}_2$, C_2^{**}, R_2^{**} denote values in the absence and presence of rationing, respectively, then the requirement that $\bar{B}_2 + C_2^{**} - R_2^{**} = B_2^* + C_2^* - R_2^*$ implies that

$$\frac{C_2^{**} - C_2^*}{\bar{B}_2 - B_2^*} = \begin{cases} -(1 - R_2^b) & \text{if } R_2^b > 0, \ R_2^c = 0 \\ -\dfrac{1}{(1 - R_2^c)} & \text{if } R_2^b = 0, \ R_2^c > 0. \end{cases}$$

That is, if B_2 is the binding constraint on cash balances then the rise in C_2 required by the imposition of $\bar{B}_2$ will be less than the fall in B_2 because of the reduction in cash balances. On the other hand, the rise in C_2 will exceed the fall in B_2 if the demand for R_2 is proportional to C_2. These results are shown in (A.15).

In the above example the lowest-cost means of transferring resources from future periods to the second period was an increase in commercial paper borrowing at constant marginal cost. Letting $\hat{C}_t'' > 0$ once again and turning to the special case in which $g_t'' \to 0$ for all t, the cheapest way of financing second-period expenditures in the face of a reduction in B_2 is to increase sales by reducing inventories at the (nearly) constant marginal cost $g_2' + p_2$. The reduction in I_2 as a proportion of the fall in B_2 will approach $(1 - R_2^b)/(g_2' + p_2)$, where $(1 - R_2^b)dB_2$ is the decline in second-period finance (adjusted for cash) available to the firm at existing interest rates. Third-period inventory holdings will fall by an amount approaching $(1 - R_2^b)(\hat{C}_2' - \hat{B}_2')$ $(dB_2)/(g_3' + p_3)$, where the numerator is the increased cost of second-period finance and $\hat{C}_2' = p_3/(g_2' + p_2)$ is the foregone marginal return from second-period inventories. All borrowing and production responses to credit rationing approach zero as $g_t'' \to 0.$[6]

If g_t'', $\hat{C}_t > 0$ but the production process approximates constant returns to scale $(Z_t'' \to 0)$, the firm will respond to the rationing of

---

[6]The special case $g_t'' \to$ and $Z_t'' \to$ are discussed in Appendices A.5 and A.6 .

bank credit by reducing purchases of inputs while maintaining inventories and other forms of borrowing unchanged. The firm reduces its holdings of cash by $R_2^b(d\bar{B}_2)$ and cuts capital spending by $k_2(dK_2) = (1 - R_2^b) (d\bar{B}_2)$. The firm responds to the contraction in B_2 by foregoing future sales through a reduction in K_2 at an opportunity cost per unit of capital equal to $\hat{C}_2' = (p_3 Z_3^K + k_3)/k_2$. Third- and fourth-period inputs, outputs, and sales are similarly reduced and the impact of rationing on terminal value is $(dV_4) = (1 - R_2^b) (\hat{C}_2' - \hat{B}_2')\hat{C}_3'(d\bar{B}_2) = \mu(d\bar{B}_2)$.

It is most unlikely, however, that constant returns to scale will be associated with perfect competition and, if p_t, w_t, and k_t are functions of S_t, X_t, and ΔK_t, respectively, interperiod shifts in production such as those described above will give rise to suboptimal movements in marginal costs relative to marginal revenues. In consequence, the firm's response to rationing will involve some reliance on alternative sources of finance and somewhat smaller reallocations of production than those shown in Appendix A.6—even when $Z_t'' \to 0$. Imperfect competition in the product and factor markets also implies a similar modification of the results obtained when $g_t'' \to 0$. However, the preceding discussion of extreme cases has illustrated that the impact of an unanticipated temporary restriction on bank lending to the large firm (1) impinges more on output the smaller are elasticities of supply of alternative forms of finance, the less are diseconomies of scale in production, the greater are increases in marginal costs of holding inventories, and the less are responses of p_t, w_t, and k_t to the firm's sales and factor purchases; (2) induces greater resort to other sources of credit the greater are the elasticities of supply of these alternative sources, the greater are diseconomies of scale in production, the greater are increases in marginal costs of holding inventories, and the greater are responses of p_t, w_t, and k_t to S_t, X_t, and ΔK_t.

IV. ANTICIPATED RATIONING

If second-period rationing is anticipated the firm will be able to soften the future impact of rationing by rearranging first-period financing, inventories and equipment purchases. Because of the rise in the expected cost of second-period borrowing, the firm will borrow less at short term in the first period (which must be refinanced in the second period) and will issue more long-term securities. The upward revision in L_1 will exceed the reduction in $B_1 + C_1$ as the firm moves from second-period to first-period borrowing in order to finance increases in K_1 and I_1—that is, it reallocates real resources from the first to the second period.[7] These results are indicated in Appendix A.2 and in the first row of the Table.

The downward revision of short-term borrowing in the first period, accompanied by expanded production and sales in the second period resulting from the increases in K_1 and I_1, makes possible a smaller rise in second-period commercial paper issues than in the case of surprise rationing. As seen in equation (A.2), $(dC_2/d\bar{B}_2)^A$ may be expressed as a proportion of $(dC_2/d\bar{B}_2)^S$, where this proportion lies between zero and unity and is inversely related to $(dC_1/dB_2)^A$.

The reduction in short-term borrowing in the first and second periods tends to reduce the need for short-term borrowing in the third period while at the same time enabling the firm to increase K_3 and I_3, which permits an increase in fourth-period sales as a contribution to the repayment of long-term debt. Furthermore, the necessity of repaying L_1 in the fourth period reduces the inclination to borrow at short term in the third period. If these forces dominate the firm's response to anticipated rationing then C_3 and B_3 fall while K_3, I_3, X_4, and Z_4 rise, the question marks in the Table being replaced by appropriate signs. These responses are the opposite of those prevailing in the case of surprise rationing. In other words, borrowing plans for the post-rationing period are revised downward while production plans are revised upward. These decisions result from increases in borrowing, inventories, and capital purchases in the pre-rationing period.

These post-rationing effects are reversed, however, if $\hat{C}_2' - \hat{B}_2'$ is large, in which case the firm may be forced to increase third-period borrowing and to reduce K_3 and I_3 as a result of the large

---

[7] Unless R_1^c or R_1^b is very large, in which case the reduction in first-period cash balances may permit a decline in first-period borrowing. See equation A.6.

increase in the financing burden as it shifts from B_2 to C_2. This will be the case if the demand for the firm's commercial paper is very inelastic during the rationing period (large $\hat{C}_2''$) and the third- and fourth-period signs in the Table will be the same in both the anticipated and surprise rationing situations. But the responses in the anticipated case will be smaller in absolute value than those in the surprise case—except in certain special cases.

In the extreme case in which commercial paper rates are independent of the firm's issues the firm will have no incentive to alter first-period decisions, even when rationing is anticipated, because of its ability to shift from B_2 to C_2 at constant cost, $\hat{C}_2'$. Consequently, the firm's response is the same in the foreseen and surprise rationing cases when $\hat{C}_t'' = 0$. This similarity of results in the two situations also holds when either $Z_t'' \to 0$ or $g_t'' \to 0$.

If $\hat{C}_t''$, g_t'', and Z_t'' are all positive and finite but the firm is able to issue long-term securities at a constant rate ℓ (i.e., $L_1'' = 0$) there will be a greater reliance on long-term borrowing in the first period. This will be accompanied by greater reductions in B_1 and C_1 but, on balance, decreases in L_1'' imply increases in total first-period debt issues and corresponding increases in I_1 and K_1. These rearrangements in the pre-rationing period make possible a more moderate response to rationing in the second period; that is, C_2 will rise and K_2 and I_2 will fall by smaller amounts than when the marginal cost of long-term borrowing is an increasing function of L_1. These adjustments in turn imply less short-term borrowing in the third period—that is, less positive or more negative changes in C_3 and B_3 with corresponding changes in K_3 and I_3 as indicated in Appendix A.2.

In summary, the correct anticipation of rationing will normally lead to a shift from short- to long-term debt and to increases in inventories and capital expenditures prior to rationing. This makes possible a more moderate response to a bank credit restriction than in the case of surprise rationing. This means smaller increases in alternative forms of borrowing and smaller reductions in capital expenditures and output during and after the rationing period—perhaps even a reversal of the post-rationing effects associated with surprise rationing. This contrast between responses in the two situations is accentuated by an increase in the elasticity of demand for the firm's long-term issues (a reduction in L_1''), but is moderated by an increase in the elasticity of demand for its commercial paper and by reductions in diseconomies of scale or the rate of increase of the cost of carrying inventories (reductions in $\hat{C}_t''$, Z_t'', g_t''. A small L_1'' encourages a greater reliance on adjustments prior to rationing, while small $\hat{C}_t''$, Z_t'', and g_t'' reduce the costs of adjustments during and after the period of rationing and therefore reduce the necessity of pre-rationing adjustments.

V. MACROECONOMIC IMPLICATIONS

Some of the special cases discussed above may occasionally be applicable to situations in which a single firm, or small group of firms, is rationed. But it is unlikely that interest rates will fail to respond to the shifts among financial assets that occur when credit restrictions are directed toward a large group of borrowers. Thus, the results obtained in the "normal" cases and set forth in Appendix A.2 may constitute a reasonably accurate description of aggregate responses to credit rationing subject to exceptions at opposite extremes from the special cases discussed in sections III and IV. Examples of such extremes are $C_t'' \to \infty$ and $L_t'' \to \infty$, which may be particularly appropriate to conditions of severe financial stress. On the one hand, if $L_1'' \to \infty$ there will not be any pre-rationing adjustments so that the firm's response will be the same in the anticipated and surprise rationing situations. On the other hand, if L_1'' is not infinitely large but $C_t'' \to \infty$, the firm will find it profitable to rearrange B_1, L_1, K_1, and I_1 in such a way as to moderate needed adjustments in later periods.

Now what are the implications of all this for policy? In particular, should the monetary authority warn economic actors of its plans regarding rationing, or what is equivalent in the long run, should it apply the same controls in the same way in the same kinds of situations so as to be predictable in its actions? Or should it "sneak up" on the market by responding differently (or similarly or randomly—in any case, unpredictably) at different times to similar situations? The answer depends upon the central bank's objectives. On the one hand, if the goal is to dismantle the financial sector, and perhaps other sectors, maximizing the number of bankruptcies along the way, surprise is called for. On the other hand, if the goal is to ensure that counterinflationary monetary policy will impinge on large firms as well as other borrowers, while at the same time avoiding credit crunches and rapid shifts in production and employment, then controls should be predictable so that credit and production responses may be distributed smoothly over time.

If there is concern that anticipated rationing will not have sufficient effect on large firms, the appropriate policy is a more stringent restriction, announced well in advance of its imposition—rather than the sudden application of less severe controls. There is little danger that firms will be able to escape completely from the effects of anticipated controls, even if account is taken of new financial institutions and instruments that may be devised to assist the evasion of those effects. The effectiveness of a limitation on bank lending to large firms depends on the elasticities of supply of alternative sources of credit. Even allowing for financial innovation, large firms will not as a group be able to evade the effects of rationing unless means can be devised to provide credit at fixed marginal costs equal to those prevailing in the absence of rationing.

APPENDIX

Definitions of the notation used in this study are listed in Section A.1. The results discussed in the text are presented in Sections A.2-A.6.

A.1—Definitions

X_t = quantity of the variable input purchased and used in the tth period.

K_t = quantity of capital equipment in the firm's possession in the tth period and contributing to production in period $t + 1$.

Z_t = quantity of output produced in the tth period.

S_{It} = quantity of sales in the tth period.

165

I_t = quantity of output carried over from the tth to the $(t + 1)^{th}$ period (gross inventory).

B_t = borrowings from banks in the tth period, in dollars; all one-period maturity.

$\bar{B}_2$ = maximum permissible bank borrowing in the second period.

C_t = commercial paper borrowings in the tth period, in dollars; all one-period maturity.

L_t = long-term (three-period) borrowings in the tth period, in dollars.

$F_t = C_t + B_t + L_t$ = total borrowing in the tth period.

b_t, c_t, ℓ_t = interest rates on B_t, C_t, and L_t, respectively.

R_t = the firm's cash balances in the tth period.

w_t = unit cost of the variable input in the tth period.

k_t = unit cost of capital equipment in the tth period.

p_t = unit price of sales in the tth period.

μ = Lagrange multiplier; shadow price of the constraint, $\bar{B}_2$.

$g(I_t)$ = the cost of carrying inventories, in dollars.

$Z(X_t, K_{t-1}) = Z_t$ = the production function.

$R(B_t, C_t) = \max[R_b(B_t), R_c(C_t)]$ = demand for cash balances.

$$g'_t = \frac{dg(I_t)}{dI_t}; \quad B'_t = \frac{d[(1 + b_t)B_t]}{dB_t}; \quad C'_t = \frac{d[(1 + c_t)C_t]}{dC_t};$$

$$L'_t = \frac{d[(1 + \ell_t)^3 L_t]}{dL_t}; \quad R^b_t = \frac{dR_t}{dB_t}; \quad R^c_t = \frac{dR_t}{dC_t};$$

$$\hat{g}'_t = g'_t + p_t; \quad \hat{C}'_t = \frac{[C'_t - (1 + r_t)R^c_t]}{(1 - R^c_t)};$$

$$\hat{B}'_t = \frac{[B'_t - (1 + r_t)R^b_t]}{(1 - R^b_t)}$$

$$g_t'' = \frac{dg_t'}{dI_t}; \quad \hat{C}_t'' = \frac{d\hat{C}_t'}{dC_t}; \quad \hat{B}_t'' = \frac{d\hat{B}_t'}{dB_t}; \quad L_t'' = \frac{dL_t'}{dL_t};$$

$$Z_t'' = [Z_t^{xx} Z_t^{KK} - (Z_t^{xK})^2]$$

$$\frac{\partial Z_t}{\partial X_t} = Z_t^x; \quad \frac{\partial Z_t}{\partial K_{t-1}} = Z_t^K; \quad \frac{\partial^2 Z_t}{\partial X_t^2} = Z_t^{xx}; \quad \frac{\partial^2 Z_t}{\partial K_{t-1}^2} = Z_t^{KK}; \quad \frac{\partial^2 Z_t}{\partial X_t \partial K_{t-1}} = Z_t^{xK}$$

$$C_t^\alpha = \frac{\hat{C}_t''}{\hat{C}_t'}; \quad B_t^\alpha = \frac{\hat{B}_t''}{\hat{B}_t'}; \quad L_t^\alpha = \frac{L_t''}{L_t'}; \quad \hat{g}_t^\alpha = \frac{g_t''}{\hat{g}_t'}; \quad Z_t^\alpha = -\frac{P_t Z_t''}{k_{t-1} Z_t^{KK}}$$

$$\Delta_t = C_t^\alpha \left[\frac{(1 - R_t^c)}{C_t^\alpha} + \frac{(1 - R_t^b)}{B_t^\alpha} + \frac{\hat{g}_t'}{g_t^\alpha} + \frac{\hat{C}_t' k_t}{Z_{t+1}^\alpha} \right], \quad t = 1, 3.$$

$$\Delta_2 = C_2^\alpha \left[\frac{(1 - R_2^c)}{C_2^\alpha} + \frac{g_2'}{g_2^\alpha} + \frac{C_2' k_2}{Z_3^\alpha} \right]; \quad \Delta_{ijk} = \Delta_i \Delta_j \Delta_k$$

All of the above terms except Z_t^{xx} and Z_t^{KK} are nonnegative.

The A and S superscripts in the following sections indicate responses of the variables to alterations in the constraint $\bar{B}_2$ in the anticipated and surprise cases, respectively. When no such superscript appears, the statement applies to both cases.

A.2—The General Case

(A.1) $$\left(\frac{dC_1}{d\bar{B}_2} \right)^A = \frac{(1 - R_2^b)[C_2^\alpha \Delta_3 + C_3^\alpha (\hat{C}_2' - \hat{B}_2')\Delta_2]}{L_1^\alpha \Delta_{123} + C_1^\alpha \Delta_{23} + \hat{C}_1' C_2^\alpha \Delta_{13} + \hat{C}_1' \hat{C}_2' C_3^\alpha \Delta_{12}}$$

$$= - \left[\left(\frac{dC_2}{d\bar{B}_2} \right)^S - \left(\frac{dC_2}{d\bar{B}_2} \right)^A \right] \frac{\Delta_2}{C_1' \Delta_1} > 0$$

(A.2) $$\left(\frac{dC_2}{d\bar{B}_2} \right)^A = \left[1 - \frac{\hat{C}_1' \Delta_1}{(1 - R_2^b)} \left(\frac{dC_1}{d\bar{B}_2} \right)^A \right] \left(\frac{dC_2}{d\bar{B}_2} \right)^S < 0;$$

$$\left(\frac{dC_2}{d\bar{B}_2} \right)^S = - \frac{(1 - R_2^b)}{\Delta_3} < 0$$

where

$$0 < \left[1 - \frac{\hat{C}_1' \Delta_1}{(1 - R_2^b)} \left(\frac{dC_1}{d\bar{B}_2} \right)^A \right] < 1.$$

(A.3) $$\left(\frac{dC_3}{d\bar{B}_2} \right)^A = \left[1 - \frac{L_1' \Delta_1}{\mu} \left(\frac{dC_1}{d\bar{B}_2} \right)^A \right] \left(\frac{dC_3}{d\bar{B}_2} \right)^S \gtreqless 0; \quad \left(\frac{dC_3}{d\bar{B}_2} \right)^S$$

$$= - \frac{(\hat{C}_2' - \hat{B}_2')(1 - R_2^b)}{\Delta_3} < 0$$

where

$$0 \begin{array}{c} \leq \\ = \\ > \end{array} \left[1 - \frac{L_1' \Delta_1}{\mu} \left(\frac{dC_1}{d\bar{B}_2} \right)^A \right] < 1.$$

(A.4) $\quad \dfrac{dB_t}{d\bar{B}_2} = \dfrac{C_t^\alpha}{B_2^\alpha} \left(\dfrac{dC_t}{d\bar{B}_2} \right), \ t = 1, 3; \ \dfrac{dB_2}{d\bar{B}_2} = 1$

(A.5) $\quad \left(\dfrac{dL_1}{d\bar{B}_2} \right)^A = - \Delta_1 \left(\dfrac{dC_1}{d\bar{B}_2} \right)^A < 0$

(A.6) $\quad \left(\dfrac{dF_1}{d\bar{B}_2} \right)^A = \left(1 + \dfrac{C_1^\alpha}{B_1^\alpha} - \Delta_1 \right) \left(\dfrac{dC_1}{d\bar{B}_2} \right)^A$

$$= C_1^\alpha \left(\frac{R_1^c}{C_1^\alpha} + \frac{R_1^b}{B_1^\alpha} - \frac{\hat{g}_1'}{g_1^\alpha} - \frac{\hat{C}_1' k_1}{Z_2^\alpha} \right) \left(\frac{dC_1}{d\bar{B}_2} \right)^A \gtreqless 0$$

(A.7) $\quad \left(\dfrac{dF_2}{d\bar{B}_2} \right)^A = 1 + \left(\dfrac{dC_2}{d\bar{B}_2} \right)^A < 1; \ \left(\dfrac{dF_2}{d\bar{B}_2} \right)^S = 1 + \left(\dfrac{dC_2}{d\bar{B}_2} \right)^S$

$$= \frac{C_2^\alpha}{\Delta_2} \left[\frac{(R_2^b - R_2^c)}{C_2^\alpha} + \frac{g_2'}{g_2^\alpha} + \frac{C_2' k_2}{Z_3^\alpha} \right] \gtreqless 0$$

(A.8) $\quad \dfrac{dF_3}{d\bar{B}_2} = \left(1 + \dfrac{C_3^\alpha}{B_3^\alpha} \right) \left(\dfrac{dC_3}{d\bar{B}_2} \right)$

(A.9) $\quad \left(\dfrac{dX_1}{d\bar{B}_2} \right)^A = \left(\dfrac{dZ_1}{d\bar{B}_2} \right)^A = 0; \ \left(\dfrac{dX_2}{d\bar{B}_2} \right)^S = \left(\dfrac{dZ_2}{d\bar{B}_2} \right)^S = 0$

(A.10) $\quad \left(\dfrac{dX_t}{d\bar{B}_2} \right)^A = \dfrac{\hat{C}_{t-1}'' Z_t^{xK}}{Z_t^\alpha Z_t^{KK}} \left(\dfrac{dC_{t-1}}{d\bar{B}_2} \right)^A; \ \left(\dfrac{dZ_t}{d\bar{B}_2} \right)^A = \dfrac{(Z_t^x Z_t^{xK} - Z_t^K Z_t^{xx}) \hat{C}_{t-1}''}{Z_t^\alpha Z_t^{KK}} \cdot$

$$\cdot \left(\frac{dC_{t-1}}{d\bar{B}_2} \right)^A; \ t = 2, 3, 4$$

(A.11) $\quad \left(\dfrac{dX_t}{d\bar{B}_2} \right)^S = \dfrac{\hat{C}_{t-1}'' Z_t^{xK}}{Z_t^\alpha Z_t^{KK}} \left(\dfrac{dC_{t-1}}{d\bar{B}_2} \right)^S; \ \dfrac{dZ_t}{d\bar{B}_2} = \dfrac{(Z_t^x Z_t^{xK} - Z_t^K Z_t^{xx}) \hat{C}_{t-1}''}{Z_t^\alpha Z_t^{KK}} \cdot$

$$\cdot \left(\frac{dC_{t-1}}{d\bar{B}_2} \right)^S; \ t = 3, 4$$

(A.12) $\quad \dfrac{dK_t}{d\bar{B}_t} = \dfrac{\hat{C}_t''}{Z_{t+1}^\alpha} \left(\dfrac{dC_t}{d\bar{B}_2} \right); \ t = 1, 2, 3.$

(A.13) $\quad \dfrac{dI_t}{d\bar{B}_2} = - \dfrac{C_t^\alpha}{g_2^\alpha} \left(\dfrac{dC_t}{d\bar{B}_2} \right); \ t = 1, 2, 3$

(A.14) $\quad \dfrac{d\mu}{d\bar{B}_2} = (1 - R_2^b) \hat{C}_2' \hat{C}_3' \left[C_2^g \left(\dfrac{dC_2}{d\bar{B}_2} \right) - B_2^\alpha \right.$

$$\left. + \frac{B_3^\alpha (\hat{C}_2' - \hat{B}_2')}{\hat{C}_2'} \left(\frac{dB_3}{d\bar{B}_2} \right) \right] < 0$$

Statements without A or S superscripts apply to both the anticipated and surprise cases. If, for example, we wish to know $(dB_t/d\bar{B}_2)^A$, we substitute $(dC_t/d\bar{B}_2)^A$ from A.1, A.2, or A.3 into A.4. Although the indicated signs will normally hold given the assumptions of this study, any of the expressions (A.1)-(A.14) may tend to be zero in certain extreme cases such as those set forth in Sections (A.3)-(A.6).

A.3—All $C''_t \to 0$

In the surprise case,

$$(A.15) \quad \left(\frac{dC_2}{d\bar{B}_2}\right)^S \to -\frac{(1 - R^b_2)}{(1 - R^c_2)}; \quad \left(\frac{dF_2}{d\bar{B}_2}\right)^S \to 1 - \frac{(1 - R^b_2)}{(1 - R^c_2)}$$

$$= \frac{(R^b_2 - R^c_2)}{(1 - R^c_2)}$$

$$(A.16) \quad \left(\frac{dC_3}{d\bar{B}_2}\right)^S \to \frac{dF_3}{d\bar{B}_2} \to -\frac{(1 - R^b_2)\,(\hat{C}'_2 - \hat{B}'_2)}{(1 - R^c_3)}$$

$$(A.17) \quad \left(\frac{d\mu}{d\bar{B}_2}\right)^S \to -(1 - R^b_2)\hat{B}'_3\hat{B}''_2$$

All of the other terms in Section A.2 approach zero. In the anticipated case all of the first-period responses approach zero and the second-to-fourth-period responses are identical to those in the surprise case.

If all $\hat{C}''_t \to \infty$, $(dC_t/d\bar{B}_2) \to 0$ and the other responses (A.1)-(A.14) are accentuated in both the surprise and anticipated cases.

A.4—$L'' \to 0$

The surprise case is independent of L''_1. In the anticipated case,

$$(A.18) \quad \left(\frac{dC_1}{d\bar{B}_2}\right)^A \to \frac{(1 - R^b_2)[C^\alpha_2\Delta_3 + C^\alpha_3(\hat{C}'_2 - \hat{B}'_2)\Delta_2]}{(C^\alpha_1\Delta_{23} + C'_1C^\alpha_2\Delta_{13} + \hat{C}'_1\hat{C}'_2C^\alpha_3\Delta_{12})}$$

and the other responses may be expressed as in equation (A.2)-(A.14), where the results are limiting values as $L''_1 \to 0$. The response $(dC_1/d\bar{B}_2)^A$ increases so that $(dC_2/d\bar{B}_2)^A$ and $(dC_3/d\bar{B}_2)^A$ also rise as L''_1 declines.

If $L''_1 \to \infty$ all first-period responses approach zero and the later responses in the anticipated case approach those in the surprise case.

169

A.5—All $g_t'' \to 0$

All first-period responses approach zero and the later responses are identical in the anticipated and surprise cases. Those not shown below tend toward zero.

(A.19) $\quad \dfrac{dI_2}{d\bar{B}_2} \to \dfrac{(1 - R_2^b)}{g_2' + p_2} ; \dfrac{dI_3}{d\bar{B}_2} \to \dfrac{(1 - R_2^b)\,(\hat{C}_2' - \hat{B}_2')}{g_3' + p_3}$

(A.20) $\quad \dfrac{d\mu}{d\bar{B}_2} \to - (1 - R_2^b)\hat{B}_3'\bar{B}_2''$

If all $g_t'' \to \infty$ the responses of I_t tend toward zero and the responses of the other variables are accentuated.

A.6—All $Z_t'' \to 0$

All first-period responses approach zero and the later responses are identical in the anticipated and surprise cases. Those not shown below tend toward zero.

(A.21) $\quad \dfrac{dK_2}{d\bar{B}_2} \to \dfrac{(1 - R_2^b)}{k_2} ; \dfrac{dK_3}{d\bar{B}_2} \to \dfrac{(1 - R_2^b)\,(\hat{C}_2' - \hat{B}_2')}{k_3}$

(A.22) $\quad \dfrac{dX_3}{d\bar{B}_2} \to - \dfrac{(1 - R_2^b)Z_3^{xк}}{k_2 Z_3^{xx}} ; \dfrac{dX_4}{d\bar{B}_2} \to - \dfrac{(1 - R_2^b)\,(\hat{C}_2' - \hat{B}_2')Z_4^{xк}}{k_3 Z_4^{xx}}$

(A.23) $\quad \dfrac{dZ_3}{d\bar{B}_2} \to - \dfrac{(1 - R_2^b)\,(Z_3^x Z_3^{xк} - Z_3^к Z_3^{xx})}{k_2 Z_3^{xx}} ;$

$\qquad\qquad \dfrac{dZ_4}{d\bar{B}_2} \to - \dfrac{(1 - R_2^b)\,(\hat{C}_2' - \hat{B}_2')\,(Z_4^x Z_4^{xк} - Z_4^к Z_4^{xx})}{k_3 Z_4^{xx}}$

(A.24) $\quad \dfrac{d\mu}{d\bar{B}_2} \to - (1 - R_2^b)\hat{B}_3'\hat{B}_2''$

If all $Z_t'' \to \infty$ the responses of X_t, K_t, and Z_t tend toward zero and the responses of the other variables are accentuated.

D. C. RAO is Economist at the International Bank for Reconstruction and Development. He holds a Ph.D. from the University of Pennsylvania, specializing in monetary economics. Author of a chapter on urban target groups in *Redistribution with Growth* (edited by Hollis R. Chenery), he has contributed to the *Journal of Finance*.

IRA KAMINOW is Vice President and Economic Adviser of the Federal Reserve Bank of Philadelphia on leave at the London School of Economics and Political Science (1975-76). He holds a Ph.D. from the University of Rochester, specializing in monetary economics and public finance. He has taught at Ohio University, Temple University, and the University of Pennsylvania, and his articles have appeared in professional and popular journals as well as in a number of anthologies.

The authors are grateful to Richard G. Davis, Irwin Friend, Duane G. Harris, Dale Henderson, Donald R. Hodgman, Robert Rasche, Mark H. Willes, and John H. Wood for helpful comments, but accept responsibility for all remaining errors. The views expressed herein are the authors' and do not necessarily reflect those of the International Bank for Reconstruction and Development.

172

Selective Credit Controls And the Real Investment Mix: A General Equilibrium Approach

D. C. RAO

IRA KAMINOW

I. INTRODUCTION

The idea of selective credit controls periodically captures the minds of public policymakers and even, from time to time, of economists. The most recent manifestation of this interest has resulted from the disproportionate effect of tight credit markets on housing, and, to a lesser extent, state and local governments. Typically, policymakers and other "men of affairs" show greater interest in the issue of selective credit controls than members of the academic community.[1] While some economists would debate whether policymakers should intervene in allocations as

---

[1]Statements on these issues have been made by Wright Patman (House Committee on Banking and Currency), U. S., Congress, House Committee on Banking and Currency, *Activities by Various Central Banks. A Staff Report*, December 1970; Andrew F. Brimmer, "The Banking Structure and Monetary Management" (mimeographed), Board of Governors of the Federal Reserve System, 1 April 1970; David P. Eastburn (Federal Reserve Bank of Philadelphia), "Federal Reserve Policy and Social Priorities," *Business Review* of the Federal Reserve Bank of Philadelphia, November 1970, pp. 2-8; Frank E. Morris (Federal Reserve Bank of Boston), "Housing and Monetary Policy," *New England Economic Review* of the Federal Reserve Bank of Boston, May/June 1970, pp. 23-27.

determined in the market,[2] there has been little systematic investigation of the general problem of selective credit controls or the ones specifically at issue. This paper is an attempt to set up a theoretical framework in which the effectiveness of selective credit policies may be examined.

Seeing a need to redistribute the burden of adjustment caused by tight monetary policy, Andrew Brimmer of the Federal Reserve Board of Governors suggested the imposition of supplemental reserves on the assets of banks. The basic idea underlying the proposal is that by levying different reserve requirements on different kinds of assets held by financial intermediaries, the monetary authority might influence the sectoral composition of real investment in the economy.

Two major criticisms have been leveled against the proposal to use selective monetary policies.

(a) Credit is "fungible" and it is therefore likely that selective controls will not influence the allocation of real investment in the way anticipated by policymakers. "The ability of borrowers to switch channels from one credit source to another and the difficulty of determining borrower purpose on the basis of the particular channel or borrowing instrument employed make control of *use* far more uncertain than control of *channel* and *instrument*."[3]

(b) The Federal Reserve Board, being a nonelective body, ought not to be entrusted with the responsibility of determining priorities for allocating capital resources.

We will not concern ourselves with (b) since it is essentially a question of finding a politically satisfactory method of specifying the objectives. It has been pointed out that the Federal Reserve Board "does not need to *set* priorities in order to help *achieve* them."[4]

This paper uses a general equilibrium framework to investigate hypothesis (a). Using this framework we learn that selective credit controls will have the impact on interest rates that policymakers would generally anticipate. Despite this, how-

---

[2]For example, Thomas Mayer, "Financial Guidelines and Credit Controls," *Journal of Money, Credit and Banking* 4 (1972): 360-74.

[3]Donald R. Hodgman, "Selective Credit Controls," *Journal of Money, Credit and Banking* 4 (1972); 342-59.

[4]Eastburn, op. cit., p. 7.

ever, the selective credit controls examined will not necessarily have the anticipated effect on the real investment mix. The paper, therefore, examines the conditions under which such a policy would influence the composition of real investment in the way anticipated by policymakers. In essence, these conditions state that the degree of substitution among holdings of different types of real capital is not high and that each real asset can be matched with a financial asset on the basis of interest sensitivity. The plausibility of these conditions is seen to be seriously affected by the presence of disintermediation. To the extent that some intermediaries are not subject to reserve requirements, the quantitative impact of the policy on the real investment mix will be smaller but the qualitative, or "directional," impact will not change. The specific policy investigated here is the proposal to levy reserve requirements on the assets of financial intermediaries, but it is shown that the conclusions also hold for a broader class of selective credit controls.

II. THE MODEL

In the basic model there are six types of assets: two kinds of loans by intermediaries, reserves, deposits, and two real capital goods. The model has one financial intermediary sector (which may, nevertheless, have many operating institutions) and one sector holding real capital. The nonfinancial sector is subdivided into a household and a corporate sector.

For expositional purposes only, we have designated the two financial assets "mortgages" (M) and "bonds" (B) and the two real capital goods, "houses" (H) and "other capital goods" (K).

The balance sheet of the system is given below, liabilities being designated by a (−) sign:

	G	F	E	Total
Reserves	−R	R		0
Deposits		−D	D	0
Mortgages		M	−M	0
Bonds		B	−B	0
Houses			H	H
Other capital			K	K
Net worth	−R	R	W	$W \equiv H + K$

175

DEFINITIONS

Sectors

G: Government, including monetary authority.

F: Financial intermediaries, defined to be homogeneous in the nature of their deposit liability and types of loans they offer.

E: Everyone other than G and F; this includes both the household and corporate sectors.

Assets

R: Reserves. The supply of reserves is assumed to be exogenous.

D: Deposits. We assume there is only one type of deposit liability issued by all intermediaries.

M and B: Financial assets supplied by the public and demanded by intermediaries.[5]

H and K: Stock of two types of real capital, measured in terms of current market value.

Rates

i_m, i_b: Rates of interest earned by intermediaries on loans made to the public.

r_h, r_k: Rates of return on real capital.[6]

a_m, a_b: The legal reserve requirements expressed as a fraction of outstanding mortgage and bond assets held by financial intermediaries.

We assume that the interest rate on deposits (id) is exogenously fixed (e.g., when the rate stays at the ceiling fixed by Regulation Q), and that the general level of prices is fixed.

---

[5]To avoid the complications caused by unrealized capital gains/losses resulting from fluctuations in market prices of these assets, we assume that these financial assets are of the "variable rate" variety.

[6]For an elaboration of the concepts underlying these definitions, the reader is referred to James Tobin, "A General Equilibrium Approach to Monetary Theory," *Journal of Money, Credit and Banking* 1 (1969): 15-29.

A. EQUATIONS

The market clearing equations are:[7] (For convenience, the partial derivative of each function with respect to each of its arguments appears above the variables. These signs are discussed below.)

$$D_f(\overset{+}{i_m}, \overset{+}{i_b}, \overset{+}{i_d}, \overset{-}{a_m}, \overset{-}{a_b}, \overset{+}{R}) = D_e(\overset{-}{i_m}, \overset{+}{i_b}, \overset{-}{r_h}, \overset{-}{r_k}, \overset{+}{i_d}) \qquad (1)$$

$$M_e(\overset{-}{i_m}, \overset{+}{i_b}, \overset{+}{r_h}, \overset{+}{r_k}, \overset{+}{i_d}) = M_f(\overset{+}{i_m}, \overset{+}{i_b}, \overset{-}{a_m}, \overset{+}{a_b}, \overset{-}{R}, \overset{+}{i_d}) \qquad (2)$$

$$B_e(\overset{+}{i_m}, \overset{-}{i_b}, \overset{+}{r_h}, \overset{+}{r_k}, \overset{+}{i_d}) = B_f(\overset{-}{i_m}, \overset{+}{i_b}, \overset{+}{a_m}, \overset{-}{a_b}, \overset{-}{R}, \overset{+}{i_d}) \qquad (3)$$

$$H(\overset{-}{r_h}) = H_e(\overset{-}{i_m}, \overset{-}{i_b}, \overset{+}{r_h}, \overset{+}{r_k}) \qquad (4)$$

$$K(\overset{-}{r_k}) = K_e(\overset{-}{i_m}, \overset{-}{i_b}, \overset{-}{r_h}, \overset{+}{r_k}) \qquad (5)$$

The rates to be determined in the system are i_m, i_b, r_h, and r_k. These rates influence the portfolio composition chosen by the public. The portfolio composition of the intermediaries is influenced directly by the rates of interest, i_m and i_b, and the legal reserve requirements a_m and a_b.

The notation $H(r_h)$ and $K(r_k)$ is used to express the fact that the market value of existing capital stock is determined by the market rate of return, given the existing stock valued at replacement cost and an unchanged technology.

Each intermediary is constrained by the identity between assets on the one hand and liabilities plus net worth on the other.

$$R + M + B \equiv D + R \qquad (6)$$

For each unit in the nonfinancial sector as well as for the sector as a whole, holdings of assets must equal liabilities plus net worth, i.e.,

$$D + H + K \equiv M + B + W. \qquad (7)$$

We have assumed that the stock of reserves is exogenously determined by the monetary authority and that the intermediaries passively accept whatever quantity is made avail-

---

[7]The subscripts of the function names refer to the sector whose portfolio decisions are described. In particular, f and e refer to the behavior of the financial and nonfinancial sectors, respectively.

able. Thus the reserves market is always in equilibrium. There are no open-market operations in the usual sense; rather the monetary authority is able to change R without directly influencing any of the other variables in the model.

The application of the balance sheet identities (6) and (7) enables us to drop one out of the equations (1)-(5); we choose to drop the Deposit equation. We are thus left with equations 2, 3, 4, and 5 to determine the four rates i_m, i_b, r_h, and r_k. The specification of the Deposit equation, which is now the "missing equation," is consistent with the requirement that the effect of a change in a variable or parameter, summed over the whole balance sheet or portfolio, must be zero for both banks and the public.

The signs of the partial derivatives are specified by the assumption that (a) all assets are gross substitutes and (b) each real asset is "financed" by both financial assets so that, for example, a rise in either financial interest rate will discourage demand for both real assets. The partial derivative of each equation with respect to its own rate of interest is positive for demand and negative for supply relationships; the opposite holds for derivatives with respect to cross rates. Intermediary demand for each financial asset is negatively related to the reserve requirement on that asset and positively related to the reserve requirement on the other asset, while the supply of deposits is inversely related to both reserve requirements.

An increase in the reserve requirement against one asset has two distinct effects on bank behavior. First, it induces a reallocation of the portfolio away from that asset. Second, a given volume of reserves will now support a smaller total quantity of assets at any given composition of the portfolio. For the present purposes, we are primarily interested in isolating the composition effects of the change in reserve requirement from the scale effects. We, therefore, assume that the supply of reserves is simultaneously altered in such a way that the stock of deposits in the new equilibrium is the same as in the previous equilibrium.[8] In incorporating this assumption in the mathematical

---

[8]Such a compensation mechanism is employed merely as a pedagogic device analogous to the full employment assumption used to sort out the allocational from stabilization effects of fiscal policies.

formulation of the model, we have further assumed that the demand for mortgages and bonds by financial intermediaries is homogeneous of degree one in reserves.

The objective of the policy change we are investigating is to encourage investment in H relative to K. It is commonly postulated that the rate of investment is proportionately related to the gap between actual capital stock and desired equilibrium capital stock. In this model, the rate of investment may be related directly to the gap between the market price and replacement cost of a unit of capital. Assuming no change in technology and in the general price level, the influence on investment can be seen directly from the change in the required rate of return on capital.

The following condition:

$$\dot{r}_k = \frac{dr_k}{r_k} > 0 \; ; \; \dot{r}_h = \frac{dr_h}{r_h} < 0 \tag{8}$$

is necessary and sufficient to ensure that investment in H will rise and investment in K will decline. But it is possible for the objective regarding *relative* rates of investment to be met even when r_h and r_k move in the same direction, in which case a plausible criterion for success would be

$$\dot{r}_k - \dot{r}_h > 0. \tag{9}$$

The system of equations obtained by taking the total differential of the market clearing equations may be written in the form:

$$Tx = q$$

where T is a 4×4 matrix and x and q are 4-vectors. Both T and q are defined to include the assumption that a compensating change in total reserves accompanies any change in a required reserve ratio. The precise mathematical definitions of T, x, and q appear in the Appendix.

To facilitate interpretation of the resulting expressions, we make two simplifying assumptions which will be relaxed later.

(i) *Specialization:* To the extent that borrowing from financial intermediaries has to be supported by specific collateral, one might expect a close connection between the mortgage rate and the demand for houses and between the bond rate and the demand for other capital. An extreme form of this association between demand for real capital and specific modes of borrowing would obtain if we could write $\partial H_e/\partial i_b = 0$ and $\partial K_e/\partial i_m = 0$. This state is defined as "specialization." It must be recognized, however, that the collateral provision of loan agreements is not sufficient to ensure "specialization." A change in one of the financial interest rates would lead to a reorganization of the asset portfolios in the nonfinancial sector, affecting the demands for *both* capital goods despite rigid collateral provisions.

(ii) *Dichotomy:* A further simplification is provided by the assumption that there is no substitution between H and K in the portfolios of nonfinancial units. For instance, the nonfinancial sector may be divided into two categories of economic agents, one set holding H but no K and the other set holding K and no H. In terms of the balance sheet of the system, the household sector holds all houses and supplies all the mortgages while the corporate sector holds all the K and supplies all the bonds.
Dichotomy implies

$$\frac{\partial K_e}{\partial r_h} = 0 \text{ and } \frac{\partial H_e}{\partial r_k} = 0.$$

B. Model I: *Dichotomy and Specialization*

We impose both the assumptions of "specialization" and of "dichotomy." The solutions[9] for $\dot{r}_h/\dot{a}_b$ and $\dot{r}_k/\dot{a}_b$ can then be written as:

$$\frac{\dot{r}_k}{\dot{a}_b} = P \, Y \, S_1 \tag{10}$$

$$\frac{\dot{r}_h}{\dot{a}_b} = P \, X \, Z_1 \tag{11}$$

---

[9]Details of the method of solution may be found in a mathematical appendix available from the Research Department of the Federal Reserve Bank of Philadelphia.

where

$$P = \frac{M_f B_f}{D} \left(\frac{\partial M_f}{\partial a_b} \frac{a_b}{M_f} - \frac{\partial B_f}{\partial a_b} \frac{a_b}{B_f} \right) > 0$$

$$Y = - \frac{1}{r_k \Delta} < 0$$

$$X = - \frac{1}{r_h \Delta} < 0$$

$\Delta = |T| > 0$; the matrix T is defined in the Appendix[10]

$$S_1 = \frac{\partial K_e}{\partial i_b} \frac{\partial D_e}{\partial i_m} \frac{\partial (H - H_e)}{\partial r_h} + \frac{\partial K_e}{\partial i_b} \frac{\partial H_e}{\partial i_m} \frac{\partial D_e}{\partial r_h}$$

$$Z_1 = - \frac{\partial H_e}{\partial i_m} \frac{\partial D_e}{\partial i_b} \frac{\partial (K - K_e)}{\partial r_k} - \frac{\partial H_e}{\partial i_m} \frac{\partial K_e}{\partial i_b} \frac{\partial D_e}{\partial r_k}.$$

From our initial assumption of gross substitution, it follows directly that S_1 is negative and Z_1 is positive, which guarantees that (8) is satisfied. We can thus conclude that, in this simple model where we have both specialization and dichotomy, the asset reserve plan is bound to succeed. It is of considerable interest that the total effect of a change in the asset reserve requirement on the rates of return on real capital can be clearly separated into: (i) the impact of the policy change on the behavior of the financial sector, embodied in "P" and (ii) the "structure" of the economy as represented by the responses of the nonfinancial sectors to changes in interest rates, embodied in YS_1 and XZ_1. It will be seen that this pattern persists in the models subsequently analyzed.

C. Model II: *Specialization*

We now drop the assumption of dichotomy but retain the assumption of specialization. The solutions of the system of equations are thereby modified and we now have the following:

---

[10]The matrix T is a general formulation for all economies, but the particular values of its elements will vary from system to system. The value of |T| will therefore be different in an economy that exhibits dichotomy and specialization than in one that does not. It should be borne in mind, therefore, that as other economies are analyzed in the text, the value (but not the expression or sign), of |T| will change.

$$\frac{\dot{r}_k}{\dot{a}_b} = P \ Y \ S_2 \tag{12}$$

$$\frac{\dot{r}_h}{\dot{a}_b} = P \ X \ Z_2 \tag{13}$$

where

$$S_2 = S_1 - \frac{\partial H_e}{\partial i_m} \frac{\partial D_e}{\partial i_b} \frac{\partial K_e}{\partial r_h}$$

$$Z_2 = Z_1 + \frac{\partial K_e}{\partial i_b} \frac{\partial D_e}{\partial i_m} \frac{\partial H_e}{\partial r_k}.$$

P, Y, and X have been defined previously.

In this model, nonfinancial sectors hold both types of real capital and can therefore substitute between them in their portfolio in response to movements in the real rates of return. Provided the degree of substitutability is small (i.e., provided $\frac{\partial K_e}{\partial r_h}$ and $\frac{\partial H_e}{\partial r_k}$ are small), the new forces are unlikely to dominate the results. More precisely,

$$S_2 < 0 \text{ if } \frac{\frac{\partial D_e}{\partial r_h}}{\frac{\partial D_e}{\partial i_b}} \cdot \frac{\partial K_e}{\partial i_b} > \frac{\partial K_e}{\partial r_h} \tag{14}$$

$$Z_2 > 0 \text{ if } \frac{\frac{\partial D_e}{\partial r_k}}{\frac{\partial D_e}{\partial i_m}} \cdot \frac{\partial H_e}{\partial i_m} > \frac{\partial H_e}{\partial r_k}. \tag{15}$$

A priori, one would expect a close relationship between mortgage rates and housing demand and between bond rates and demand for other capital, i.e., $\frac{\partial K_e}{\partial i_b}$ and $\frac{\partial H_e}{\partial i_m}$ are probably fairly large. It, therefore, seems plausible that the inequalities in (14) and (15) are satisfied. These conditions are sufficient to ensure that the increase in the reserve requirement against bonds will lead to an increase in r_k and a decrease in r_h.

D. Model III: *General*

We now examine the consequences of dropping both the assumptions of dichotomy and specialization. The nonfinancial sectors may now hold both types of real capital and use both mortgages and bonds to finance each of them. This results in further amplification of the structural terms in the solution and we now have

$$\frac{\dot{r}_k}{\dot{a}_b} = P\ Y\ S_3 \tag{16}$$

$$\frac{\dot{r}_h}{\dot{a}_b} = P\ X\ Z_3 \tag{17}$$

where

$$S_3 = \begin{vmatrix} \dfrac{\partial D_e}{\partial i_m} & \dfrac{\partial D_e}{\partial i_b} & \dfrac{\partial D_e}{\partial r_h} \\[2mm] -\dfrac{\partial H_e}{\partial i_m} & -\dfrac{\partial H_e}{\partial i_b} & \dfrac{\partial(H - H_e)}{\partial r_h} \\[2mm] -\dfrac{\partial K_e}{\partial i_m} & -\dfrac{\partial K_e}{\partial i_b} & -\dfrac{\partial K_e}{\partial r_h} \end{vmatrix} \qquad Z_3 = \begin{vmatrix} -\dfrac{\partial D_e}{\partial i_m} & -\dfrac{\partial D_e}{\partial i_b} & -\dfrac{\partial D_e}{\partial r_k} \\[2mm] -\dfrac{\partial H_e}{\partial i_m} & -\dfrac{\partial H_e}{\partial i_b} & -\dfrac{\partial H_e}{\partial r_k} \\[2mm] -\dfrac{\partial K_e}{\partial i_m} & -\dfrac{\partial K_e}{\partial i_b} & \dfrac{\partial(K - K_e)}{\partial r_k} \end{vmatrix}$$

It is easily seen that

$$S_3 = S_2 - \frac{\partial K_e}{\partial i_m}\frac{\partial D_e}{\partial i_b}\frac{\partial(H - H_e)}{\partial r_h} - \frac{\partial K_e}{\partial i_m}\frac{\partial H_e}{\partial i_b}\frac{\partial D_e}{\partial r_h} + \frac{\partial H_e}{\partial i_b}\frac{\partial D_e}{\partial i_m}\frac{\partial K_e}{\partial r_h}$$

$$Z_3 = Z_2 + \frac{\partial H_e}{\partial i_b}\frac{\partial D_e}{\partial i_m}\frac{\partial(K - K_e)}{\partial r_k} + \frac{\partial H_e}{\partial i_b}\frac{\partial K_e}{\partial i_m}\frac{\partial D_e}{\partial r_k} - \frac{\partial D_e}{\partial i_b}\frac{\partial K_e}{\partial i_m}\frac{\partial H_e}{\partial r_k}.$$

To interpret these expressions, let us consider a situation where nonfinancial units are completely indifferent between mortgages and bonds in financing their holdings of real capital. The two assets are not identical from the point of view of the financial intermediaries and we might, therefore, define indifference as being the situation in which the demands by the nonfinancial sector for the various assets is equally responsive to the interest rates on mortgages and bonds, i.e.,

$$\frac{\partial H_e}{\partial i_m} = \frac{\partial H_e}{\partial i_b}; \quad \frac{\partial K_e}{\partial i_m} = \frac{\partial K_e}{\partial i_b}; \quad \frac{\partial D_e}{\partial i_m} = \frac{\partial D_e}{\partial i_b}. \tag{18}$$

Given such a situation, and given the fact that $(M + B)$ remains unchanged in the new equilibrium, one would expect that a compensated change in the reserve requirement should have absolutely no effect on the required rates of return in the real capital goods markets, i.e.,

$$\frac{\dot{r}_h}{\dot{a}_b} = 0 \; ; \; \frac{\dot{r}_k}{\dot{a}_b} = 0. \tag{19}$$

This result is obtained directly from (16) and (17) by the imposition of the conditions for "indifference."

But "indifference" as defined above and "specialization" as in Model II are both polar cases. A more realistic situation would be one in which nonfinancial units do engage in a moderate degree of substitution between mortgages and bonds. If we assume that the demand for deposits is approximately equally sensitive to the interest rates on the two financial liabilities and the real assets, and if

$$\left| \frac{\partial K_e}{\partial i_b} \right| \geqslant \left| \frac{\partial K_e}{\partial i_m} \right| \tag{20}$$

$$\text{and} \quad \left| \frac{\partial H_e}{\partial i_m} \right| \geqslant \left| \frac{\partial H_e}{\partial i_b} \right| \tag{21}$$

with the strict inequality holding in at least one of the above, then

$$S_3 < 0 \quad \text{and} \quad Z_3 > 0.$$

It is very plausible that the demand for houses is more responsive to the mortgage rate than to the rate on bonds, and that the demand for other capital is more responsive to the bond rate than to the mortgage rate. Thus (20) and (21) are probably satisfied. We can, therefore, conclude that the asset reserve plan will be successful unless there is complete indifference in the sense defined above, or unless the demand for deposits is very much more sensitive to one financial rate than to another.

E. Model IV: *Uncontrolled Intermediaries*

The efficacy of a selective asset reserve requirement imposed on banks alone has been questioned on the grounds that intermediaries not subject to reserve requirements would act to compensate for the changes in the portfolios of banks.

To investigate this problem we have set up Model IV, which modifies Model III by allowing some of the intermediaries to lie outside the control of the monetary authorities. Let the set of intermediaries (F) in Model III be divided into two subsets F_1 and F_2, only the former being subject to asset reserve requirements. We assume that both F_1 and F_2 deal in the same financial assets (mortgages and bonds) but do not necessarily issue identical deposit liabilities.

The balance sheet of the economy is shown below:

	G	F_1	F_2	E	Total
Reserves	−R	R			0
Deposit 1		−D_1		D_1	0
Deposit 2			−D_2	D_2	0
Mortgages		M_1	M_2	−M	0
Bonds		B_1	B_2	−B	0
Houses				H	H
Other capital				K	K
Net Worth	−R	R	0	W	W ≡ H + K

Noting that each institution in F_2 is also subject to a balance sheet constraint, we can reduce the system to four equations as in Model III. We can then examine the effect of a compensated change in the reserve requirement against bonds, assuming that the supply of reserves is simultaneously altered such that the total value of mortgages and bonds in the new equilibrium is the same as in the previous equilibrium.

The solution of the system of equations then yields

$$\frac{\dot{r}_k}{\dot{a}_b} = P_1 \, Y \, S_3 \tag{22}$$

$$\frac{\dot{r}_h}{\dot{a}_b} = P_1 \, X \, Z_3 \tag{23}$$

where
$$P_1 = \frac{M_{f_1} B_{f_1}}{D_1} \left(\frac{\partial M_{f_1}}{\partial a_b} \frac{a_b}{M_{f_1}} - \frac{\partial B_{f_1}}{\partial a_b} \frac{a_b}{B_{f_1}} \right).$$

Since we know that P_1 is positive, the conditions that will ensure the success of the asset reserve plan are precisely the same as those derived for Model III. The relative magnitudes of the effects of the policy in the two regimes defined by Model III and Model IV can be observed directly by comparing P_1 and P.

Noting that the set of intermediaries F has been divided into two mutually exclusive subsets F_1 and F_2, we can write

$$\begin{aligned} P &= \frac{M_f B_f}{D} \left(\frac{\partial M_f}{\partial a_b} \frac{a_b}{M_f} - \frac{\partial B_f}{\partial a_b} \frac{a_b}{B_f} \right) \\ &= \frac{M_f B_f}{D} \left[\left(\frac{\partial M_{f_1}}{\partial a_b} \frac{a_b}{M_{f_1}} - \frac{\partial B_{f_1}}{\partial a_b} \frac{a_b}{B_{f_1}} \right) \right. \\ &\quad - \frac{B_{f_2}}{B_f} \left(\frac{\partial B_{f_2}}{\partial a_b} \frac{a_b}{B_{f_2}} - \frac{\partial B_{f_2}}{\partial a_b} \frac{a_b}{B_{f_1}} \right) \\ &\quad + \left. \frac{M_{f_2}}{M_f} \left(\frac{\partial M_{f_2}}{\partial a_b} \frac{a_b}{M_{f_2}} - \frac{\partial M_{f_1}}{\partial a_b} \frac{a_b}{M_{f_1}} \right) \right]. \end{aligned}$$

The above expression is considerably simplified if the sensitivity of a particular institution to asset reserve requirements in Model III is not related to whether it happens to fall in F_1 or F_2 in Model IV. In this special case,

$$\frac{P_1}{P} - \frac{\dfrac{M_{f_1} B_{f_1}}{D_1}}{\dfrac{M_f B_f}{D}} \tag{24}$$

This ratio lies between zero and one and reflects the extent of coverage of reserve requirements over financial intermediaries. As the coverage of the asset reserve plan is restricted, so is the magnitude of the effect reduced. If all intermediaries are subject to the asset reserve requirements, $P_1 = P$, i.e., the magnitude of the impact of the policy change on the real rates of return is the same in Model IV as in Model III.

As a further generalization we have examined the consequences of allowing the deposit rate on uncontrolled intermediaries' liabilities to vary as a function of the financial interest rates i_b and i_m, the purpose being to reflect the variability of rates on savings and loan shares, mutual savings bank deposits, etc. There is a second order effect on the movement of the real rates of return which depends, essentially, on the *difference* in sensitivity of the deposit rate to i_m and i_b. In terms of criterion (9), the effects tend to offset each other and the conditions for success are almost unaltered.[11]

In summary, one can draw the following conclusions from an analysis of Model IV:

(i) The necessary and sufficient conditions for the success of the asset reserve plan are not changed even if some intermediaries are not subject to asset reserve requirements.

(ii) If both intermediary classes have the same behavioral elasticities, the magnitude of the effect is directly proportional to the width of coverage of reserve requirements.

(iii) The reduction in the magnitude of the effect of the policy change is directly related to the sensitivity that the uncontrolled intermediaries might display to asset reserve requirements if they were brought under coverage of the plan.

F. Model V: *Disintermediation*

An important limitation of policies operating on the financial intermediary sector is the possibility that borrowers are able to finance their requirements outside the intermediary sector if they choose to do so. In this model, we examine the consequences of permitting corporations to borrow directly from the household sector by selling them bonds. The balance sheet of the economy in this regime is shown below, distinguishing

---

[11]Details of this case appear in a mathematical appendix (see footnote 9).

between households (N) and corporate (C) components of the nonfinancial sector. Bonds are now an asset of the household sector instead of a liability.

	G	F	N	C	Total
Reserves	$-R$	R			0
Deposits		$-D_f$	D_n	D_c	0
Mortgages		M_f	$-M_n$	$-M_c$	0
Bonds		B_f	B_n	$-B_c$	0
Houses			H_n	H_c	H
Other capital			K_n	K_c	K
Net Worth	$-R$	R	W_n	W_c	$W \equiv H + K$

The market clearing equations must now be slightly modified. Equations (1), (2), (4), and (5) remain unchanged. Equation (3) is replaced by (3a):

$$B_c(i_m, i_b, r_h, r_k, i_d) = B_n(i_m, i_b, r_h, r_k, i_d)$$
$$+ B_f(i_m, i_b, a_m, a_b, R, i_d) \quad (3a).$$

The solution of the model then yields

$$\frac{\dot{r}_k}{\dot{a}_b} = P\ Y\ S_3\ ;\ \frac{\dot{r}_h}{\dot{a}_b} = P\ X\ Z_3 \qquad (25)$$

which is identical to the solution of Model III given in equations (16) and (17). It therefore follows that the inequalities (20) and (21) are sufficient to ensure that the change in asset reserve requirements will have the desired effect on the real rates of return, even under a regime of disintermediation.

The crucial difference, however, is that the partial derivative $\frac{\partial H_e}{\partial i_b}$ (which comprises the effect of the bond rate on the demand for houses by the household and corporate sector) now reflects a completely different behavioral relationship. In Model III, it represented the response of the demand for housing to a change in one of the modes of financing that might be used. Using the argument that house purchases are closely related to the mortgage rate, we are able to assert that condition (21) would probably be satisfied. However, in Model V, bonds and houses are competing assets in the portfolio of a part of the nonfinancial

188

sector. If households regard the holding of corporate bonds as a close substitute for the holding of houses, it is less clear that condition (21) will be satisfied. While noting that (21) is a sufficient, not necessary, condition for the asset reserve plan to have the desired effect on the real rates of return, the analysis of Model V does point up the possibilities of failure. A resolution of this issue will have to await satisfactory empirical estimates of the parameters involved.

G. RATES OF RETURN ON FINANCIAL ASSETS

Since our main concern is the real investment mix, we have concentrated on the rates of return to real assets. However, the discussion may easily be extended to include the rates of return on the financial assets. The marginal effects of a change in a_b on the financial rates are given by:

$$\frac{\dot{i}_b}{\dot{a}_b} = P \frac{1}{i_h \Delta} \Sigma > 0 \tag{26}$$

and

$$\frac{\dot{i}_m}{\dot{a}_b} = P \frac{1}{i_m \Delta} \Xi < 0 \tag{27}$$

where

$$\Sigma = - \frac{\partial D_e}{\partial i_m} \left\{ \frac{\partial (H - H_e)}{\partial r_h} \frac{\partial (K - K_e)}{\partial r_k} - \frac{\partial K_e}{\partial r_h} \frac{\partial H_e}{\partial r_k} \right\}$$
$$- \frac{\partial D_e}{\partial r_h} \left\{ \frac{\partial H_e}{\partial i_m} \frac{\partial (K - K_e)}{\partial r_k} + \frac{\partial K_e}{\partial i_m} \frac{\partial H_e}{\partial r_h} \right\}$$
$$- \frac{\partial D_e}{\partial r_k} \left\{ \frac{\partial H_e}{\partial i_m} \frac{\partial K_e}{\partial r_h} + \frac{\partial K_e}{\partial j_m} \frac{\partial (H - H_e)}{\partial r_h} \right\} > 0$$

and

$$\Xi = \frac{\partial D_e}{\partial i_b} \left\{ \frac{\partial (H - H_e)}{\partial r_h} \frac{\partial (K - K_e)}{\partial r_k} - \frac{\partial K_e}{\partial r_h} \frac{\partial H_e}{\partial r_k} \right\}$$
$$+ \frac{\partial D_e}{\partial r_h} \left\{ \frac{\partial H_e}{\partial i_b} \frac{\partial (K - K_e)}{\partial r_k} + \frac{\partial K_e}{\partial i_b} \frac{\partial H_e}{\partial r_h} \right\}$$
$$+ \frac{\partial D_e}{\partial r_k} \left\{ \frac{\partial H_e}{\partial i_b} \frac{\partial K_e}{\partial r_h} + \frac{\partial K_e}{\partial i_b} \frac{\partial (H - H_e)}{\partial r_h} \right\} < 0.$$

189

The signs of Σ and Ξ and hence of $\dfrac{\dot{i}_b}{\dot{a}_b}$ and $\dfrac{\dot{i}_m}{\dot{a}_b}$ follow immediately from the facts that all the partial derivatives in the expansions of Σ and Ξ are negative and that $\dfrac{\partial(H - H_e)}{\partial r_h}$ and $\dfrac{\partial(K - K_e)}{\partial r_k}$ are dominant diagonal terms.[12]

The expressions (26) and (27) suggest that regardless of the ambiguities surrounding the real investment mix, the financial rates will respond to asset reserve policies in the way qualitatively suggested by partial equilibrium analysis.

H. OTHER SELECTIVE POLICIES

With minimal modification, the models we have analyzed can be used to investigate the effectiveness of *any* selective policy that operates by shifting the demand curves of the financial intermediaries for different financial assets without directly affecting the behavior of the nonfinancial sector. The demand for each asset would then be a function of interest rates, the volume of reserves and a shift parameter (say, "s") controlled by the policymakers. Asset reserve ratios are simply specific examples of such shift parameters. Other examples are government guarantee schemes that reduce the risk quality of specific financial assets, legislation that permits certain assets to be counted toward the conventional reserve requirements, etc. We can simply reinterpret the above models, replacing a_b with the relevant "s."

---

[12] The terms Σ and Ξ were derived under the assumption of a fixed deposit rate. Under a variable rate scheme the term $\dfrac{\partial D_e}{\partial i_m}$ would be replaced by $\dfrac{\partial D_e}{\partial i_m} + \dfrac{\partial D_e}{\partial i_d}$ $\dfrac{\partial i_d}{\partial i_m}$, $\dfrac{\partial H_e}{\partial i_m}$ by $\dfrac{\partial H_e}{\partial i_m} + \dfrac{\partial H_e}{\partial i_d} \dfrac{\partial i_d}{\partial i_m}$, etc. A sufficient condition to insure that these changes will leave the qualitative conclusions unchanged is:

$$\left| \frac{\partial D_e}{\partial i_m} \right| > \left| \frac{\partial D_e}{\partial i_d} \frac{\partial i_d}{\partial i_m} \right| \text{ and } \left| \frac{\partial D_e}{\partial i_b} \right| > \left| \frac{\partial D_e}{\partial i_d} \frac{\partial i_d}{\partial i_b} \right|.$$

For any such selective monetary policy, $\frac{\dot{r}_k}{s} > 0$ and $\frac{\dot{r}_h}{s} < 0$ are sufficient to ensure that the policy would encourage investment in H relative to K. The necessary and sufficient conditions for these inequalities to be satisfied are identical to those expressed in (20) and (21). This remarkable result follows from our ability to separate the "policy" terms from the "structural" terms in the solution of the system of equations, as described in our discussion of Model I.

It is instructive to regard $\frac{\dot{r}_k}{s}$ and $\frac{\dot{r}_h}{s}$ as policy multipliers associated with the policy "s," i.e., the change in the rates of return on real capital associated with a change in the policy parameter "s." If s_1 and s_2 are any two selective policies, both operating on the same "world" as symbolized by the equations of our model, their relative effectiveness can be measured by the ratio of the policy multipliers. This ratio is given by

$$\frac{P_{s_1}}{P_{s_2}}$$

where

$$P_{s_1} = \frac{\partial M_f}{\partial s_1} \frac{s_1}{M} - \frac{\partial B_f}{\partial s_1} \frac{s_1}{B}$$

$$P_{s_2} = \frac{\partial M_f}{\partial s_2} \frac{s_2}{M} - \frac{\partial B_f}{\partial s_2} \frac{s_2}{B}.$$

Recalling that a selective monetary policy will tend to shift the two functions M_f and B_f in opposite directions, it follows that the policy that has the greatest initial impact on bank behavior will also achieve the maximum change in the rates of return on real capital when equilibrium is restored.

By suitable modification, the above models can also be used to examine the impact on the composition of real investment of selective policies that influence the behavior of nonfinancial units in the financial markets. Examples of such policies are tax credits or deductibility of interest payments on specific types of borrowing. This analysis is not undertaken here.

191

III. CONCLUSIONS

The efficacy of selective credit controls has traditionally been debated in a partial equilibrium context or, at best, in an intuitively formulated general equilibrium framework. The results of the current paper allow us to sharpen our theoretical understanding of the operation of selective controls in a general equilibrium framework. It is heartening to know that the model confirms many of our intuitive expectations. But it goes beyond this by pinpointing the interrelationships between the relevant elasticities. This allows policymakers the opportunity to check their *a priori* expectations about the component elasticities with their *ad hoc* feelings about the efficacy of selective credit controls. It also points out elasticities that must be estimated if we are to have more systematic predictions about the effectiveness of these controls.

The following points summarize the specific conclusions that can be drawn from the detailed analysis of the models set up in the text:

(1) Success of the selective asset reserve requirement in influencing the composition of real investment depends on a low degree of substitution in demand for different types of real capital goods and on the demand for each type of capital being more sensitive to the rate on one financial instrument than another.

(2) The ability of the corporate sector to by-pass the financial intermediaries and borrow directly from households raises the possibility that the asset reserve plan may fail to have the desired impact. The crucial conditions for success are stated in (20) and (21), which turn on the relative magnitudes of four elasticities of demand. Evaluation of these, however, would require careful empirical investigation. Despite the ambiguity generated by disintermediation *vis-à-vis* the real investment mix, it does not alter the qualitative conclusions regarding interest rates in the financial markets.

(3) If all financial intermediaries are not directly covered by the asset reserve plan, the magnitude of the ultimate effect on the real rates of return resulting from a given change in the reserve requirement will be reduced. The reduction in the mag-

nitude of the effect is directly proportional to the gap in coverage. But the plausibility of success of the asset reserve plan is unaltered.

(4) The above conclusions apply with equal strength to all selective monetary policies that operate on bank preferences for different assets.

(5) The policy multipliers associated with different selective credit controls on financial intermediaries can be compared directly by comparing the initial impact of these policies on bank demands for alternative assets.

Appendix

Ignoring the compensation mechanism described in the text, the General Model may be represented by the following equations.

$$(A1)$$

$$
\begin{bmatrix}
\dfrac{\partial(M_e - M_f)}{\partial i_m} & \dfrac{\partial(M_e - M_f)}{\partial i_b} & \dfrac{\partial M_e}{\partial r_h} & \dfrac{\partial M_e}{\partial r_k} \\[2mm]
\dfrac{\partial(B_e - B_f)}{\partial i_m} & \dfrac{\partial(B_e - B_f)}{\partial i_b} & \dfrac{\partial B_e}{\partial r_h} & \dfrac{\partial B_e}{\partial r_k} \\[2mm]
-\dfrac{\partial H_e}{\partial i_m} & -\dfrac{\partial H_e}{\partial i_b} & \dfrac{\partial(H - H_e)}{\partial r_h} & -\dfrac{\partial H_e}{\partial r_k} \\[2mm]
-\dfrac{\partial K_e}{\partial i_m} & -\dfrac{\partial K_e}{\partial i_b} & -\dfrac{\partial K_e}{\partial r_h} & \dfrac{\partial(K - K_e)}{\partial r_k}
\end{bmatrix}
\begin{bmatrix}
di_m \\[2mm] di_b \\[2mm] dr_h \\[2mm] dr_k
\end{bmatrix}
$$

$$
=
\begin{bmatrix}
\dfrac{\partial M_f}{\partial a_b}\, da_b + \dfrac{\partial M_f}{\partial R}\, dR \\[2mm]
\dfrac{\partial B_f}{\partial a_b}\, da_b + \dfrac{\partial B_f}{\partial R}\, dR \\[2mm]
0 \\[2mm]
0
\end{bmatrix}
$$

By virtue of the compensation mechanism, however, we can write

$$dM + dB \equiv 0 \qquad (A2)$$

or, equivalently,

$$\left(\frac{\partial M_f}{\partial i_m} + \frac{\partial B_f}{\partial i_m}\right) di_m + \left(\frac{\partial M_f}{\partial i_b} + \frac{\partial B_f}{\partial i_b}\right) di_b \qquad (A3)$$

$$+ \left(\frac{\partial M_f}{\partial a_b} + \frac{\partial B_f}{\partial a_b}\right) da_b + \left(\frac{\partial M_f}{\partial R} + \frac{\partial B_f}{\partial R}\right) dR \equiv 0.$$

Recalling that the M_f and B_f functions are assumed homogeneous in R (so that $\frac{\partial M_f}{\partial R} + \frac{\partial B_f}{\partial R} = \frac{M_f}{R} + \frac{B_f}{R} = \frac{D}{R}$), we can solve (A3) for dR and substitute that expression into (A1) to yield the set of equations.

$$Tx = q \qquad (A4)$$

where

$$T = \begin{bmatrix} \left[\dfrac{\partial M_e}{\partial i_m} - \dfrac{B}{D}\dfrac{\partial M_f}{\partial i_m} + \dfrac{M}{D}\dfrac{\partial B_f}{\partial i_m}\right] & \left[\dfrac{\partial M_e}{\partial i_b} - \dfrac{B}{D}\dfrac{\partial M_f}{\partial i_b} + \dfrac{M}{D}\dfrac{\partial B_f}{\partial i_b}\right] \\ \left[\dfrac{\partial B_0}{\partial i_m} + \dfrac{B}{D}\dfrac{\partial M_f}{\partial i_m} - \dfrac{M}{D}\dfrac{\partial B_f}{\partial i_m}\right] & \left[\dfrac{\partial B_e}{\partial i_b} + \dfrac{B}{D}\dfrac{\partial M_f}{\partial i_b} - \dfrac{M}{D}\dfrac{\partial B_f}{\partial i_b}\right] \\ -\dfrac{\partial H_e}{\partial i_m} & -\dfrac{\partial H_e}{\partial i_b} \\ -\dfrac{\partial K_e}{\partial i_m} & -\dfrac{\partial K_e}{\partial i_b} \end{bmatrix}$$

$$\begin{matrix} \dfrac{\partial M_e}{\partial r_h} & \dfrac{\partial M_e}{\partial r_k} \\ \dfrac{\partial B_e}{\partial r_h} & \dfrac{\partial B_e}{\partial r_k} \\ \dfrac{\partial(H - H_e)}{\partial r_h} & -\dfrac{\partial H_e}{\partial r_k} \\ -\dfrac{\partial K_e}{\partial r_h} & \dfrac{\partial(K - K_e)}{\partial r_k} \end{matrix} \Bigg] = [t_{ij}]$$

$$x = \begin{bmatrix} \dfrac{di_m}{da_b} \\[2mm] \dfrac{di_b}{da_b} \\[2mm] \dfrac{dr_h}{da_b} \\[2mm] \dfrac{dr_k}{da_b} \end{bmatrix} = [x_i], \text{ and } q = \begin{bmatrix} \dfrac{B}{D}\dfrac{\partial M_f}{\partial a_b} - \dfrac{M}{D}\dfrac{\partial B_f}{\partial a_b} \\[2mm] -\left(\dfrac{B}{D}\dfrac{\partial M_f}{\partial a_b} - \dfrac{M}{D}\dfrac{\partial B_f}{\partial a_b}\right) \\[2mm] 0 \\[2mm] 0 \end{bmatrix} = [q_i]$$

JAMES M. O'BRIEN is a Senior Economist at the Federal Reserve Bank of Philadelphia. He holds a Ph.D. from the University of Illinois, specializing in monetary economics. He has contributed to the *Review of Economics and Statistics*, the *Journal of Money, Credit and Banking,* and the Philadelphia Fed's *Business Review.*

The author is grateful to Rudolph G. Penner for his helpful comments. The views expressed therein are the author's and do not necessarily reflect those of Mr. Penner.

Household Asset Substitution
And the Effectiveness
Of Selective Credit Policies

JAMES M. O'BRIEN

The use of selective credit policies to influence the allocation of capital among different activities has become of increasing interest to U. S. Congressmen, other public officials, and still others concerned with an allocation of resources in accordance with "national priorities." The desirability of such policies depends on a number of issues concerning the effects on equity, the costs of regulation, and the ability of credit controls to alter the pattern of capital flows. At least in a comparative static framework, the ability of credit controls to affect the pattern of capital flows is determined by the sensitivity of the demands and supplies of financial and real assets to changes in asset prices or yields. The appropriate conditions for the success of selective credit controls have been most generally specified by D. C. Rao and Ira Kaminow.[1] These conditions have been further elaborated on and applied to housing credit programs

---

[1]"Selective Credit Controls and the Real Investment Mix: A General Equilibrium Approach," *Journal of Finance* 28 (1973): 1103-18; also reprinted in this volume on pp. 173-95.

197

by Rudolph Penner and William L. Silber[2] and earlier discussed by Donald R. Hodgman.[3]

This study deals with the efficacy issue in the same context as dealt with in these earlier studies. Its particular focus is the role of household financial asset substitution as it relates to the ability of credit policies to affect the composition of financial flows. Section I identifies the theoretical conditions which determine the relation between household's financial asset substitution and the ability of credit controls to affect financial flows. Section II provides empirical information on household asset substitution across a spectrum of financial assets. This empirical analysis attempts to apply a technique developed by Henri Theil and others for measuring substitution among commodities. Section III considers the implications of the empirical results for the effectiveness of selective credit controls as they relate to household portfolio behavior. Results and conclusions are summed up in section IV.

I. THEORETICAL CONSIDERATIONS

Suppose the Federal Government were to subsidize the interest cost of borrowers floating new issues of a particular type of debt instrument in order to encourage investment in a particular real activity. For simplicity, assume further that the subsidy was financed by general taxes on citizens. The effectiveness of the policy will depend on the investment response in the favored activity as well as that in other activities to the interest rate subsidy. The policy's effectiveness will also depend on the investment responses to interest rates on other debt instruments as well. A presumption is that the interest elasticity of investment demand in the favored activity is greater with respect to the subsidized debt instrument than it is with other debt instruments and vice-versa for investment demand in other activities. Under this presumption, the credit control will be more successful the more willing are lenders to absorb new issues of the subsidized debt instrument into their portfolios.

---

[2]"The Interaction between Federal Credit Programs and the Impact on the Allocation of Credit," *American Economic Review* 63 (1973): 838-52.

[3]"Selective Credit Controls," *Journal of Money, Credit and Banking* 4 (1972): 343-59.

Suppose instead of a subsidy to borrowers, the Government subsidized all holders of new issues of this particular debt instrument. Initially, this can be expected to raise the price of new issues in proportion to the subsidy.[4] The rise in price lowers the cost to borrowers of financing investment through this instrument in a manner exactly the same as when the borrower was directly subsidized. Thus, the various conclusions cited above concerning the determinants of effectiveness are also applicable to this situation. In particular, we can say that when the lender is subsidized, the selective credit control will be more successful the more willing is the lender to absorb new issues of the subsidized debt instrument. Moreover, these conclusions can be expected to apply in an analogous way when the objective of the selective credit policy is to reduce investment in a certain activity by taxing the lenders or borrowers holding or issuing the designated debt instrument.

The last case to consider is when the Government subsidizes only a particular group of lenders, say financial institutions. Activities of the financial institutions will tend to drive up the price of new issues. This, in turn, will cause nonsubsidized lenders to reduce their demands for new issues below what they otherwise would have been. The smaller their offsetting reduction in demand for the designated debt instrument, the more effective the selective credit control will be. However, there are several qualifications which follow from the fact, and to the degree, that the financial institutions will issue more liabilities to purchase the subsidized debt instrument. One is that if the reduction in demand for this instrument is largely offset by purchases of institutions' liabilities, there will only be a small

---

[4]By "initially" is meant "after a marginal increase in new issues." The subsidy might be assumed to be some fixed proportion of the interest return. The expected proportional increase in the price of the new issue assumes (a) citizens properly evaluate the present value of the taxes needed to cover the subsidy and (b) an absence of wealth redistribution effects on asset demands. Note that (a) presumes that the subsidy, while it changes the price of the particular debt instrument, has no aggregate wealth effect. Moreover, it also presumes that the aggregate supply of the income stream yielded by the subsidized debt instrument is (initially) unaltered. These presumptions along with (b) are sufficient to conclude that the price of new issues of the subsidized debt instrument must rise in proportion to the subsidy. In addition, this result would be completely unaffected if previously outstanding issues of this debt instrument were also subsidized (either purposely or if somehow borrowers were able to trade in old debt issues for subsidized new issues.).

negative impact on the effectiveness of the selective credit policy. Second, if there is a large elasticity between the nonsubsidized holdings of nondesignated debt instruments and institutional liabilities, the effectiveness of the credit policy will be greater than otherwise.

These considerations suggest the following generalizations regarding subsidy—tax types of selective credit policies aimed at credit reallocation and household asset behavior:

1. A policy applied uniformly to either all borrowers or all lenders utilizing a particular debt instrument will be more successful the *greater* is the elasticity of substitution between the designated financial instrument and other financial assets in the portfolios of households.

2. A policy applied only to assets purchased by financial institutions will be more successful the *lower* is the substitutability of those assets with other financial assets in households' portfolios.

In addition, there is the corollary:

3. A policy applied only to the assets purchased by institutional lenders will be more effective the greater is the substitution between its liabilities and other financial assets in the portfolios of households.

II. COVARIANCE ESTIMATES OF HOUSEHOLD ASSET SUBSTITUTION

The empirical analysis is concerned with applying to household asset data a technique originally developed by Theil to estimate substitution among commodities.[5] He has shown that under certain conditions the covariance between the variation in the demands for two goods, holding constant prices and income, would measure the substitutability of the two goods (more precisely, their Slutsky-Hicks substitution effects up to a negative scalar). This theorem and the framework behind it

---

[5]*Economics and Information Theory* (Chicago: Rand McNally and Company, 1967).

have subsequently been used in further studies of commodity substitution.[6]

The potential usefulness of the covariance technique, when applied to time series data in estimating substitution, has been discussed elsewhere.[7] An additional advantage here is that it can be applied across a spectrum of assets (or commodities) in using cross-section data. Unlike the traditional price or yield procedure, covariance estimates of substitutability do not depend on variability in prices or yields across sample units.

We will now briefly consider the underpinnings of this method, the information it provides, and how the covariance measure relates to the more traditional asset-yield measure of substitution.

A. THE COVARIANCE MEASURE

Theoretical Underpinnings. The theoretical framework developed and used by Theil and others assumes the household maximizes a quadratic utility function with respect to a vector of N goods, y, and subject to a budget constraint, that is, max $u(y) = a'y + \frac{1}{2}y'Zy$ and s.t. $-\acute{p}y + w = 0$. It is then assumed that the preference parameter vector, a, is subject to random shocks, Δa. This gives rise to covariances among commodities of the form $cov(\Delta y) = V cov(\Delta a)V$. The (N,N) symmetric matrix V is shown to contain the Slutsky-Hicks substitution effects among the N commodities except for a multiplicative constant.[8]

A critical assumption is then made that
(1) $cov(\Delta a) = c \partial^2 U/\partial y^2$
where c is a negative scalar. With this assumption it becomes

---

[6]See A. P. Barten, "Estimating Demand Equations," *Econometrica* 36 (1968): 213-51; Z. A. Hassan, S. R. Johnson, and R. M. Finley, "Further Evidence on the Structure of Consumer Demand in the U. S.: An Application of the Separability Hypothesis," *Southern Economic Journal* 41 (1974): 245-57; Louis Phlips, "Substitution, Complementarity, and the Residual Varion around Dynamic Demand Equations," *American Economic Review* 61 (1971): 586-97; and Louis Phlips and Philippe Rouzier, "Substitution, Complementarity, and the Residual Variation: Some Further Results," *American Economic Review* 62 (1972): 747-51.

[7]Phlips, op. cit., p. 597.

[8]Ibid., pp. 588-90; and Theil, op. cit., pp. 229-33.

only a mathematical exercise to derive the desired commodity covariance structure

(2) $\quad \text{cov}(\Delta y) = cV.$

Thus, the commodity demand covariance matrix is proportional to the matrix of Slutsky-Hicks substitution effects under assumption (1). It should be noted that the reasonableness of the assumption depends on the structure of individual preference functions and the source of variation of preferences.[9]

Asset Yield and Price Measures of Substitution. It will be assumed that the utility maximization problem regarding assets can be viewed as being analogous to that with respect to goods where y becomes a vector of asset quantities (which might be measured as the expected dollar value of holdings in each asset at the end of one period). The constraint $-\acute{p}y + w = 0$ becomes a wealth constraint where p is a vector of asset prices (the ith element of which might indicate the current cost of purchasing a promissory note or share denoted asset i which is expected to be exchangeable for one dollar one period hence) and w is the current market value of the household's wealth.

With this model we can derive

(3) $\quad \partial y_i / \partial e_j = k_j(v_{ij} + 1_j \partial y_i / \partial w)$

where e_j is the expected one period yield on asset j, v_{ij} (as before) is the Slutsky-Hicks substitution effect between i and j, k_j is a constant that depends on the initial expected rate of return on asset j, and 1_j depends on the stock of asset j held and the marginal utility of wealth.[10]

Comparing (2) and (3) indicates that the covariance measure and the more traditional measure of substitution between asset j and some other asset would provide the same ranking of relative substitutability as determined by the substitution effect, although the latter includes a wealth effect term. As a first approximation, it may be reasonable to treat the wealth effect on asset demand as negligible. For one thing, if e_j is the yield on a

---

[9]For the initial arguments behind (1) see Theil, pp. 230-31; and for further analysis, see James M. O'Brien, "The Information Value of Demand Equation Residuals: A Further Analysis," Philadelphia Fed Research Papers (Federal Reserve Bank of Philadelphia, 1975).

[10]This approach to asset behavior and consequent derivation of (3) is in the spirit of G. O. Bierwag and M. A. Grove. See their "Slutsky Equations for Assets," *Journal of Political Economy* 76 (1968): 114-27.

deposit then the wealth effect is zero since its price is always $1. Moreover if, say, an increase in the yield on j reduced the wealth of holders of j because of a lower price, it identically raises the wealth of the issuers of j. If this *redistribution* of wealth did not affect the demand for asset i then the wealth effect would also be zero.

B.   EMPIRICAL ANALYSIS

Data and Statistical Model. The empirical analysis will utilize the Federal Reserve System's 1962 Survey of Financial Characteristics of Consumers.[11] The analysis will examine the substitutability among nine financial assets: checking accounts, savings bonds, bonds, savings deposits of commercial banks, savings deposits in savings institutions, stock, life insurance, mutual funds, and "other assets." The sample units were divided into a low- and high-wealth group—those with financial assets less than $50,000 but greater than zero (1658 units), and those with greater than or equal to $50,000 (393 units). The substitution analysis is carried out separately for each wealth group.

It will be assumed that for each household the demand for asset i takes the general form

(4) $y_i = f_i w$ $(i = 1, \ldots, N)$

The term f_i reflects the household's preference for asset i given its wealth. The wealth variable, w, is defined as the sum of the household's holdings in the nine assets.[12] Under the assumption that asset yields are constant, random variations in f_i imply variations in y_i resulting from randomly shifting preferences for the underlying wants or motives that assets satisfy. The resulting covariances among the random shifts in asset preferences,

[11]Dorothy S. Projector and Gertrude S. Weiss, *Survey of Financial Characteristics of Consumers* (Washington: Board of Governors of the Federal Reserve System, 1966).

[12]The definition of wealth as the sum of financial asset holdings assumes that the problem of the composition of the financial portfolio can be separated from the wider problem of the allocation of total wealth (human, physical, and financial). Also, to remain consistent with the quadratic formulation of the utility function assumed in section 1, the formulation of the demand function in (5) assumes that the household's asset utility function is quadratic with respect to the *share* of wealth held in each asset.

(5) $\text{cov}(\Delta f_i, \Delta f_j) = \text{cov}[\Delta(y_i/w), \Delta(y_j/w)]$ (all i, j),

constitute Theil's covariance measure of substitution as developed in section I and specified in (2).

The theoretical development of the covariance measure of substitution does not dictate how the Δf_i's are to be generated except to require that the underlying behavioral condition defined by (1) be satisfied. The procedure here was to regress the asset proportions on a vector of socioeconomic characteristics for each of the two wealth groups. A formulation of Δf_i is then the estimated residual, $e_i = (y_i/w - d_i)$, where d_i is the predicted value of asset proportion i based on the ith regression.[13]

There are several sources of potential bias which stem from the use of cross-section data which ought to be noted. One is that households tend to underreport their asset holdings with the underreporting being more serious among higher wealth households.[14] A second source of distortion is the existence of regional differences in pecuniary yields paid on some assets such as savings deposits and possibly other attributes (the effects of these differences on asset composition could not be controlled because the data are not classified by region). Finally, the comparative statics behind the theory of the covariance measure implies that actual variations in observed asset composition reflect desired variations. The fact that at least some households will not have their desired portfolio—that is, will be in a state of disequilibrium—may account for at least some asset composition differences among households. These three potential sources of observed variation in asset composition violate the condition set out in (1) that observed asset variations reflect variations in asset preferences. The empirical analysis implicitly assumes that these several distorting influences on asset

---

[13]In terms of the actual results, this procedure comes fairly close to that where Δf_i was simply the difference between asset proportion i held by the individual and its average value for the sample. For a further discussion of why the asset residuals were used, see James M. O'Brien, "The Covariance Measure of Substitution: An Application to Financial Assets," *Review of Economics and Statistics* 56 (1974): 458-69.

[14]See Robert Ferber, John Forsythe, Harold W. Guthrie, and E. Scott Maynes, "Validation of a National Survey of Consumer Financial Characteristics," *Review of Economics and Statistics* 51 (1969): 436-44; and Robert Ferber, John Forsythe, Harold W. Guthrie, and E. Scott Maynes, "Validation of Consumer Financial Characteristics: Common Stock," *Journal of the American Statistical Association* 64 (1969): 415-32.

composition are relatively minor and that the determining differences in asset composition among households are differences in households' asset preferences.

Empirical Results. The predominance of negative correlation coefficients among the asset equation residuals (Tables 1A and 1B) indicates that for both wealth groups there is a general absence of complementarity among assets.[15] Using the Fisher test for significance of correlation coefficients, the several positive correlations that do occur are not significant at the 0.05 level. The magnitudes of the correlations (covariances) provide an indication of relative substitutability among assets.

These bivariate correlations are determined by what may be called the "total" substitution effects, the elements in V as defined above. Houthakker has decomposed the total substitution effect into two additive parts called the specific and the general substitution effects.[16] The component which comprises the specific substitution effect is determined by the elements in the Hessian utility matrix, $\partial^2 U/\partial y^2$, and, in particular, $\partial^2 U/\partial y_i \partial y_j$. The general substitution effect component which is always positive arises from the linear dependency imposed by the budget constraint on the total substitution effects. And, as Theil has suggested, "this part of the total substitution effect can be regarded as describing the general competition of all commodities (assets) for the consumer's dollar."[17] The significance of this decomposition of the substitution effect, as was originally shown by Houthakker, is that *the household's utility function is additive if and only if the specific substitution effects are zero.*

---

[15]The interested reader may use the standard deviations presented in the row headings of Tables 1A and 1B to compute the respective covariances. The ranking of assets according to their substitutability with other assets to be reported and analyzed in this study is the same whether the correlations or covariances are used. In the several specific cases where a substitution ranking according to covariances would differ from that according to correlations, the differences in the respective covariances (correlations) are sufficiently small to prohibit any meaningful distinction in substitution ranking—and none is made in this study. The advantages of analyzing the correlation coefficients is that some indication of their significance is possible and they are amenable to separating the importance of the general from the specific substitution effects (see below).

[16]Hendrik S. Houthakker, "Additive Preferences," *Econometrica* 28 (1960): 248.

[17]Theil, op. cit., p. 192.

TABLE 1

Bivariate Asset Residual Correlations*

A. Sample Units With Financial Assets < $50,000

	Demand Deposits	Savings Bonds	Bonds	Savings Deposits Commercial Banks	Savings Deposits Savings Institutions	Stock	Life Insurance Reserves	Mutual Funds	Other Assets
Demand Deposits .289									
Savings Bonds .177	−.129								
Bonds .057	−.013	−.019							
Savings Deposits Commercial Banks .259	−.208	−.076	−.036						
Savings Deposits Savings Institutions .270	−.213	−.123	−.062	−.241					
Stock .157	−.080	−.087	−.033	−.088	−.124				
Life Insurance Reserves .327	−.409	−.170	−.041	−.270	−.243	−.136			
Mutual Funds .093	−.044	−.061	−.024	−.066	−.079	−.025	−.078		
Other Assets .126	−.025	−.081	−.021	−.072	−.113	−.110	−.096	−.054	

B. Sample Units With Financial Assets ≥ $50,000

	Demand Deposits	Savings Bonds	Bonds	Savings Deposits Commercial Banks	Savings Deposits Savings Institutions	Stock	Life Insurance Reserves	Mutual Funds	Other Assets
Demand Deposits .068									
Savings Bonds .086	.004								
Bonds .152	−.016	−.086							
Savings Deposits Commercial Banks .091	−.001	−.079	−.047						
Savings Deposits Savings Institutions .143	−.013	−.051	−.127	−.011					
Stock .291	−.168	−.194	−.281	−.202	−.318				
Life Insurance Reserves .131	.027	−.079	−.091	−.089	−.099	−.298			
Mutual Funds .137	−.059	−.023	−.058	−.069	−.061	−.344	−.055		
Other Assets .178	−.060	−.104	−.105	−.050	−.076	−.393	−.064	−.083	

*Numbers in the row headings are the standard deviations of the asset proportions, and asset residual proportions, respectively. The Fisher test of significance for correlation coefficients with 1656 degrees of freedom gives critical values of ± .063 and ± .048 at the .01 and .05 levels of significance, respectively. With 391 degrees of freedom, the critical values are ± .131 and ± .099. For a discussion of conditions underlying the use of the Fisher statistics see G. W. Snedecor, *Statistical Methods* (5th ed.; Ames: Iowa State University Press, 1956), pp. 170-80.

Assets: Demand deposits—checking account balances for personal use; savings bonds—U.S. Savings Bonds at their face value; bonds—U.S., state and local, corporate and foreign bonds, bills or notes at par value (state and local obligations dominate bond holdings); savings deposits in commercial banks—time deposits, certificates of deposit, Christmas and vacation club accounts; savings deposits in savings institutions—savings shares and deposits in savings and loan associations, mutual savings banks and credit unions; stock—publicly traded common and preferred stock at market value; life insurance reserves—cash surrender value of life insurance policies; mutual funds—shares in mutual funds and investment clubs; other assets—mortgage assets, loans to businesses in which no family member has an active or nonactive part, oil royalties, patents, commodity contracts, net credit balances at brokers. For further information on asset categories see Dorothy S. Projector and Gertrude S. Weiss, *Survey of Financial Characteristics of Consumers* (Washington: Board of Governors of the Federal Reserve System, 1966), pp. 45-49.

In the present analysis, the budget constraint is captured by the linear constraint among the residuals of the asset equations, $\Sigma_i e_i = 0$. The corresponding linear constraint on the (total) substitution effects is empirically captured by the linear dependency among asset residual covariances, $\Sigma_i \sigma_{ij} = 0$. Using this dependency, Phlips and Rouzier have derived a statistical measure of the part of the correlation due to the general substitution effect.[18] For the asset substitution analysis of this study, estimates of the Phlips-Rouzier measure have been made and are presented in Tables 2A and 2B above the diagonals.[19] When the part of the correlation estimated to be due to the general substitution effect is subtracted from the correlation coefficient, the remainder is the part of the correlation due to the specific substitution effect. The elements below the diagonals of Tables 2A and 2B are the corresponding estimates of specific substitution effect correlation components.

The most striking aspect of Tables 2A and 2B is that the estimates of the general substitution effects are, as a rule, appreciably more important than the specific substitution effects in their determination of the correlation coefficients. For the lower wealth group the dominating influence of the general substitution effects is most pronounced (the average absolute value of the estimated general substitution correlations is .108 and for the specific substitution correlations is .030). Besides being mostly insignificant, the specific correlations appear to be randomly distributed about zero. In the high wealth group there is still a significant tendency for the general substitution effects to dominate over the specific substitution effects, but the tendency is somewhat less discernible because of the greater variability in the specific correlations (the average absolute

---

[18]See their "Substitution, Complementarity, and the Residual Variation: Some Further Results," op. cit., pp. 747-51.

[19]The Phlips-Rouzier measure for estimating the part of the correlation due to the general substitution effect is

$-[(p_i \partial y_i/\partial w \, p_j \partial y_j/\partial w) \, / \, (1 - p_i \partial y_i/\partial w)(1 - p_j \partial y_j/\partial w)]^{1/2}$.

According to (5), $\partial y_i/\partial w = f_i(\ ) + (\partial f_i/\partial w)w$ in our model. The $\partial y_i/\partial w$ was estimated and evaluated at the mean value of w and $f_i(\ )$ for each asset (for each of the two samples). However, no explicit account was taken of p_i and p_j in the calculation (the wealth constraint is expressed simply as $\Sigma y_i = w$).

value of the estimated general substitution correlations is .104 and for the specific substitution correlations is .039). The relatively greater variability in the specific correlations of the high wealth group, and the accompanying greater variability of the (total) correlation coefficients, may simply reflect the much smaller sample size compared to that of the low wealth group.

In sum, a major result of the empirical testing is that, by and large, the only significant covariation that could be found among the asset categories was that imposed by the constraint on the total value of assets. From Houthakker's consumer analysis, this implies that the asset categories may enter households' utility functions in an approximately additive manner.

III. IMPLICATIONS FOR SELECTIVE CREDIT POLICIES

That household asset preferences may be approximately additive has direct implications for the *relative* response of household asset owners to selective credit policies. In particular, it implies that the relative asset price or yield elasticities will equal the relative wealth elasticities.[20] Estimates of the wealth elasticities for each sample group from empirical estimates of (4) have been calculated and also used to compute the elasticities for the entire household sector (see Table 3).

There is a general tendency for variable priced assets to be wealth elastic and fixed price assets to be wealth inelastic (savings bonds and mutual funds being exceptions). As an example of the implications, we might consider the income tax exemption on municipal bonds as it applies to households. According to Table 3, increased purchases of municipals as a result of higher after-tax yields would induce the household sector to make relatively large percentage decreases in marketable securities and relatively small shifts out of deposits. However, the relative differences should not be overemphasized as all the wealth elasticities for the household sector have been estimated

---

[20] See Houthakker, op. cit., pp. 244-55.

TABLE 2
Estimated Decomposition of Correlation Coefficients into General and Specific Substitution Effects

SPECIFIC / GENERAL

A. Sample Units with Financial Assets < $50,000

	Demand Deposits	Savings Bonds	Bonds	Savings Deposits Commercial Banks	Savings Deposits Savings Institutions	Stock	Life Insurance Reserves	Mutual Funds	Other Assets
Demand Deposits		−.144	−.050	−.187	−.208	−.167	−.260	−.088	−.095
Savings Bonds	.015		−.030	−.113	−.125	−.101	−.157	−.053	−.057
Bonds	.037	.011		−.036	−.040	−.032	−.050	−.017	−.018
Savings Deposits Commercial Banks	−.021	.037	.000		−.173	−.139	−.217	−.073	−.079
Savings Deposits Savings Institutions	−.005	.002	−.022	−.068		−.160	−.250	−.085	−.091
Stock	.087	.014	−.001	.051	.036		−.187	−.063	−.068
Life Insurance Reserves	−.149	−.013	.009	−.053	.007	.051		−.120	−.129
Mutual Funds	.044	−.008	−.007	.007	.006	.038	.042		−.033
Other Assets	.070	−.024	−.003	.007	−.022	−.042	.033	−.021	

B. Sample Units with Financial Assets ≥ $50,000

	Demand Deposits	Savings Bonds	Bonds	Savings Deposits Commercial Banks	Savings Deposits Savings Institutions	Stock	Life Insurance Reserves	Mutual Funds	Other Assets
Demand Deposits		-.035	-.068	-.042	-.051	-.160	-.061	-.051	-.056
Savings Bonds	.039		-.052	-.032	-.038	-.122	-.046	-.038	-.043
Bonds	.052	-.034		-.067	-.081	-.256	-.097	-.081	-.090
Savings Deposits Commercial Banks	.041	.111	.020		-.046	-.147	-.056	-.046	-.052
Savings Deposits Savings Institutions	.038	.089	-.046	.035		-.181	-.068	-.057	-.064
Stock	-.008	-.072	-.025	-.055	-.137		-.449	-.374	-.417
Life Insurance Reserves	.088	-.033	.006	-.033	-.031	.151		-.070	-.078
Mutual Funds	-.008	.015	.023	-.023	-.004	.030	.015		-.065
Other Assets	-.004	-.061	-.015	.002	-.012	.024	.014	-.018	

to be fairly close to "one." Thus, any asset shifting would still be broadly based. This, of course, refers to the asset categories defined here. There might, for example, be much more shifting within, say, the bond category in response to the tax exemption on municipal bonds.

TABLE 3

Estimated Wealth Elasticities*

	Wealth Groups		Entire Household Sector
	<50,000	≥50,000	
Demand Deposits	.88	.90	.88
Savings Bonds	1.08	.79	1.02
Bonds	1.29	1.20	1.21
Savings Deposits Commercial Banks	.95	.86	.93
Savings Deposits Savings Institutions	1.02	.79	.96
Stock	1.62	1.07	1.17
Life Insurance Reserves	.89	.82	.87
Mutual Funds	1.03	.81	.90
Other Assets	1.42	1.22	1.29

*For estimates of equation (4) see James M. O'Brien, "The Covariance Measure of Substitution: An Application of Financial Assets," *Review of Economics and Statistics* 56 (1974): 461, Table 2. On the basis of the estimated value of (4) for each asset, the wealth elasticity was calculated for each wealth group as

$$\Sigma_{iw} = f_i + \frac{\partial f_i}{\partial w} w/f_i$$

where f_i and w were put at their means for the respective sample. For the entire household sector, a weighted average of the asset elasticities of the two wealth groups was obtained. The weights were the proportions of the entire household sector's holdings of asset i as held by the respective wealth groups (as calculated from Tables A10, A31, and A36 in Projector and Weiss, op. cit.).

The asset covariances technically provide information only concerning *relative* asset substitutability. However, it may be that something can also be said about the absolute degree of asset substitution and, hence, the effectiveness of selective credit controls. In particular, there have been a number of studies which have examined commodity substitution within an additive preference framework.[21] The estimated direct price elasticities have invariably been very low, always less than 1.0 and more often than not less than .50. Of course, the individual cross-price elasticities were lower still. In analyzing the results, the authors have noted that the low price elasticities are to be expected given the (presumed) additive preference function.

It would not seem unreasonable to suppose that where asset preferences are additive the substitution elasticities are also likely to be low. With this presumption, the results of section II would imply that, for the asset categories examined, selective credit policies may elicit relatively little absolute response on the part of household asset owners. According to the theoretical considerations of section I, this implication can cut several ways. To the extent that credit policies were applied directly to assets purchased by households, their effectiveness would be relatively small. However, if the policies applied only to institutional asset purchasers, there may be relatively little offset substitution by households. Again, these implications apply only to the asset categories as studied here. One might expect that within a given category asset substitution would be greater.

It will be useful to return to the example of the municipal bond tax exemption as applied to households. For the average household owner of municipals, the effective after-tax yield is estimated to be somewhere in the neighborhood of fifty percent higher than that on comparable bonds.[22] According to the Fed-

---

[21]See Theil, op. cit., pp. 237-50; Barten, op. cit., pp. 213-51; and Hassan, Johnson, and Finley, op. cit., pp. 245-57.

[22]This is based on a marginal tax rate of slightly under 50 percent for the average household owner of municipals (see Susan Ackerman and David Ott, "An Analysis of the Revenue Effects of Proposed Substitutes for Tax Exemption of State and Local Bonds," *National Tax Journal* 23 [1970]: 397-406) and the yield on comparable corporate bonds being somewhere around 130 percent of municipals (see Harvey Galper and John Petersen, "An Analysis of Subsidy Plans to State and Local Borrowing," *National Tax Journal* 24 [1971]: 205-34).

eral Reserve Survey of Financial Characteristics of Consumers in 1962, municipals comprise about half of households' holdings of marketable bonds (the remainder being split almost equally between U. S. Government and corporate issues).[23] Suppose we now take our suggested finding of a low-asset substitutability for the categories examined to the limit, that is, no substitutability. We further assume that in the absence of the tax exemption on municipals, bond holdings would be equally divided among the three bond categories. This would imply that the tax exemption increases households' municipal holdings by 50 percent (and correspondingly reduces U. S. and corporate bond holdings each by 25 percent). The implied direct yield elasticity is one. For this rather narrowly defined asset, the elasticity is not very high. Moreover, as long as we continue to hold to the assumption that households would be roughly indifferent between municipals, U. S. and corporate issues in the absence of the tax exemption, the direct elasticity cannot be greater than two. And this maximum results only if there were absolutely no substitution away from other marketable bond issues to municipals.

This example is very specific and involves a number of important parameters which have been only roughly estimated. Not disregarding these limitations, it does seem interesting that it largely agrees with the more general conclusion argued earlier of a possible weak response by households to the yield effects of selective credit policies.

IV. SUMMARY

This study has attempted to examine the role of household portfolio behavior and the effectiveness of selective credit policies. It was argued that a high degree of substitution among assets in household portfolios will tend to enhance the effectiveness of selective credit policies when they are applied to issues of the designated financial instruments purchased by households. The opposite tends to be true when the policies are applied only to issues of the designated instruments purchased

[23]See Projector and Weiss, op. cit., pp. 61-62.

214

by other sectors, particularly, financial institutions. This holds whether they are applied directly to the borrower or lender.

The empirical analysis found that preferences for financial assets—as divided into nine asset categories—appeared to be approximately additive. Thus, the relative substitutability of one asset for another can be calculated from the relative wealth effects on asset demands. It also was suggested that the lack of specific substitutability among the asset categories might imply a generally low absolute degree of substitution among these asset groups for households. According to this interpretation, selective credit policies will elicit relatively little substitution response across the nine asset categories. A rough assessment of the effects on households' portfolios of the income tax exemption on municipal bonds did not seem at odds with this suggestion.

This study is only a limited start toward examining the role of households' portfolio behavior in determining the effectiveness of selective credit policies in reallocating real resources. The analysis was applied not to resource flows, but rather to credit flows. Moreover, the final impacts of households' asset demand elasticities on credit and resource reallocations must be determined in conjunction with other asset demand and supply elasticities in a general equilibrium context. The empirical analysis used a novel technique for determining asset substitutability. This technique rests on a number of underlying assumptions whose validity is, at present, subject to some degree of uncertainty.

Nonetheless, the analysis and results were at least suggestive of possible impacts of household portfolio behavior on the effectiveness of selective credit policies. Further testing of the results arrived at in this study—particularly the general absence of specific substitutability—could reduce the tentativeness of the conclusions. Empirically examining some of the other untested issues—particularly the degree of substitutability within any given asset category—could also significantly help in determining the effects of households' portfolio behavior on selective credit policies and, in particular, the tax exemption of municipal bonds.

R. M. YOUNG is an Economist at Wharton EFA, Inc., Philadelphia, Pennsylvania. He holds a Ph.D. from the University of Pennsylvania, specializing in econometrics and macroeconomic theory. Formerly a Lecturer in the Department of Econometrics at the University of Birmingham (England), he served as an Economist at the Federal Reserve Bank of Philadelphia from 1971 to 1973, with primary responsibility for preparing an economic forecast and analysis for monetary policy formulation. He has published in *Econometrica* and the Philadelphia Fed's *Business Review*.

The Distribution of Stabilization Responsibility: A Possible Role for Structural Instruments

R. M. YOUNG

The side effects [of monetary restraint] point to the need for active fiscal policy to avoid placing a disproportionate share of the burden of economic stabilization on monetary policy—*Economic Report of the President* (1969).

Properly used, fiscal policy can reduce—or even eliminate—the need for cyclical changes in interest rates that give rise to disruptions in mortgage credit flows. . . . It is widely believed that the single most important contribution to more stable credit markets would be more active use of fiscal policy—Lyle E. Gramley, "Short-Term Cycles in Housing Production," *Federal Reserve Staff Study: Ways to Moderate Fluctuations in Housing Construction* (1972).

. . . The basic solution to the cycles in the housing sector, however, is to make greater use of fiscal policy as a stabilizing force so that monetary policy is free to maintain an even flow of credit at reasonable rates of interest—*Report of the Commission on Mortgage Interest Rates to the President of the United States and to the Congress* (1969).

Tradeoffs between stabilization activity on the part of monetary and fiscal authorities appear to have become a part of the conventional wisdom concerning macroeconomic policy. Im-

217

plicit in this notion is the idea that stabilization responsibility can be shifted from monetary to fiscal authorities with no loss in the stabilizing effect. The observation that a model of economic policy which views the policy process as an extremum problem leaves no room for such tradeoffs is perhaps superfluous. The purpose of this study is to use a simple model of policy which allows such tradeoffs to discuss the possible effects of a class of policy instruments which includes selective credit controls on the solution of the policy problem. It is argued that manipulation of these types of policy instruments may be used to alter the feasible tradeoffs among more traditional stabilization tools.

Development of this proposition is based on a simple model of stabilization presented in section I. Section II employs the model to investigate the optimal division of stabilization activity between fiscal and monetary policy from the point of view of an extremum problem. Section III argues that an alternative to the extremum model may better explain current division of stabilization activity. Section IV develops the theme that the class of policy instruments which includes selective credit controls is unique among stabilization tools and that within the model developed in section III they may be used to influence the feasible set of relative stabilization activity between fiscal and monetary authorities.

I. MODEL FOR DETERMINING RELATIVE LEVELS OF STABILIZATION ACTIVITY

In an early discussion of stabilization activity, Milton Friedman used a simple model to demonstrate (1) that the stability characteristics of policy actions depend on the correlation of their impact with the impact of the exogenous shocks which the economy receives and (2) that for some values of that correlation no stabilizing action should be attempted by the policy authority.[1] An extension of that model is used to analyze the current problem.

---

[1] See his "The Effects of a Full Employment Policy on Economic Stability," Milton Friedman, ed., *Essays in Positive Economics* (Chicago: University of Chicago Press, 1953), pp. 117-32.

218

It is assumed that minimizing the variance of a single variable, X, is the only goal of stabilization policy. Depending on the terms of reference this may be a level, percentage change, first difference, or deviation from desired path. Possible candidates include real and nominal output measures and unemployment or inflation rates. Moreover, it is assumed that the value of X is determined as a simple sum of the effects of monetary policy, M; fiscal policy, F; and all variables exogenous for the purposes of the policy decision, E.

(1) $$X = M + F + E$$

The relationship in (1) may be viewed as a compact representation of a reduced or solution form of a linear model or world. More specifically, M will be the sum of the effect of all monetary policy decisions on the current value of X; F, the same value for fiscal actions; and E, for all other reduced form variables influencing the current value of X.[2] It is assumed that each of M, F, and E are random variables with known moments.

While sections II and III below discuss alternative models of the policy process, each of them is concerned with the variance of X which may be represented by

(2) $$\sigma_X^2 = \sigma_M^2 + \sigma_F^2 + \sigma_E^2 + 2\rho_{MF}(\sigma_M^2\sigma_F^2)^{\frac{1}{2}} + 2\rho_{ME}(\sigma_E^2\sigma_M^2)^{\frac{1}{2}} + 2\rho_{FE}(\sigma_F^2\sigma_E^2)^{\frac{1}{2}}$$

where ρ_{ij} is the correlation between i and j, σ_i^2 is the variance of i with i, j = F, M, E. These variances and covariances may be interpreted in various ways. For the purposes of this study, σ_M^2

---

[2] If the reduced form equation underlying (1) takes the form

$$X = a_1m_1 + a_2m_2 + a_3f_1 + a_4f_2 + a_5e + v$$

where m_1 and m_2 are specific monetary policy variables, say free reserves and the discount rate; f_1 and f_2, fiscal policy variables; e an exogenous variable and v a disturbance term; then

$$M = a_1m_1 + a_2m_2$$
$$F = a_3f_1 + a_4f_2$$
$$E = a_5e + v$$

and σ_F^2 are regarded as the objects of policy choice, measuring the stabilization activity levels of the two policy components.

Using the variance of the impact of all policy actions as the measure of the level of stabilization policy has several advantages over possible alternatives such as the variance or coefficient of variation of the instruments of policy. First, the unit of measurement in terms of the objective variable facilitates comparison of the levels of stabilization activity. Second, the variance of impact on the objective variable permits distinguishing between adjustments of policy variables for stabilization and nonstabilization purposes. For example, two instruments of monetary policy may affect both the variance of X and Y, where X is a stabilization target and Y is not. The policy instruments may be adjusted to influence Y without affecting the variance of their impact on X, i.e., without changing stabilization policy. Use of any measure of the variance of individual instruments could not distinguish between this type of adjustment and one made for stabilization purposes.

Variances of the impacts of the policy and of all exogenous effects may be regarded as arising either from a world with stochastic parameters or as a specification of our knowledge of a world with constant but unknown parameters.[3]

[3]There is an alternative possibility in which the parameters of the world are known and constant, but the world is subject to random shocks. In this case, variances may arise because optimal control of the economic system results in instrument movements determined as a function of the random shocks to the system and are therefore random variables themselves. (See Gregory C. Chow, "Optimal Stochastic Control of Linear Economic Systems," *Journal of Money, Credit and Banking* 2[1970]: 291-302.) While this specification is not uninteresting, the specification in the text seems closer to the information structure facing policy units.

To illustrate the situation for a world with stochastic parameters using the notation of footnote 1, if

$$a = \begin{bmatrix} a_1 \\ a_2 \\ \cdot \\ \cdot \\ \cdot \\ a_5 \end{bmatrix} \sim N(\alpha, \Sigma), \quad \Sigma = \begin{pmatrix} \sigma_{11} & \sigma_{12} \\ \sigma_{21} & \sigma_{22} \end{pmatrix}$$

then $\sigma_M^2 = m_1^2 \sigma_{11} + m_2^2 \sigma_{22} + m_1 m_2 \sigma_{12}$. The decision process here could be viewed as taking place in two stages. The first would choose σ_M^2 and the second would select levels for specific instruments, possibly to satisfy some secondary considerations, subject to the constraint that σ_M^2 equal its chosen level.

For the purposes of the ensuing discussion, the three correlations that appear in (2) are viewed as parameters of the system at any point in time. The idea that ρ_{FE} and ρ_{ME} are parameters has some intuitive appeal. Friedman in exploiting this refers to the correlation between the effect of the policy instrument and exogenous factors as a measure of the timing or fit of counter-cyclical policy. From this viewpoint these correlations would be determined by the ability to foresee and adjust to the exogenous forces affecting the target variable—that is, the state of knowledge and institutional arrangements. Forecasting accuracy, the decision structure, and the validity of our current view of the economy will all evolve through time, but it seems unlikely that serious error is involved in assuming them to be fixed over the policy horizon. Accepting this view of the correlations implies that there exists some relationship between M and E and between F and E, such as

$$M = a_1 + b_1E + u$$
$$F = a_2 + b_2E + v$$

where a's and b's are constants and u and v stochastic terms. For σ_M^2 and σ_F^2 to be objects of choice and for constant b's, the policy authority must in some way be free to choose the variances of u and v; perhaps by the manner in which policy effects are distributed among individual instruments. Note, however, that this does not mean that the correlation ρ_{MF} is an object of choice. It does mean that for ρ_{MF} to be constant the covariance of u and v must bear a functional relationship to their variances.[4] While no attempt is made to develop such a relationship in the present

---

[4] If, for example,

$$M = a_1 + b_1E + u$$
$$F = a_2 + b_2E + v$$

$$\binom{u}{v} \sim (0,\Sigma), \qquad \Sigma = \begin{pmatrix} \sigma_{11} & \sigma_{12} \\ \sigma_{21} & \sigma_{22} \end{pmatrix},$$

then $\sigma_{12} = \rho_{MF}[b_1^2\sigma_E^2 + \sigma_{11} + \text{cov}(Eu)]\ [b_2^2\sigma_E^2 + \sigma_{22} + \text{cov}(Ev)]$
$\qquad - [b_1b_2\sigma_E^2 + b_1\text{cov}(Ev) + b_2\text{cov}(Eu)]$

context, a stochastic version of the model developed by Carl F. Christ seems likely to exhibit such a property.[5]

Whatever else is implied by the assumption that these correlations are constant over the policy horizon it seems clear that the probability distribution attached to the reduced form parameters underlying (1) must be constant over the policy horizon. The simplest example to demonstrate this is to assume $X = b_1 m + b_2 f + E$ where m and f are particular policy instruments and b, a random vector. If

$$b \sim (\beta, \Sigma) \qquad \Sigma = \begin{pmatrix} \sigma_{11} & \sigma_{12} \\ \sigma_{21} & \sigma_{22} \end{pmatrix}$$

it follows that

$$\rho_{MF} = \frac{\sigma_{22}}{(\sigma_{11}\sigma_{22})^{\frac{1}{2}}}.$$

If policy can change this covariance matrix over the policy horizon, then ρ_{MF} becomes a choice variable rather than a parameter. As we shall see below, this suggests a natural dichotomy among policy instruments.

II. EXTREMUM SOLUTIONS OF THE POLICY PROBLEM

Recent work on modeling the policy process has concentrated on analyzing a decision unit which is concerned with maximizing some objective function or minimizing some loss function. Although this approach is consistent with that economists have used in the theory of consumer behavior and the theory of the firm, the proposition that macroeconomic policy units behave in this manner does not appear to have yielded any meaningful theorems concerning their behavior which could be empirically refuted. In section III an alternative model is proposed, but it is useful to first present the results of an extremum-type approach.

---

[5]See his "A Simple Macroeconomic Model with a Government Budget Constraint," *Journal of Political Economy* 76 (1968): 53-67.

If we first assume there is a single policy unit or that policy choices are perfectly coordinated and that the goal of policy is to minimize σ_X^2, then it is possible to show, if an internal solution to the policy problem exists, that

$$(3) \qquad \sigma_M^2 = [(\rho_{MF}\rho_{FE} - \rho_{ME})/(1 - \rho_{MF}^2)]^2 \; \sigma_E^2$$
$$\sigma_F^2 = [(\rho_{MF}\rho_{ME} - \rho_{FE})/(1 - \rho_{MF}^2)]^2 \; \sigma_E^2.$$

Within this framework, or indeed within any extremum type problem with a unique solution, there is no room for trading off one type of stabilization policy against another. There exists an optimum level of activity for both types of policy and any deviation from that level will result in an increase in the loss associated with the problem. This approach then fails to explain the continuous negotiations, implicit (if not explicit) in public statements, through which one policy agency attempts to get the other to increase its stabilization activity, claiming this will enable them to reduce their own and not affect the level of stabilization.[6]

A more realistic, and perhaps more promising, approach is to assume that each policy unit takes the activity level of the other as given and attempts to minimize σ_X^2 by choosing the level of stabilization activity of its policy. Using the monetary authority as an example, the appropriate level of σ_M^2 is given by

$$(4) \qquad \sigma_M^2 = [\rho_{MF}(\sigma_F^2)^{1/2} + \rho_{ME}(\sigma_E^2)^{1/2}]^2.$$

Without specifying the procedure for assigning a value to the variance of the other policy for decision purposes, it can be assumed that the correlation between the actual variance and that used for decision purposes by the other agency is positive. Then it is clear that without any change in the probability

---

[6]This writer has examined the situations in which parametric variations in the model could result in a movement from one optimum to another giving the appearance of this type of policy shift. (See his "A Note on Relative Levels of Monetary and Fiscal Stabilization Activity," mimeographed, available from the author.) However, if we maintain the assumption that the distributions associated with the parameters of the world are constant, true tradeoffs cannot be explained within the above model.

distributions, which the monetary authority associates with the parameters of the policy problem, it is possible for a change in σ_E^2 to generate a situation wherein σ_M^2 and σ_F^2 move in opposite directions to decrease σ_X^2, since

$$(5) \qquad \frac{\partial \sigma_M^2}{\partial \sigma_E^2} = (\sigma_M^2)^{\frac{1}{2}} [\rho_{MF}(\sigma_F^2)^{-\frac{1}{2}} \frac{\partial \sigma_F^2}{\partial \sigma_E^2} + \rho_{ME}(\sigma_E^2)^{-\frac{1}{2}}]$$

It should be emphasized here that this is a movement from one optimum to another, not a tradeoff. The rhetoric which we observe may be generated by attempts of one body to impose on the other an optimum perceived through its superior wisdom; however, the sense of most such statements seems to envision a real tradeoff in stabilization activity.

III. SATISFICING SOLUTIONS OF THE POLICY PROBLEM

A simple alternative to the extremum approach to the policy problem is to assume that the policy authorities are attempting to maintain some given level of σ_X^2, say $\bar{\sigma}_X^2$, and that this is feasible for some set of σ_M^2, σ_F^2. The idea is similar to Jan Tinbergen's notion of fixed targets and the value of $\bar{\sigma}_X^2$ may be reached by some form of consensus which the policymakers help to shape.[7] A more realistic view of the problem perhaps is to specify that $\bar{\sigma}_X^2$ is some maximum variation in the variable of interest and the objective is to keep the actual variance below this. If we ascribed some costs to lowering the variance and no additional benefit, then for the univariate case the solution reduces to keeping $\sigma_X^2 = \bar{\sigma}_X^2$.

From this view of the policy process, the arguments that one type of stabilization activity should be increased and another type reduced become more than semantical confusion. A tradeoff is available and the public statements concerning who

---

[7]See his On the Theory of Economic Policy (Amsterdam, The Netherlands: North-Holland Publishing Company, 1970).

should take stabilization responsibility may be interpreted as negotiating postures. Relative responsibility might be negotiated between the two policy bodies, each attempting to reduce its share of the burden of stabilization in order to facilitate the achievement of nonstabilization-type goals. The outcome of the negotiating process cannot be predicted within the confines of the simple model posed here. However, the possibilities for substitution between σ_M^2 and σ_F^2 can be examined if it is assumed that the policy bodies have agreed on the level of stabilization to be achieved, $\bar{\sigma}_X^2$.

From (2) we see that if σ_M^2 and σ_F^2 are adjusted to maintain σ_X^2 at any agreed level then

$$
(6) \quad \frac{\partial \sigma_M^2}{\partial \sigma_F^2} = - \left[\frac{1 + \rho_{MF}(\sigma_M^2/\sigma_F^2)^{\frac{1}{2}} + \rho_{FE}(\sigma_E^2/\sigma_F^2)^{\frac{1}{2}}}{1 + \rho_{MF}(\sigma_F^2/\sigma_M^2)^{\frac{1}{2}} + \rho_{ME}(\sigma_E^2/\sigma_M^2)^{\frac{1}{2}}} \right]
$$

We might in the first instance be willing to assume that the two policy variances are of approximately the same order of magnitude and that both are small relative to σ_E^2. In this case the slope of the isoquant will be determined by the sign of ρ_{FE}/ρ_{ME}. In the case where the correlations have the same sign, the isoquant will slope downward over the relevant interval and there will be room for substitution of one type of policy for another. If, however, these correlations should happen to be of opposite sign, the isoquant will have a positive slope and maintaining a given level of σ_X^2 will require that they rise and fall together.

Alternatively, we might suppose that the three variances are all of roughly the same order of magnitude and that

$$
\text{sign } \frac{\partial \sigma_M^2}{\partial \sigma_F^2} = \text{sign } - \frac{(1 + \rho_{MF} + \rho_{FE})}{(1 + \rho_{MF} + \rho_{ME})}.
$$

If we assume that M and F are positively correlated and that both have a negative correlation with E, this would mean that the slope of the isoquant is negative and policy substitution could occur. Moreover, note that in general if ρ_{MF} is large relative to

225

ρ_{FE} and ρ_{ME}, an assumption which seems not completely unwarranted, there will tend to be substitution possibilities since the sign of both numerator and denominator of the fraction in brackets will tend to take the sign of ρ_{MF}.

Within the confines of this satisficing approach to policy there appears to be a great deal of scope for the type of policy tradeoffs often urged before Congressional committees. The tradeoff is an actual substitution of one policy for another and not a movement from one optimum to another, necessitated by changes in the parametric structure or data of the policy problem.

Finally, note that the range of substitution possible in the normal case, that is the range of σ_M^2/σ_F^2 over which the sign of (6) will be negative for any given values of σ_X^2 and σ_E^2 assuming $1 > \rho_{MF} > 0 > \rho_{ME}, \rho_{FE} > -1$, will depend on the size of ρ_{MF}. The closer to 1 the value of ρ_{MF}, the greater the range of variation of σ_M^2/σ_F^2 over which the bracketed term on the RHS if (6) will be positive. As ρ_{MF} becomes smaller, *ceteris paribus*, the possible range of substitution will become smaller since the last term in the numerator or denominator will more quickly dominate the sign as σ_M^2/σ_F^2 varies.

The alternate situations are shown in the following Figure. The rays b and b' and a and a' touch their respective isoquants B and A at the points at which an increase in one type of stabilization activity will require an increase in the other to maintain σ_X^2. The set of values of σ_M^2/σ_F^2 for which it is possible to reduce one form of stabilization activity and maintain $\bar{\sigma}_X^2$ by increasing the other is bounded by the slopes of a and a' when the isoquant is shaped as A, and by b and b' when the relevant isoquant is B. As the isoquants are drawn, B would be associated with a value of ρ_{MF} nearer to 1 than A.

The sense of this is clear. As ρ_{MF} approaches unity, it becomes more difficult to discern any difference between the two types of policy in affecting the variance of X and they can be freely substituted for one another without affecting σ_X^2. As ρ_{MF} approaches zero the substitution possibilities move in the opposite direction. Moreover, if we assume that positive stabilization activity imposes costs on policy bodies, then the ratios of

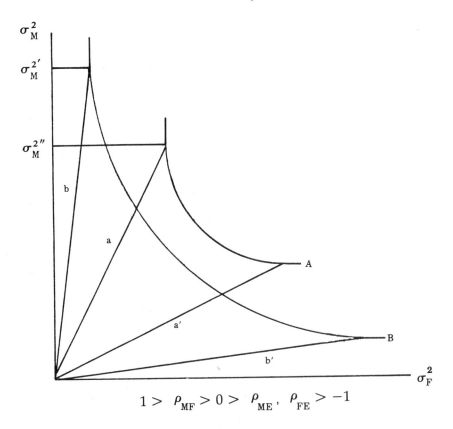

$$1 > \rho_{MF} > 0 > \rho_{ME}, \ \rho_{FE} > -1$$

stabilization activity which are observed will be bounded by rays such as a and a'. No group of policy bodies would negotiate a division of activity at which each could gain by reducing their activities with no loss of stabilization effects.

IV. STRUCTURAL POLICY UNDER A SATISFICING REGIME

It has become fashionable to analyze selective credit controls in terms of their static general equilibria effect on GNP, categorizing them with more traditional tools of economic policy such as Government expenditures, monetary aggregates,

227

and interest rates.[8] On a theoretical level this literature has largely concentrated on whether the effects of such controls, when they are binding, will be expansionary or contractionary with respect to aggregate income. This appears to be an outgrowth of the extremum approach to policy. The idea is that if the effect of the policy instrument on the variables of interest can be identified, its appropriate value will fall out of the maximization or minimization process being followed.

The foregoing discussion seems, however, to suggest an alternative view. If rather than affecting σ_M^2, selective credit controls have their primary impact on ρ_{MF}, ρ_{ME} and ρ_{FE}, then these instruments could be adjusted to change the feasible set of stabilization responsibility. For example, if we refer back to the Figure, a monetary authority which felt itself overburdened with stabilization responsibility at $\sigma_M^{2\prime}$ on isoquant B might prefer to shift negotiations to an isoquant shaped like A where the maximum activity level is $\sigma_M^{2\prime\prime}$, if it were in its power to do so. This might be accomplished if it could affect the values of the correlations, particularly ρ_{MF}.

For the moment, let us assume that a class of policy instruments, distinct from those related to σ_M^2 and σ_F^2, exist which can, if not determine, at least affect the correlations. We might term them structural instruments. Under what conditions would a legitimate dichotomy exist between these structural instruments and the stabilization instruments reflected in policy variances which would justify a decision model that regards the structural instruments as constant?

If the structural instruments are such that their efficacy depends on their intermittent use, or if their value can be altered only at discrete intervals because of cost or custom, it would seem legitimate to accept a division in which the policy

---

[8]See, for example, James Tobin and William C. Brainard, "Financial Intermediaries and the Effectiveness of Monetary Controls," *American Economic Review* 53 (1963): 383-400; Karl Brunner, "Monetary Analysis and Federal Reserve Policy," and Patric H. Hendershott, "Open Market Operations, the Money Stock, and Various Policy Issues," Karl Brunner, ed., *Targets and Indicators of Monetary Policy* (San Francisco: Chandler Publishing Company, 1969), pp. 250-82 and 283-99; Gordon Pye and Ian Young, "The Effect of Deposit Rate Ceilings on Aggregate Income," *Journal of Finance* 28 (1972): 1023-34; and Richard G. Davis, "An Analysis of Quantitive Credit Controls and Related Devices," *Brookings Papers on Economic Activity* No. 1 (1971): 65-104.

body regards them as fixed while conducting stabilization policy in terms of σ_M^2 and σ_F^2. Certain types of policy instruments do seem to fulfill this criterion. In particular one thinks of wage-price controls, quantitative credit controls, and interest rate ceilings. Discussions of these types of instruments often refer to their eroding effect and to the notion that one can only use them intermittently if they are to be effective.[9]

The literature on interest rate ceilings and credit controls also indicates that these policy instruments will not enter the reduced form simply as a variable but will affect the parameters of the reduced form directly. Richard Davis argues that one view of the effect of quantitative credit controls is that they speed credit rationing and increases in interest rates leading to a quickened response of aggregate demand to policy actions.[10] Gordon Pye and Ian Young analyze the effect of interest rate ceilings on aggregate income within the confines of a comparative statics, certainty framework.[11] They demonstrate that an effective interest rate ceiling changes the slope of the LM relationship. That is, a binding constraint will affect the reduced form relationships for income and the interest rates. Both of these arguments take the view that the effect of a binding control is simply to suspend one or more structural relationships. This will alter the probability distribution assigned to the reduced form parameters altering the correlations in (2) as demonstrated above.

Suppose the relevant structural system takes the form:

$$By + Cx = u$$

$$B = \begin{bmatrix} 1 & B_{12} & B_{13} & 0 \\ B_{21} & 1 & B_{23} & 0 \\ 0 & B_{32} & 1 & B_{33} \\ 0 & B_{42} & B_{43} & 1 \end{bmatrix} \qquad C = \begin{bmatrix} \gamma_{11} & \gamma_{12} & 0 \\ \gamma_{21} & 0 & \gamma_{23} \\ \gamma_{31} & \gamma_{32} & 0 \\ \gamma_{41} & 0 & 0 \end{bmatrix}$$

---

[9]See John H. Wood's contribution to this volume (pages 147-70) for an analysis of quantitative credit controls along these lines.
[10]See his "An Analysis of Quantitative Credit Controls and Related Devices", pp. 65-104.
[11]See their "The Effect of Deposit Rate Ceilings on Aggregate Income", pp. 1023-34.

y = a vector of endogeneous variables.

x = a vector of exogenous variables including variables with $x_1 = 1$.

u = a stochastic disturbance term.

This pattern might arise if we were modeling two related financial markets. The first two equations can be thought of as the supply and demand for one debt instrument and the last two for a second where y_1 and y_4 are the quantity variables. If our knowledge of the parameters of this system takes the form of a probability distribution over the elements of B and C we can approximate the distribution of the reduced form parameters, $\pi = -B^{-1} C$, where

$$y = \pi X + v$$
$$v = B^{-1}u$$

Now suppose a binding constraint is imposed on issuing the debt instrument y_1, such that rather than the first equation we have $y_1 = y_1^0$.

The structural system which results from this is

$$B^*y^* + C^*X = u^*$$

$$B^* = \begin{bmatrix} 1 & \beta_{23} & 0 \\ \beta_{32} & 1 & \beta_{33} \\ \beta_{42} & \beta_{43} & 1 \end{bmatrix} \quad C^* = \begin{bmatrix} \gamma_{21}+\beta_{21}y_1 & 0 & \gamma_{23} \\ \gamma_{31} & \gamma_{32} & 0 \\ \gamma_{41} & 0 & 0 \end{bmatrix}$$

with y^* and u^* the y and u vectors with the first element deleted. Clearly the reduced form matrix derived from this relationship will differ both in mean and in covariance matrix even if the moments of the surviving elements of B and C have not changed. As was demonstrated in section I, the constancy of the correlations cannot survive this alteration in the probability distribution of the elements of π.

The satisficing view of policy suggests then that policy instruments might be dichotomized into those which appear as explanatory variables in the reduced form and those which have the effect of altering reduced form relationships.

Within the framework of the simple model described above there does not appear to be any *a priori* reason to suspect that the imposition of a specific selective credit control would either increase or decrease a correlation. For a given structural form, however, it would be possible to estimate the effect of a specific control conditional on the distribution of parameters of all other structural relations remaining constant. Thus, the policy body involved could forecast the effect of a structural policy move on the feasible set of relative stabilization responsibility, σ_M^2/σ_F^2. In the case of the example in the Figure, the policy authority with the strongest negotiating position would be interested in finding a structural policy which would place negotiations on B while the weaker party would search for instruments that would place negotiations on A.

The view of the policy process described in this and the previous section suggests that one might find increasing responsibility for stabilization policy associated with an increasing commitment to structural policy. Indeed, it appears that in recent years the Federal Reserve has assumed greater responsibility for stabilization and has also been one of the primary sources for the structural policies which have been implemented or suggested.